21 DAYS
TO BAGHDAD

OSPREY
PUBLISHING

HEATHER MARIE STUR

21DAYS
TO BAGHDAD

GENERAL BUFORD BLOUNT
AND THE 3RD INFANTRY DIVISION
IN THE IRAQ WAR

OSPREY PUBLISHING
Bloomsbury Publishing Plc
Kemp House, Chawley Park, Cumnor Hill, Oxford OX2 9PH, UK
29 Earlsfort Terrace, Dublin 2, Ireland
1385 Broadway, 5th Floor, New York, NY 10018, USA
E-mail: info@ospreypublishing.com
www.ospreypublishing.com

OSPREY is a trademark of Osprey Publishing Ltd

First published in Great Britain in 2023

A catalog record for this book is available from the British Library.

ISBN: HB 978 1 4728 5363 9; PB 978 1 4728 5361 5; eBook 978 1 4728 5360 8;
ePDF 978 1 4728 5362 2; XML 978 1 4728 5359 2

23 24 25 26 27   10 9 8 7 6 5 4 3 2 1

Maps by www.bounford.com, previously published in *Blood, Metal and Dust* (Osprey, 2020)
Index by Zoe Ross

Typeset by Deanta Global Publishing Services, Chennai, India
Printed and bound in Great Britain by CPI (Group) UK Ltd, Croydon, CR0 4YY

Osprey Publishing supports the Woodland Trust, the UK's leading woodland conservation charity.

To find out more about our authors and books visit www.ospreypublishing.com.
Here you will find extracts, author interviews, details of forthcoming events and the
option to sign up for our newsletter.

Contents

List of Illustrations

General Blount briefing the final attack plan for Baghdad. The original invasion plans did not have the 3rd ID going into the city, but Blount convinced his superiors at V Corps that his division was the one for the job. (General Blount's personal archive)

ABC news anchor Diane Sawyer talking with General Blount while on assignment in Kuwait. The Army's embedded media program gave journalists close access to the war. (General Blount's personal archive)

3rd ID Bradley fighting vehicles from 3-7 Infantry take a brief stop during their move deeper into Iraq, March 21, 2003. (Photo by Scott Nelson/Getty Images)

A 3rd ID M1/A1 Abrams tank rolls deeper into Iraqi territory on March 23, 2003, south of the city of An Najaf. (Photo by Scott Nelson/Getty Images)

3rd ID vehicles navigate their way through "the mother of all sandstorms." The sandstorm temporarily slowed the division's progress but also created time for tank crews to conduct maintenance on their vehicles. (General Blount's personal archive)

A U.S. soldier practices drinking water from a canteen while wearing a chemical suit. 3rd ID personnel wore chemical suits during the entirety of the invasion due to concerns about Hussein having chemical weapons. (General Blount's personal archive)

The 3rd ID's armored column approaching Baghdad. The division made history when it arrived in Baghdad only three weeks after it invaded Iraq. (General Blount's personal archive)

Division Operations Officer Peter Bayer, General Blount, and Major Erik Berdy, Blount's aide-de-camp, in front of Blount's M113, which he nicknamed Zeus. (General Blount's personal archive)

Iraqi people welcoming American soldiers on the outskirts of Baghdad. From Blount's perspective, locals viewed U.S. troops as liberators when they arrived. (General Blount's personal archive)

Soldiers of the 1st Brigade Combat Team (BCT), under the command of Colonel William Grimsley, wait for 2nd BCT troops at the end of the first thunder run at Saddam International Airport. (General Blount's personal archive)

2nd BCT tactical operations center at Objective Saints after an Iraqi missile attack. The attack occurred as Colonel David Perkins was leading 2nd BCT troops into the heart of Baghdad on the second thunder run. (General Blount's personal archive)

An Iraqi orphan tries to sell a pack of cigarettes. U.S. soldiers were told to avoid buying items from locals they encountered during Operation *Iraqi Freedom*. (General Blount's personal archive)

U.S. soldiers at Saddam Hussein's VIP Parade Field in central Baghdad after the second thunder run, which solidified the 3rd ID's control of Iraq's capital city. (General Blount's personal archive)

3-7 Infantry soldiers use a Bradley fighting vehicle for cover as they conduct a neighborhood patrol on the outside perimeter of Baghdad International Airport, April 8, 2003. (Photo by Scott Nelson/Getty Images)

Brigadier General Lloyd Austin, General Buford Blount, and Colonel Jack Sterling on Easter Sunday 2003 in Baghdad. (General Blount's personal archive)

On Firdos Square in central Baghdad, in front of the Shahid mosque, a U.S. Marines tank helps the population to take down a statue of Saddam Hussein. (Photo by Patrick ROBERT/Corbis via Getty Images)

Private First Class William Mersereau of the HHC 2-69 AR Scout Platoon, 3rd ID, helps an Iraqi woman as troops assist in the distribution of household gas canisters in Baghdad, May 25, 2003. (Photo by PATRICK BAZ/AFP via Getty Images)

A soldier reads a letter included in a long-awaited care package from home. Delivery of mail to U.S. troops was a logistical challenge but also an important morale booster. (General Blount's personal archive)

Republic Bridge over the Tigris River after the thunder runs. Highways in and out of Baghdad served as transportation conduits even as troops fought on them. (General Blount's personal archive)

A memorial to Private Gregory Huxley, who was killed when a rocket-propelled grenade penetrated the M113 personnel carrier in which he was riding. (General Blount's personal archive)

Memorial service in Baghdad for fallen 3rd ID soldiers. The division lost 44 soldiers, with more than 300 wounded. (General Blount's personal archive)

Infantry soldiers shifting from desert warfare to clearing a jungle-like area along the Tigris River. The palm trees and lush greenery were a jarring contrast to the brown dry desert conditions U.S. soldiers experienced during the attack into Baghdad. (General Blount's personal archive)

Iraqis look on as U.S. Army soldiers keep watch after an attack killed one U.S. soldier and wounded five others on June 5, 2003 in Fallujah. The 3rd ID moved into the town in an effort to quell anti-American attacks in the area. (Photo by Mario Tama/Getty Images)

General Blount leads a group of soldiers back from Iraq on August 22, 2003, at Fort Stewart in Hinesville, Georgia. Blount returned with the division's colors, signaling the return of most of the unit based at Fort Stewart. (Photo by Erik S. Lesser/Getty Images)

General Blount (left) and Lieutenant General David Mc Kiernan, commander of all coalition ground forces in Iraq, walk in front of Iraq's Hands of Victory monument as they tour territory captured by the Army during the U.S.-led war against Iraq. (Photo by Rick Loomis/Los Angeles Times via Getty Images)

General Blount gives up command of the 3rd ID in 2003. The change of command ceremony was held at Fort Stewart, the division's home in Georgia. (General Blount's personal archive)

Iraq, 2003

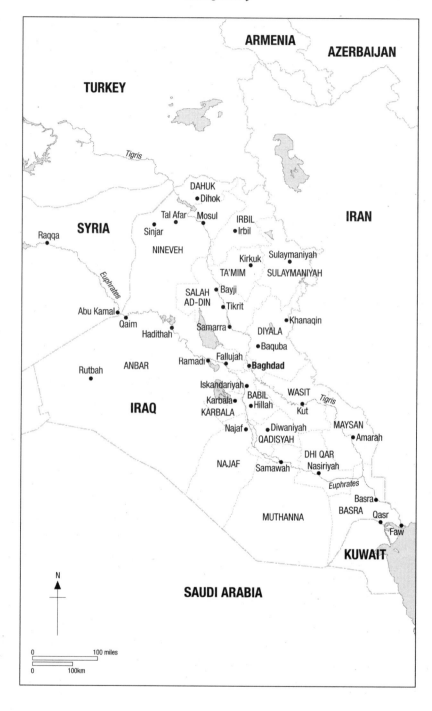

COALITION ATTACK ON IRAQ, MARCH 20–APRIL 9, 2003

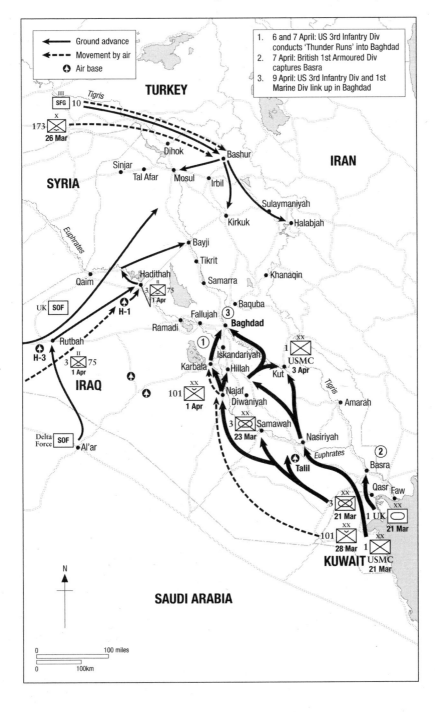

Ground advance
Movement by air
Air base

1. 6 and 7 April: US 3rd Infantry Div conducts 'Thunder Runs' into Baghdad
2. 7 April: British 1st Armoured Div captures Basra
3. 9 April: US 3rd Infantry Div and 1st Marine Div link up in Baghdad

TURKEY

IRAN

SYRIA

Tigris

SFG 10

173   26 Mar

Dihok   Bashur

Sinjar   Tal Afar   Mosul   Irbil

Sulaymaniyah

Kirkuk   Halabjah

Euphrates

Bayji

Qaim   Hadithah   Tikrit

Samarra   Khanaqin

UK SOF   H-1   75   1 Apr

Baquba

Fallujah   ③ Baghdad

Ramadi

H-3   Rutbah   75   1 Apr   Iskandariyah   1 USMC 3 Apr

Karbala   ① Hillah   Kut

IRAQ   101   1 Apr

Najaf   Tigris

Delta Force SOF   Diwaniyah   Amarah

Al'ar   3   Samawah   23 Mar

Nasiriyah

Talil   Euphrates   ② Basra

Qasr   Faw

3   21 Mar   1 UK   21 Mar

101   28 Mar   1 USMC 21 Mar

KUWAIT

N

SAUDI ARABIA

0   100 miles

0   100km

Introduction

Somewhere in the middle of the Kuwaiti desert, it was ten minutes to four in the morning when General Buford "Buff" Blount, commander of the U.S. Army's 3rd Infantry Division, rolled over in his bed and looked at the clock. President George W. Bush was set to go live on television at 4am Kuwait time and deliver an ultimatum to Saddam Hussein. Blount jumped out of bed, realizing he had overslept. He had set an alarm, or thought he had, but if he had set it, it had failed to wake him up. Blount dressed quickly and made it into the command center right at four as the broadcast began. ABC's Ted Koppel was there waiting for him. Koppel was in Kuwait on assignment, embedded with the division, and Blount had invited him to watch Bush's address with him at division headquarters. "General, I thought you were going to miss it," Koppel remarked as Blount sauntered into the room. Blount smiled as he stood in front of the TV. Not a chance would he have missed it. His entire military career had led him to this moment, and the president's words would determine what came next for Blount and his soldiers.

The day was March 17, 2003, and Bush's ultimatum demanded that Hussein leave Iraq within 48 hours or U.S. troops would invade. If it came to that, the 3rd Infantry Division (3rd ID) would lead the invasion as the "tip of the spear" that was U.S. land forces. The entire division was in Kuwait, and for six months, the soldiers of the 3rd ID had trained for a war in the Middle East. Before arriving in the Middle East, units had completed rotations at the National Training Center in the California desert.

Even before invasion orders came down, Blount knew that the operation was imminent. Units had cut back on their training so as to not put more wear and tear on their tanks and Bradley fighting vehicles. Soldiers knew what it meant, and they had begun to get anxious. Then the 101st and 82nd Airborne divisions started arriving. General David McKiernan, commander of Third Army Combined Forces Land Component Command (CFLCC), which would oversee Army actions in Operation *Iraqi Freedom*, called Blount and told him that 3rd ID soldiers had to move out of their camps to make room for the airborne units. Blount initially balked at the order. The camps had hot water, showers, and dining facilities offering three meals a day. Soldiers slept on cots in tents that had real wooden floors. As far as they were concerned, they had been in Kuwait for half a year, and these were their quarters. Some of Blount's soldiers suggested that the new arrivals go sleep in the open desert to get used to their surroundings.

But Blount understood why McKiernan had ordered the 3rd ID to move out. CFLCC wanted the division to get into tactical mode, ready to attack. 3rd ID units moved closer to the Iraqi border where their attack positions would be. Tension was high as Blount's soldiers left the camp and headed for the border. They knew it was only a matter of time before President Bush gave them the go-ahead to start rolling.

Air Force commanders had pushed for two weeks of "shock and awe" air strikes before the ground invasion began, but Blount disagreed. He advocated for air strikes and the ground invasion to occur simultaneously. Blount's soldiers were trained and ready to go. The days would get hotter the longer they waited, and air strikes would tip off the Iraqis that the 3rd ID was coming, eliminating any element of uncertainty or surprise. Air strikes were akin to announcing that the U.S. was about to invade.

What's more, Blount had observed Operation *Southern Watch* closely from his office in Riyadh, where he had been program manager for the Saudi Arabian National Guard modernization project. For more than a decade, since the end of the first Persian Gulf War, Operation *Southern Watch* consisted of joint U.S. air patrols enforcing the no-fly zone over southern Iraq. A two-star Air Force general had been in charge of the operation from Riyadh, and Blount met with him weekly. The Air Force general explained which targets were priorities and which they'd hit that particular week. Military sites and communications centers were the primary targets during *Southern Watch*, the same targets Air Force planners proposed to hit at the start of Operation *Iraqi Freedom*, but Blount knew U.S. missiles had probably already taken them out or caused them to move.

Targets of *Southern Watch* had been structural, but the new air attack would hit human ones. The U.S. Defense Intelligence Agency (DIA) had created a deck of 52 playing cards, each one bearing a picture of one of Iraq's most wanted, all high-level Ba'ath Party officials and close advisors to Hussein. U.S. defense planners hoped to capture or kill everyone in the deck of cards, but no missiles fired had found any of them. They had all gone into hiding, and Hussein had ordered his palaces to be packed up and cleared out. If U.S. missiles had already hit the main military and communications targets, and all the Ba'athists were in hiding, Blount questioned what shock and awe would accomplish. United States Central Command (CENTCOM) and V Corps commanders eventually agreed, and they slated missiles to begin firing as the 3rd ID began its charge into Iraq.[1]

When it came time to cross the berm separating Kuwait from Iraq, Blount was confident in his commanders and soldiers. They had trained, choreographed, and rehearsed their operations for months. What awaited them across the border they didn't know, but they were as prepared for the contingencies of war as they could be. If the Iraqis fired on them, they had their armor. If Hussein unleashed chemical weapons on them, they had their chemical suits. The chance of dying exists for everyone about to enter a war zone, but the thunder of 10,000 vehicles as their engines roared to life and they moved into position offered what might have been a sense of comfort or assurance. Blount had told his soldiers that the way to get home was to get to Baghdad, and the road to Baghdad started at the berm.

The Making of a Seventh-Generation Soldier

When the Anglo-Saxon king Edward the Confessor died in January 1066, William, Duke of Normandy saw an opportunity to seize the English throne. That summer, he assembled his forces, drawing men from throughout Normandy, Brittany, and Flanders. Two brothers, one in William's navy and one in his infantry, carried the surname Blount. The Blount brothers landed at Sussex as part of the Norman invasion in late September, and they fought at the battle of Hastings as part of the Norman Conquest, which earned William the nickname "the Conqueror."[1] The two medieval soldiers named Blount were a branch on a family tree that became deeply rooted in military service and produced General Buford C. Blount III. On the Blount family crest is the motto "*Lux tua via mea*" – "Thy light is my way."

More than half a millennium later, Blount ancestors arrived in North America, and some of them settled in Duplin County, North Carolina. One was Warren Blount, Sr. Born in the 1750s, he served in the 6th Regiment of the North Carolina militia, three years as a sergeant, as part of the Continental Army during the American Revolution. When the war was over, Warren Blount received a payment of about 13 pounds sterling for his service in the militia, but it was only a partial payment. The government issued him an IOU in 1792, and, still waiting on payment three years later, Blount petitioned the court in Duplin County for his remaining pay.[2] Like many soldiers of the Continental Army, he had to demand payment from a cash-strapped government struggling to find its financial footing after the war.

Meanwhile, in the 1760s in Ireland, the Hathorn brothers made the decision to go to America, where they set down another set of Blount's ancestral roots. The three young men secured passage on a ship bound for South Carolina, and from there, they trekked to Georgia in search of work. As they moved farther south, they encountered General Andrew Jackson's troops marching out of Spanish Florida. The brothers joined the unit, and as the soldiers passed through Mississippi, the Hathorns fell in love with the territory's wild beauty. Choctaw and Chickasaw tribes still controlled most of the land at that time. After fighting in the battle of New Orleans, the final contest of the War of 1812, the brothers returned to Mississippi and stayed.[3]

Warren Blount's five sons also served in the War of 1812, mustering into regiments of the North Carolina militia as their father had during the American Revolution. One of the sons, Edmund, married a woman from Indiana after the war, and the couple settled in the new Mrs. Blount's hometown of Posey. It was there that William Blount was born in 1817. As a young man, William took a raft down the Mississippi River to get in on the cotton boom as the U.S. federal government dispossessed tribes from their land and pushed them west of the river. English textile factories drove the U.S. cotton economy, and Mississippi's fertile soil and proximity to ports at New Orleans and Mobile made the area important to that trade. William Blount eventually established the town of Blountville in what was then Lawrence County in the south-central part of Mississippi. In the late 19th century, a land speculator named Prentiss Berry offered to sell his land for a railroad to be built through the area if officials agreed to change the town's name to Prentiss.[4]

William Blount was in his early 40s when the Civil War erupted, and he enlisted in the summer of 1862 when he was 44. He was mustered into Company D of the Covington Farmers, a militia raised in Covington County. Blount's 15-year-old son, Thomas

Cupit Blount, also joined the Confederates, serving as a private with the 1st Regiment of the Mississippi Light Artillery. He was discharged in July 1862, just three months after he enlisted, but he joined up again in 1863 and served as a private in Company B of Yerger's Regiment of the Mississippi Cavalry. The unit surrendered at Citronelle, Alabama, in May 1865, and Blount and other soldiers in his unit were held prisoner for a time at Ship Island off the coast of Mississippi. Thomas Blount, along with his father and the captain of his unit, signed loyalty oaths to the United States so that Union troops would release them.

The "B" in B Company was for Nathan Barnes, the company captain. Barnes had been born in Georgia but migrated to Mississippi and settled in Covington County. His daughter, Amelia, captivated the young Thomas Blount, and after the war, he asked his former captain for Amelia's hand in marriage. Barnes agreed, and the couple wedded. Thomas and Amelia remained in Covington County and had five children before Amelia died.

Estes Nathan Blount, General Buford Blount's grandfather, was born to Thomas and Amelia Blount in 1874 and carried the Blount family's military tradition into the 20th century. Estes was in medical school in Tennessee when war broke out in the Philippines in 1899. U.S. forces had defeated Spain the previous year, and Filipino insurgents who had fought alongside the Americans against the Spanish assumed independence would be their reward. When American troops remained on the islands after the war ended, the Filipinos who had fought the Spanish went to war with them. The war lasted until 1902 and made the Philippines a U.S. colony, an arrangement that lasted until the end of World War II.

Since he had medical training, Estes Blount became a captain with the U.S. Army Hospital Corps. He contracted tuberculosis while in the Philippines but survived the illness. When his service was up, Blount returned to Mississippi and settled in the small town of Bassfield in Jefferson Davis County. Bassfield, a cotton farming community, was a stop on the Mississippi Central Railroad that connected the lumber town of Hattiesburg to Natchez on the Mississippi River. Estes Blount married Leola Hathorn, a descendent of the Irish Hathorns who had sailed to the U.S. and fought in the War of 1812, and set up as the town doctor.

Two of Estes Blount's sons, Robert Estes Blount and Buford Charles Blount, carried on the family's military lineage. Robert, the older of the two, enlisted in the Army in the 1930s after earning his medical degree from Tulane University in New Orleans. He served as General Douglas MacArthur's doctor in World War II and rose to the rank of major general. After 36 years of service, Robert Blount left the Army but continued practicing medicine and eventually became the dean of the University of Mississippi Medical Center.

The younger Blount brother, Buford Charles, was a student at Millsaps College in Jackson when Japanese bombers attacked Pearl Harbor on the morning of December 7, 1945. He joined the Army, became a pilot, and was assigned to the Army Air Corps 13th Troop Carrier Squadron in the South Pacific. The "Thirsty 13th," as the unit was nicknamed, arrived at New Caledonia in time to support U.S. Marines in the Guadalcanal campaign. The unit's C-47 planes supported American soldiers in additional battles in the Northern Solomon Islands, New Guinea, and the Philippines. In a story that could be straight out of James Michener's *Tales of the South Pacific*, Blount used his plane to make a liquor run for one of the island camps. He did not imbibe, but he did a favor for some of his fellow soldiers who enjoyed the sauce.

While in flight training, Blount also used his C-47 to impress a girl back home. He was smitten with Cecil Dickson, a young woman who had grown up around the corner from him in Bassfield. Cecil and her mother, Beulah Dickson, were college-educated women who had attended the University of Southern Mississippi. Hoping to get Cecil's attention, Blount buzzed the town's Main Street, soared past the water tower, and accidentally grazed some pecan trees as he put on his one-man air show. When he came home from the war, Buford Charles proposed to Cecil in July 1945. She said yes, and they married in December of that year.

His ancestors had mostly settled into civilian life after their tours of military service, but Buford Charles Blount made his career in the military. He and Cecil raised six children as they moved through the U.S. and the world following Blount's assignments. Not only did Blount serve in World War II, but he also fought in Korea and Vietnam and was the deputy base commander of Keesler Air Force Base in Biloxi, Mississippi, when he retired as a colonel. The family built a house in Bassfield in 1971, and Blount entered local politics. He was elected mayor of Bassfield in 1973 and served nine terms, earning the distinction of being the longest serving mayor in Mississippi when he died in 2009.

From this lineage came the man who would lead the U.S. Army's 3rd Infantry Division into Baghdad in the spring of 2003. Buford Charles Blount III was born in Texas in 1948, the second of Cecil and Buford's six children. The younger Buford, known as Buff, spent his high school years in London and attended London Central High School, a U.S. Defense Department school for American students. The day after he graduated, he hopped on an Air Force C-130 bound for Charleston, South Carolina, and then caught a Greyhound bus to Hattiesburg, Mississippi, to begin his studies at the University of Southern Mississippi. He enrolled in the Reserve Officers' Training Corps (ROTC) program there, carrying on the Blount family military legacy that dated back to the battle of Hastings and made him a seventh-generation soldier.

When Blount was at Southern Mississippi, he had his eye on his lab partner, an attractive divorcee who did not reciprocate the interest. Blount kept trying, if for no other reason than to borrow her class notes. One evening, in need of notes, Blount walked to the home economics house on campus where his lab partner lived. When he entered the house, he saw Anita, a petite brunette, and it was love at first sight.

They wasted no time starting their life together, marrying in 1969 when he was 20 and she was 22. Blount's mother had to sign their marriage license since he wasn't 21 yet. Anita also graduated in that year and stayed on at Southern Mississippi working on a master's degree and then as a home economist for the Mississippi Power Company. Later, she earned a master's degree in early childhood education. Blount graduated in 1971, the same year their first child, Wendy, was born. A second daughter, Megan, arrived in 1974 while the family was stationed in Germany.

It was a happy time for Buff and Anita, but it was marred by tragedy in Blount's extended family. In October 1972, Buff's brother David, the fourth of the Blount siblings, was killed in a car wreck. He was 20 and a student at the University of Southern Mississippi, and he had been driving on a local highway with his 19-year-old wife, Marsha, when his car collided with a truck. A Rescue 7 helicopter airlifted them to Forrest General Hospital in Hattiesburg, where David was pronounced dead. Marsha lay in critical condition but eventually survived her injuries.[5]

Buff Blount, an Army lieutenant at that point, was going through chemical warfare training in Garmisch-Partenkirchen, Germany. Located in the Bavarian Alps, Garmisch-Partenkirchen was known for its skiing, and on a Saturday evening, Blount had just come off the slopes when he got the call about David. He immediately arranged a transport home. Blount Sr. had instilled a strong sense of connection and love in his family. Throughout the years on the road as a military family, all they had was each other. When one of their own was taken from them, their natural reaction was to come together and hold one another in their sorrow.

When Blount's assignment in Germany was up, he and Anita and the girls returned to the U.S., where he was to command two companies at Fort Polk, Louisiana, and a third command of a separate armored cavalry troop at Fort Benning, Georgia. From Fort Benning, the Army sent Blount to the Command and General Staff College at Fort Leavenworth, Kansas. Upon completion of the program in 1984, Blount had the opportunity to choose his next assignment. On the list was Saudi Arabia, and it sounded interesting to him. He had grown up traveling the U.S. and the world as his family followed his father's military postings, and going to Saudi Arabia would be another adventure. Blount discussed it with Anita first, as their marriage was always a partnership, and she was game. The move set Blount on a path that defined much of his military career and set him on the road to Baghdad long before invading Iraq was a U.S. strategic focus.

The Arabist: Blount in Saudi Arabia

U.S. oil companies had been paying attention to the Kingdom of Saudi Arabia since oil was discovered there in the 1930s. Diplomatic relations, as well as military and economic ties, between the U.S. and Saudi Arabia date back to World War II. In 1944, Saudi Arabia sent its first diplomatic representatives to the U.S., and the two countries established the Arabian American Oil Company (ARAMCO). The following year, U.S. President Franklin D. Roosevelt met Saudi King Abdul Aziz ibn Saud for the first time aboard the USS *Quincy* in the Suez Canal. The meeting resulted in an agreement wherein Saudi Arabia promised to fund Western-supported insurgencies and political movements throughout the Third World in exchange for U.S. military protection against regional threats. Among the terms of the military agreement was a provision for modernizing the Saudi Arabian National Guard.[1]

Not long after World War II ended, the U.S. began getting involved in Middle Eastern affairs. Oil access and concerns about regional security as Britain reduced its commitments in the area motivated U.S. policymakers to pay attention to the Middle East. U.S.–Saudi relations solidified in 1945, and the U.S. recognized Israel upon its founding in 1948. When Iranian Prime Minister Mohammad Mosaddegh moved to nationalize Iran's oil, the CIA facilitated a coup against him that resulted in the installation of Shah Reza Pahlavi, a monarch friendly to the U.S. In 1956, the Eisenhower administration intervened in the Suez Crisis by threatening financial retribution against Britain and France for their attempts to occupy the Suez Canal, countering Egyptian President Gamal Abdel Nasser's announcement that Egypt was nationalizing the canal. The Suez Crisis signaled the end of Western Europe's primacy in the Middle East and America's ascendancy.

America's international relations included foreign military sales, which facilitated billions of dollars in contracts between foreign governments and U.S. companies. The Defense Department negotiated sales with foreign governments and then contracted with private firms to deliver goods and related training and technical assistance. During the early Cold War, the U.S. reserved foreign military sales contracts primarily for NATO and other "free world" allies, but by the 1970s, the Pentagon offered agreements to any friendly anticommunist government, including those in the developing world. The expansion of U.S. military sales to the Middle East and elsewhere in the Third World began during Richard Nixon's presidency. Earlier Cold War administrations had sold arms to foreign countries with minimal Congressional oversight, but in the 1970s, opposition to the executive "blank check" to wage war in Vietnam motivated some legislators to push for limits on the president's power to sell weapons. Yet central to the Nixon Doctrine was the idea that well-equipped allies were important components of U.S. security. As Vietnam War spending and production declined, U.S. arms manufacturers looked to the volatile Middle East for new customers. In May 1973, the Pentagon agreed to sell F-4 Phantom bombers and F5-E Tiger II supersonic jets to Saudi Arabia.[2]

Beginning in 1975, Vinnell Corporation contracted with the Department of Army Materiel Development and Readiness Command (DARCOM) to train and modernize the Saudi Arabian National Guard. The U.S. Army Office of the Program Manager–Saudi Arabian National Guard (OPM-SANG) was the military unit that worked with Vinnell on the Saudi guard project. In 1973, Crown Prince Abdullah entered into an agreement with the U.S. government to modernize the Saudi Arabian National Guard, and the Army established OPM-SANG as the arm through which to facilitate the partnership. Vinnell Corporation was a heavy contractor that ran dry dock facilities for South Vietnam and operated South Vietnamese and South Korean air bases and power systems. It did not get involved in tactical military training until the mid-1970s, when Vietnam veterans formed a pool of experienced military labor from which Vinnell drew employees willing to go to work in Saudi Arabia.[3] U.S. advisors employed by the Vinnell Corporation worked to train and equip the Saudi Arabian National Guard.[4] By 1982, Vinnell employees had organized and trained a mechanized infantry brigade consisting of four combined arms battalions as well as field artillery, logistical support, and combat engineer battalions. Vinnell also established the Guard's logistical and maintenance base.[5] It was not uncommon for foreign military sales contracts to include provisions for training, but OPM-SANG's contract between Vinnell and Saudi Arabia was the first to employ a contractor to directly train the troops using the equipment. Vinnell's hiring of Vietnam veterans was of interest to governments looking to employ counterinsurgency strategy and tactics in their approach to local opposition movements. Combat and counterinsurgency experience in Vietnam was a highly desirable qualification.

U.S. companies held contracts with every branch of the Saudi military by the end of the 1970s. In addition to Vinnell's contract with the Saudi Arabian National Guard, Bendix Corporation worked with the regular army, Lockheed and Raytheon contracted with the air force, and AVCO Corporation worked with the coast guard. By 1979, approved U.S. arms sales to the Saudi government approached $26 billion. Along with private contracts, the U.S. Army Corps of Engineers supervised 20 billion dollars' worth of construction projects in Saudi Arabia in 1979.[6] Saudi Arabia had contracted with Northrop for F-5 fighter jets as well as flight and maintenance training and supply support. Bendix entered into an eight-year contract to build and operate a logistics system for the Saudi Regular Army Ordnance Program.

A $755 million contract in 1977 between Northrop and Saudi Arabia was more expensive than all the contracts in 1975 combined.[7] In 1977, there were more than 2,000 American employees of private contracting firms working in Saudi Arabia. Saudi Arabia and Iran had entered into the largest contracts with U.S. firms, and the rise in oil prices in 1973 allowed the two oil-rich nations to be able to afford expensive contracts. With the British withdrawal of all points east of Suez beginning in 1971, U.S. security experts worried that the British exit would lead to instability. Loath to step in as a regional police force, the U.S. instead anointed Iran and Saudi Arabia the protectors of order and prioritized the two countries for defense contracts.

Defense contracts were broad in scope and went beyond the acquisition of military equipment. In 1982, a U.S. contract built the Saudi Arabian National Guard Hospital, a state-of-the-art 500-bed hospital and medical complex in Riyadh. Job advertisements sought experienced American nurses to move to Saudi Arabia and work in the new hospital. Benefits included free transportation, furnished lodging, 30 days' paid vacation, bonus pay, and bonus leave in exchange for a two-year commitment. Thousands of Americans lived and worked in Saudi Arabia as a result of contracting and related employment needs in the late 1970s and early 1980s.

In the mid-1970s, the Soviet Union, France, Britain, and West Germany all joined the U.S. in selling arms to Persian Gulf nations. With U.S. military involvement in Vietnam coming to an end, American defense analysts shifted their focus to the Middle East, where continued tension between the Arab states and Israel, as well as unrest in Iran and Afghanistan, made the region particularly volatile. Europe and Japan imported most of their oil from Persian Gulf nations, and the U.S. was an increasing buyer of Middle Eastern oil. During the early Cold War, America's primary interests in the Gulf region were supporting Shah Reza Pahlavi in Iran against Soviet communist expansion, strengthening ties with Saudi Arabia, and encouraging Britain to maintain a presence in the region. America's outlook began to change by the late 1960s, as détente made the Soviet Union seem like less of a threat to U.S. interests in the Gulf. At the same time, British Prime Minister Harold Wilson announced that his country would withdraw its military and political advisors from the area.[8]

Growing demand for oil increased the power of the Organization of Petroleum Exporting Countries (OPEC) and fueled the fires of nationalism that had already begun to burn throughout the Middle East. In 1971, OPEC successfully lobbied for a greater share of oil profits with oil companies and raised oil prices. Two years later, OPEC enacted an embargo against the U.S. and other nations for their support of Israel in the Yom Kippur War. Iran and Saudi Arabia were at the center of OPEC's assertion of power and control.

Americans saw stability in the Middle East as a key to ensuring the uninhibited flow of oil to Western customers. U.S. eyes remained on the Soviet Union, too, even in the era of détente. Selling arms and American training to Gulf states was a proactive measure against Soviet encroachment from land and sea on Middle Eastern oil. Saudi Arabia was rich in oil, but with a population of only about five million, it lacked the manpower to achieve an ambitious $150-billion development plan. In 1976, Iran, having enjoyed major backing from the U.S. for two decades, was the most powerful oil nation in the Middle East. As demand for oil rose and the Arab–Israeli conflict remained unresolved, Gulf states built up their arsenals in what some American observers considered a new arms race. Senator Ted Kennedy called for a moratorium on U.S. arms sales to Persian Gulf nations, arguing that if an arms race led to instability in the region, it could hinder the flow of oil to importing nations.[9]

Saudi Arabia's relationship with Iraq was unstable throughout the Cold War and into the post-Cold War era. In the 1960s and 1970s, Saudi leaders worried that Baghdad was offering clandestine support to groups that opposed the royal family and its interests. To counter perceived Iraqi threats, the Saudis strengthened ties with Syria, Iran, and Kuwait. Saudi's regional relations changed sharply in the wake of the Iranian Revolution. Concerned royals hoped to avoid a similar religious-influenced insurgency in their kingdom, and the Saudi government poured billions of dollars into Iraq during the Iran–Iraq War. Iraq's invasion of Kuwait in 1990 turned the Saudi–Iraq relationship adversarial again as Saudi leaders wondered if their kingdom was next on Saddam Hussein's list. Saudi Arabia was a main base for Operation *Desert Storm*, and the kingdom deployed Saudi combat units as part of coalition forces. Saudi authorities also allowed the U.S. military to use the kingdom's facilities and air space to enforce sanctions against Iraq from 1991 to 2003.

Throughout the 1960s and 1970s, Afghanistan, Iran, and Saudi Arabia faced clashes between modernity and traditionalism in their societies. When the Iranian Revolution erupted in 1979, it forced Gulf monarchs to take stock of their status and hold on their countries. If it could happen there, it could happen in Saudi Arabia or any other regional kingdom. A few weeks after Iranians seized the U.S. Embassy in Tehran in November 1979, members of a conservative Muslim organization called al-Jamaa al-Salafiya al-Muhtasiba (JSM) staged an armed takeover of the Grand Mosque in Mecca, Islam's holiest site. With 50,000 worshippers gathered at the mosque for early morning prayers, 200 JSM rebels brandished rifles, and their leader, 40-year-old Juhayman al-Otaybi, grabbed the microphone from the imam leading the prayers. He ordered his followers to shoot anyone who tried to escape the mosque. Fear rippled through the crowd as worshippers made sense of what was happening.[10]

Juhayman founded JSM in response to what he saw as the collapse of traditional Saudi values as a result of the consumerism that oil money enabled. He blamed the Saudi royal family for the kingdom's urbanization, more and more cars on the roads, and the loosening of social relations that saw men and women interacting in public. From his Bedouin home village in the center of the Arabian Peninsula, Juhayman developed a following as he preached against what he called the corruption and decadence of the royals. Having served in the Saudi Arabian National Guard, Juhayman was a trained soldier who put his military skills to work as he organized the seizure of the mosque. The day he chose to launch the attack on the Grand Mosque, neither Crown Prince Fahd bin Abdulaziz al-Saud nor Prince Abdullah was in the country. Local police dispatched a few officers to the scene, but they quickly retreated as bullets rained down on their cars. National Guard troops arrived next, but the rebels held them off. The insurgents eventually released most of the worshippers but continued to fight Saudi guardsmen and regular army soldiers for two weeks. The Saudi government sought help from French commandos who secretly entered the kingdom to offer hasty counterinsurgency training. In the end, tear gas and starvation forced Juhayman and 67 surviving militants out of the mosque and into police custody. They were all sentenced to death and beheaded in public squares throughout the kingdom.[11]

But the siege on the Grand Mosque achieved JSM's desired result. Saudi society turned sharply away from modernization and adopted ultraconservative mores. The royal family deferred to clerics on social issues and more forcefully emphasized sharia law throughout the kingdom.[12] Among those deeply influenced by Juhayman and JSM was a young man from a wealthy and well-connected family that had made billions in the Saudi construction industry. His name was Osama bin Laden.

Resistance from the left also challenged the Saudi royal family's hold on the country. Leftist Saudi expats founded Sout al-Taliah in 1973 with financial backing from Saudi students in the U.S. Sout al-Taliah opposed Islamic conservative social norms and demanded that a democratic political system replace the monarchy.[13] JSM's attack on the Grand Mosque, combined with regional unrest, motivated the Saudi government to bolster external and internal defenses. In 1981, representatives from Saudi Arabia, Kuwait, Bahrain, Oman, the United Arab Emirates, and Qatar founded the Gulf Cooperation Council (GCC). A year later, Saudi Prince Nayef bin Abdulaziz supported the creation of the Gulf Rapid Development Force to defend GCC member states.[14]

It was in this context that Blount took the assignment to be a combat arms advisor for the Saudi National Guard modernization program, OPM-SANG, which had its own foreign military sales contract with the U.S. government. Blount had just finished a graduate program at the Command and General Staff College at Fort Leavenworth, Kansas, in 1983, and the next step was to take an assignment. One of the slots available was the Saudi position, and Blount, a major at the time, took it. As the son of an Air Force officer, he had lived all over the world, and the assignment sounded interesting. Blount's wife, Anita, was supportive, and the couple decided to take on the adventure with their two daughters, who were ten and 12. It was a two-year assignment, which worked well for the family given Saudi social restrictions. The government did not allow Western teenagers to go to school in the kingdom for fear that they would influence their Saudi peers with Western culture, so the end of Blount's tour would come before his oldest daughter started high school.

A week before they were scheduled to depart for Saudi Arabia, the Blounts traveled to Washington, DC, for an orientation on the Middle East. An area expert from the State Department taught them about local customs and laws, and they learned a bit of Arabic. State Department officials also briefed them on regional hot button issues, especially regarding the Arab world's views on Israel. Media specialists ran through the different ways news outlets covered Middle East issues. Blount would eventually complete two tours with OPM-SANG, and during the second tour, he was also a military advisor to Crown Prince Abdullah, the commander of the guard.

When the Blounts arrived on the Arabian Peninsula, the desert heat hit them with an intense welcome. It took Anita's breath away as she stepped off the plane. It was nothing like the humid heat she was accustomed to in Mississippi. Saudi Arabia's heat was like a hair dryer on full blast. A car took the family to the American compound in Riyadh, the Saudi capital. All American employees of OPM-SANG lived there. A concrete wall surrounded the compound, and Saudi troops stood watch guarding it. As part of Saudi's foreign military sales case, the Saudi government paid for Blount's living arrangements, salary, benefits, travel, and family expenses.

Inside the compound, American mores ruled. Saudi nationals did not typically come onto the grounds. Women wore bathing suits at the pool, and there was a club on the property. A military chaplain held religious services on Fridays, although they were supposed to be kept secret. Most Westerners living in Saudi did not have access to Christian services, but the word got out that Sunday worship occurred in the U.S. government compound, and requests to attend flowed in. Each family in the compound received permission to invite one other family onto the compound for church, and those who came had to smuggle in their bibles in a purse or paper bag. The room where church was held also served as a community room, a theater, a library of VHS tapes, and a gymnasium for the children whose families lived in the compound. The compound itself spanned about four to five blocks, and children could run around or ride their bikes in relative safety. They had a spacious, comfortable house within the compound, and they felt safe. But there was a safe room with a bomb-proof door just in case.

What also made worship challenging was that Sunday was a regular workday in Saudi Arabia. The Muslim day of rest was Friday, so weekends were Thursday and Friday, and the American "weekend" was part of the work week. The different weekly schedule, along with the time change, made it challenging to communicate with offices in Washington, DC. Blount fielded a fair share of 2am phone calls on his weekends. It always seemed that crises happened in Washington on Friday afternoons, DC time.

Anita was a schoolteacher by trade, and she taught pre-school, kindergarten, and first grade at the international school in Riyadh. During Blount's second tour, she taught first grade. The school consisted of five two-story stucco buildings, and passage between the lower elementary building and other school buildings required walking outside, but rain wasn't a concern in the Arabian desert. The teachers were foreign nationals from the U.S., Canada, and other countries. Art teachers painted murals on the exterior walls, and student artwork decorated the hallways and classrooms. It was a well-funded, efficiently operated school with a cooperative faculty whose members worked well together despite their different nationalities and languages. Saudi Arabians were not allowed to attend.

Abiding by local customs was important to Blount, and he considered it central to his work. Only by immersing himself in local culture could he get to know the issues that affected Saudi Arabia's relations with its neighbors, the U.S., and the rest of the world. When the Blount family attended dinners at the homes of their Saudi associates, they followed the gender-segregated dining custom. Arriving at the home by car, the men entered the front door while women were escorted to the back. The men sat in the dining room while the women ate in a separate dining area. After the meal, the men retired to the front of the house for tea and coffee.

Equally tricky was reconciling Saudi dinner start times with the next morning's work start time. Anita Blount arrived at her school at six-thirty every morning, but when her husband received a dinner invitation, it often called for an 11pm start time, which would have them getting home at 3am. Knowing the Americans operated on a different time schedule, Saudi hosts usually adjusted the dinner and visiting time to accommodate the Blounts. It was all part of the family's immersion into Saudi culture, which the Blounts grew to love.

America's foreign military sales with Saudi Arabia also had a provision for Saudi officers to travel to the U.S. for military training and education. After completing an English language program in Saudi Arabia, the lieutenants and captains who passed then went to Army school, MP, Armor, Infantry, or Logistics in the U.S. on the Saudi government's dime. One or two highly qualified officers gained admission to the Command and General Staff College every year. The Saudi officers often brought their families with them, and there was the occasional Saudi baby born in a U.S. hospital.

One of the functions of the Saudi Arabian National Guard was to protect Crown Prince Abdullah. The complex and tangled family lineage of the Saudi royal family had the potential to pit brother against brother. Multiple wives of King Abdulaziz bore sons who later competed for ascendancy to the throne. Abdullah was the only son of King Abdulaziz and one of his wives, but Abdullah had seven half-brothers from Abdulaziz's favorite wife, Hussa bint Ahmed Al Sudairi. The half-brothers became known as the "Sudairi Seven" due to their link to the Sudairi clan of the Arabian desert. Competition over rights to succession made Abdullah worry that his half-brothers might attempt to push him out, so a special guard unit was created within the national guard for his security.

Abdullah functioned as the commander of the guard, and because of that, Blount developed a good relationship with him. The foreign military sales case that Blount managed gave him signature authority to enter into contracts for construction projects and equipment that Abdullah wanted for the national guard. It was a separate case from the one the Saudi secretary of defense had with the U.S. because the guard was a separate military force. Blount's group secured Abdullah's compound with the latest security technology and brought in Special Forces A-Teams to train his guards, building a 1,500-man security unit just for the crown prince.

Like Lawrence of Arabia, Blount developed a strong interest in the region. T.E. Lawrence, who attended Oxford University, wrote his senior thesis on the Crusader castles of Syria. Lawrence decided to go there and see the ruins for himself. Upon graduating from Oxford, Lawrence joined an archeological expedition to Syria sponsored by the British Museum. He spent time getting to know the villagers and tribal leaders he encountered and asked them about their families and their history. Conversations with locals instilled in Lawrence a respect for Arabs who desired independence from the Ottoman Empire.[15]

The dig ended with the outbreak of World War I in 1914, but the British Army sent Lawrence, by then commissioned a second lieutenant, back to the Middle East with an intelligence unit because of his experience in Syria. When a revolt against the Turks broke out on the Arabian Peninsula, Lawrence traveled there from Egypt to assess the situation. There he gained the trust of Faisal, son of Emir Hussein, mastermind behind the revolt. Faisal made Lawrence one of his most trusted advisors, and Lawrence, wearing the traditional robes of a sheik, attended tribal strategy sessions. He helped plan an attack on the Hejaz Railway, and the operation, launched in September 1917, killed 70 Turkish soldiers.[16]

Blount drove out to where the Arab attack on the Turkish train occurred. The remains of the train cars Lawrence and his Arab associates blew up lay in the desert, brittle and rusty. Before leaving the scene, Blount bent down and picked up a piece of the train track. He took it with him as a souvenir connecting him to a man who in some ways was his predecessor. Before going to Saudi Arabia, Blount read up on T.E. Lawrence, curious what he might learn from the Brit's experiences. While he was in Iraq, some of his superiors believed he may have gotten too close to the Arab world.

But Blount's job required it. On his first Saudi Arabian tour in the 1980s, the national guard recruited troops from the Bedouin tribes loyal to Abdullah, and the transition from tribal life to soldiering was a jarring one that required Blount's understanding. Lower-ranking U.S. officers who worked with Blount came in with gung-ho plans to train the new guardsmen to be killers, but Blount knew that the task began with small steps. In tribal life, some of the recruits had never put on boots or pants with a zipper. From what Blount observed, in the past the average Bedouin man had got up in the morning, drank a cup of coffee, and had a small breakfast of bread. He then left his tent to herd his sheep or goats, and that was his day. At dusk, the man returned to his tent, ate dinner, and went to bed. It was the same routine that had dictated the lives of their fathers and grandfathers and great-grandfathers and those before. Any deviation from that routine was new, not to mention the introduction of technology into their lives – not just weapons but computers and other mechanical devices armies use.

Yet now Blount and his team had to make them into soldiers. They built barracks with beds, which were foreign structures to the recruits who had grown up living in tents and sleeping on mats on the ground. Then they built homes for the recruits' families, complete with microwave ovens and other appliances, as well as toys for the children. But the items were strange and impractical to the locals, who needed to butcher their livestock, not heat up a frozen dinner. Abdullah wanted modern soldiers in his national guard, and that meant changing their ways of life as well as training them to use advanced weaponry.

Blount also served in Operation *Bright Star* in Egypt when he was a major and a lieutenant colonel with the 24th Infantry Division. Throughout the 1980s, the U.S. and Egyptian militaries conducted joint training exercises, and Blount went over with tank units deployed to train for war in the Middle East. *Bright Star* was the largest U.S. deployment to the region since World War II, and it originated in the Camp David Accords. The late-1970s peace negotiations that U.S. President Jimmy Carter facilitated between Egyptian President Anwar Sadat and Israeli Prime Minister Menachem Begin included a U.S. commitment of military aid to Egypt, and the *Bright Star* exercises were part of the aid package. Operation *Bright Star* also signaled America's emphasis on Middle East security given the Iranian Revolution and the Soviet invasion of Afghanistan.

Blount returned to the kingdom in 1997 for a second tour of duty, this time as program manager for the Saudi National Guard project. He'd gotten a call in the summer of 1997 asking if he was interested in returning to the Arabian Peninsula. At that time, some 40,000 Americans lived in Saudi Arabia, including 5,000 military personnel there enforcing a no-fly zone over southern Iraq to deter Iraqi and Iranian aggression against the Saudi kingdom. Congress noted that Saudi Arabia was "a strategic U.S. ally, oil supplier, and, as the largest purchaser of U.S. arms, commercial partner."[17] Abdullah assigned Blount a mentor, Sheikh Tuwaijri, who had been with the royal family since the crown prince was a child.

The Blounts' decision was not without risk. In November 1995, terrorists bombed the Saudi National Guard program manager's headquarters in Riyadh. The attack killed five Americans and two Indians and injured several others. Then, in June 1996, terrorists detonated a truck loaded with explosives and parked near Khobar Towers, a housing complex for U.S. troops stationed at King Abdulaziz Air Base in Dhahran. The bombing killed more than 20 Americans and injured nearly 500 people of various nationalities. A Congressional Research Service report from July 5 on the Khobar Towers attack concluded that it was an example of Islamic extremism opposing the Saudi royal family.[18]

Blount's first appointment to Saudi Arabia introduced him to a new world. His second stint put him on the Army Chief of Staff's radar screen and led to his taking command of the 3rd Infantry

Division. It was also during his second time in Saudi Arabia that Blount was promoted to the rank of major general. Having already spent two years in the kingdom, Blount didn't face the cultural learning curve that other generals had to overcome. When Blount arrived at Abdullah's palace, the crown prince greeted him warmly and commented that he was the only program manager to have served in the kingdom before. The two men quickly developed a good working relationship. Abdullah already trusted Blount; they got directly to work. As program manager, Blount supervised about 80 U.S. Army personnel and 100 civilians who worked for his office as well as administering the Vinnell contract of nearly 1,000 personnel.

Coordinating Abdullah's security meant that Blount always knew where Abdullah was. He had befriended the commander of the security brigade, and the commander kept track of where Abdullah was and kept Blount posted. When American diplomats realized Blount's proximity to Abdullah, they began reaching out to him when they wanted a meeting with the crown prince. Even President Bill Clinton sought Blount's help in bringing Arab leaders to the negotiating table regarding Israel. When Syrian president Hafez al-Assad refused to go to Camp David, Clinton asked Abdullah to intercede with the Syrian leader on America's behalf. Abdullah used Blount to send his feedback through diplomatic channels. Blount's relationship with Abdullah gave him diplomatic as well as military insights and let him in on the major international relations developments of the time.

Relationship-building in Saudi involved trips to the royal family's desert retreat. For about ten days to two weeks every year, Abdullah and his family went into the desert to commune with his tribal roots. They didn't rough it; hundreds of staff personnel set up large air-conditioned tents with elaborate rugs and large motor homes that amounted to a mobile palace. Living quarters included televisions among their amenities. Like any family on an annual camping trip, the Saudi royals engaged in friendly competitive games; Abdullah's game of choice was bocce ball. The winner of his tournament received a gold Rolex watch.

Blount went falcon hunting with Abdullah's brother and stayed in the royal camp. When General Anthony Zinni, commander of CENTCOM at the time, traveled to Saudi Arabia and visited U.S. ambassador Wyche Fowler, Blount arranged for them to join a royal falcon hunt. A bus took the Americans to the camp 150 miles into the desert, and royal staff set up large and well-equipped tents for each of the men. Falcon hunting in the Arabian desert was diplomacy, and Blount was the liaison between the Americans and some of the Saudi royals. Fowler usually contacted Blount if he wanted a quick audience with Abdullah. Blount realized that a key component to successful diplomacy was a sense of adventure, and if communing in the desert with Saudi royals or learning to hunt with falcons was what it took, he did it.

Frequent meetings between Abdullah and Blount gave the two men ample time to discuss politics. Blount's second assignment to Saudi Arabia was during the Clinton presidency, and the impeachment proceedings against him baffled Saudi leaders. They wanted Blount to explain why Americans would want to dethrone the most powerful man in the world when all the other heads of state had a secret girlfriend, or so they thought. In the kingdom, men had multiple wives. Saudi social conservatism did not govern the sexual dalliances of men in power.

They also talked at length about democracy. President Clinton's foreign policy centered on the expansion of democracy throughout the world, but Abdullah cautioned Blount that Western-style democracy would not work everywhere. There were other ways that leaders could respond to the needs of their constituents, Abdullah asserted. He used his kingdom as an example. Once a week, Abdullah opened his palace to the people, allowed 600 in, and shook the hands of everyone who came through. Blount observed the process wherein security guards screened each person, and scribes then wrote down the people's requests. Servants poured coffee and tea for those in the waiting area.

Some constituents came just to say hello and meet the crown prince. Many others made requests of all kinds. A Bedouin might need a new truck to replace one that broke down, or they might have a relative who needed cancer treatment, hopefully in the U.S. Blount saw more than one constituent read a poem they'd written for Abdullah or the country. Once a man came asking for a school bus. He needed a vehicle large enough to transport his 45 children.

Every week, a different group of 600 was allowed into the palace. Abdullah had Blount join him occasionally, and he insisted that Blount show up in uniform. The crown prince wanted his people to see that he had a good relationship with the U.S. military. Blount sat with Abdullah and shook hands with people, too. Some of Abdullah's associates teased Blount, telling him he should ask Abdullah for another wife since he didn't have sons with Anita. When Blount told her, they both had a good laugh and understood the joke as a way of breaking the cultural ice.

Abdullah valued Blount so much that he didn't want the general to leave when his two-year term was up. The crown prince called Vice President Al Gore and told him he wanted to keep Blount in Saudi Arabia. A few days later, Blount got a call from Army Chief of Staff Eric Shinseki asking him to stay. Blount gave the answer he was supposed to give, which was "Yes, sir," and he ended up staying in Saudi Arabia through 2001. During that time, he was promoted to the rank of two-star general, and Abdullah and Anita pinned on his second star.

Shinseki wanted to see a new light-armored vehicle that Blount and his team had trained Saudi guardsmen to operate, so he took a trip to Saudi Arabia while Blount was there and was impressed by what he saw. Because guardsmen needed to move around the kingdom quickly, they needed a light vehicle. Shinseki wanted to shift U.S. armor away from heavy tanks and toward lighter armored vehicles. Tanks were already 65 tons; any heavier and some bridges and roads might not be able to support them. It would require larger airplanes to carry larger tanks. Plus, U.S. military technology had developed to where some war planners believed intelligence and new missiles should destroy enemy tanks and vehicles, eliminating the need for head-to-head combat between tank units.

Blount had the test case for light armor in Saudi Arabia. The vehicles, a newer generation of the Marine Corps light armored vehicle (LAV), had been designed by Americans and were tested in the U.S. before being shipped to the Arabian Peninsula for guard training exercises. When Shinseki saw what the Saudi National Guard did with the new light vehicles, he knew he wanted that same things for the U.S. Army. The Army ended up going in the direction Shinseki had envisioned but with a different vehicle, yet the chief of staff remained impressed by Blount's work. While in Saudi, Shinseki and Blount talked at length about the future of U.S. armor and the possibilities of what lighter vehicles could accomplish in a war zone. The two men hit it off and quickly developed mutual respect.

It was a fortuitous meeting for Blount's career. One of the Army chief of staff's responsibilities was to select division commanders, and Shinseki chose Blount to command the 3rd Infantry Division. The 3rd ID focused on desert warfare, and not only had Blount spent years leading military training exercises in the Arabian Desert, but he also had imagined how he would conduct an invasion of Iraq if ever he had the opportunity. He had a large map of the Middle East hanging in his office in Riyadh, and he often stood at it and thought about how he would lead an armored division all the way to Baghdad. Blount wargamed an operation in his head. It was the kind of thing he had done when he commanded the 64th Armor Regiment of the 3rd ID in Germany. When he wanted to wargame an operation against the Soviet Union, he drove an Army vehicle out to a possible invasion point and thought about where to position his tanks.

Baghdad was on his mind during his second Saudi appointment because the first Gulf War had occurred but Saddam Hussein was still in power. From Blount's perspective, it wasn't out of the realm of possibility that the U.S. would invade Iraq again. Operation *Southern Watch* was also happening, and the region remained volatile. Whenever he imagined the invasion, it always featured tanks in the lead, even after hearing Shinseki's vision for light armor. Tanks had intrigued Blount since he was a boy, and by the time he was a general, he knew about their strength and lethality.

It was August 2001 when Blount learned he would take command of the 3rd ID. He met with Shinseki at the Pentagon, and as the men talked, Shinseki told Blount to prepare his division for war. Members of the Bush administration were convinced that Saddam Hussein had weapons of mass destruction and the capability to build more, even though UN weapons inspectors returned from Iraq with inconclusive reports. By not removing Hussein from power during the first Gulf War, the U.S. had not finished the job. Now it was looking as though Blount's 3rd ID might have the chance to complete the mission sometime in the near or distant future.

About a month later, Blount attended a command training event at the Air War College in Montgomery, Alabama. Blount was one of the only two-star generals in a room with many more three- and four-stars. During one of the sessions, representatives from the Army, Navy, and Air Force discussed possible scenarios in a war involving India and Pakistan. There was a projector and a screen that the presenters used to show PowerPoint slides related to the discussion. Abruptly, the projector operator switched the view to a video of the Twin Towers. Those in the room through it was part of a wargaming scenario. Then an airplane hit; later the attendees learned it was the second plane to hit the towers. The projector operator called out that it was a live broadcast, not a simulation. The day was September 11, 2001.

3

War Planning

Before Iraq was Iraq, it was Mesopotamia. The fertile crescent, blessed with the waters of the Tigris and Euphrates rivers, was home to some of the earliest known human civilizations. Engineers developed irrigation techniques that allowed communities to harness the waters of the two great rivers for agriculture, and successful harvests extended the lifespans of ancient Mesopotamians. Scribes developed the cuneiform script, using reeds to write on wet clay that dried into tablets in the desert sun. Inventors designed the wheel, used at that time to make pottery, but then revolutionizing travel, manufacturing, and movement. Great buildings like the temple at Uruk, dedicated to the goddess Inanna, were at the center of Mesopotamian cities and showed the architectural and construction skills of the locals.

Kingdoms such as Sumer, Akkad, and Babylon controlled Mesopotamia. King Hammurabi of Babylon wrote down one of the first known law codes, setting a precedent for how subsequent kingdoms and governments theorized about law and order. Hammurabi's code told the story not just of his laws but of Babylonian society and culture. Free people owned slaves, and slaves were valuable property under the law. Babylonians cared about property rights, and laws admonished those who violated their neighbors' property, whether intentionally or due to carelessness. It was a society that held men in higher regard than women and abhorred adultery. Laws dealing with extramarital dalliances punished women more harshly than men, often with the penalty of death. Throughout the course of thousands of years, empires rose and fell, communities sustained themselves, scientists developed advances in medicine and chemistry, universities educated the elite, and writers told stories that remain classics of world literature.

Baghdad rose to prominence during what scholars refer to as the golden age of Islamic civilization. After the Abbasid Caliphate deposed the Umayyads and took control of a vast Muslim empire that stretched from Persia to Spain, caliph al-Mansur "The Victorious" chose Baghdad to be the capital of his dynasty in 762. The city became a cosmopolitan hub of intellectual exchange. Muslim, Christian, and Jewish scholars discussed philosophy, religion, history, and literature in the public square and in the House of Wisdom, a library and research center. It was here that Muslim scholars translated philosophical texts from China, India, and Greece into Arabic. Mathematician al-Khwarizmi, known as the father of algebra, served as the head of the House of Wisdom, beginning in 820. Astronomers studied eclipses, the rotation of the planets, and attempted to calculate the circumference of the earth. Chemists such as Jabir ibn Hayyan and others pioneered chemical processes including distillation, which turns crude oil into fuel, makes water potable, and creates alcoholic beverages. In 1227, Abbasid leaders established Mustansiriya University in Baghdad, one of the oldest universities in the world still operating.

Travel writers took note of Baghdad's location between the Tigris and Euphrates rivers, deeming it an oasis in the desert. Mukaddasi, a 10th-century Arab geographer, noted that Baghdad's "winds are balmy and its science penetrating," and those who settle in the city will be "surrounded by palms and close to the water." The rivers stimulated agriculture and commerce, and they served as natural barriers to invasion. Yakubi, another Arab geographer, predicted that Baghdad would become "the most prosperous city in the world" as a global crossroads linking Asia, Europe, and Africa.[1] The Mongols' siege of Baghdad in 1258 brought an end to the Abbasid Caliphate and absorbed the city into the vast Central Asian empire.

Baghdad later changed hands again, falling under Persian and Turkish control and remaining part of the Ottoman Empire until the end of World War I.

The British had been interested in the city since the mid-19th century. It remained a crossroads for trade, and the advent of the railroad promised to replace camel caravans with train cars. British investment in the Euphrates Valley Railway Company on behalf of the East India Company brought Europe into Mesopotamian affairs, an influence that would have far-reaching consequences for the future of Iraq.[2] During World War I, British Army intelligence officer T.E. Lawrence led an initiative to arm and train Arab rebels to fight against the Ottoman Empire. In exchange for putting their bodies on the line, British authorities promised to recognize Arab independence in former Ottoman lands after the war. British troops entered Baghdad in March 1917, seizing the city from the Ottoman Turks. While British military officers had promised to support Arab independence, British diplomats had made a secret agreement with their French counterparts to divide Ottoman territory into Allied zones of influence after the war. The Sykes–Picot Agreement gave Britain control of Mesopotamia, igniting the anger of the betrayed Arabs who had fought with the British.

Internal arguments among British authorities over local political administration added to the tension in Baghdad. Lawrence advocated for the appointment of Faisal, leader of the Arab revolt against the Ottomans, as king of an independent Arab nation. Faisal, his brother Abdullah, and their guerrilla army of Bedouin fighters, had been instrumental in disrupting Ottoman supply lines and stranding Turkish troops in the desert. British diplomats Percy Cox and Arnold Wilson disagreed with Lawrence, preferring to install a British commissioner in Baghdad with a cabinet of Arab ministers and British advisors. In 1919, Wilson declared that Iraqi tribal leaders desired British management of an independent Arab state, and the Paris Peace Conference solidified Britain's continued role in the region. The postwar mandate system put Sykes–Picot into practice, granting Britain control of Mesopotamia and Palestine. As a result, the Arab revolt that once targeted the Turks turned its attention to the British. Local leaders issued a fatwa against British rule and declared jihad against the foreigners.[3]

By 1921, British public opinion on continued involvement in Mesopotamia had soured. T.E. Lawrence himself wrote in the *Sunday Times* that the "people of England have been led in Mesopotamia into a trap from which it will be hard to escape with dignity and honour."[4] Dwindling public support combined with a tenacious Iraqi insurgency wore the British government down. On August 23, 1921, British authorities handed control over to Faisal, king of an independent Iraq. It was a beginning long in the making, but it was not the end of Iraq's problems. British cultural influence angered conservative elements of Baghdad society, and the wealthy and well connected flaunted their expensive clothes and extravagant leisure pursuits. In the 1930s, instability in Palestine spilled over into Iraq, and Iraqi nationalists protested British influence in the region, including the status of oil-rich Kuwait as a British protectorate.[5]

After World War II, the nationalism that swept the decolonizing world erupted in Iraq, and groups including communists, Ba'athists, and pan-Arabists vied for power in Baghdad. The Ba'ath Party was founded in Syria in 1947 and purported to combine elements of socialism, nationalism, and pan-Arabism. Ba'athists armed a militia and set out to depose Prime Minister Abd al Karim Kassem. In the 1950s and 1960s, brutal street fighting between rival political factions turned Baghdad into a dangerous and bloody city. Several failed coup attempts finally led to the Ba'athist takeover of Iraq in 1968. Ahmed Hassan al Bakr seized the presidency and appointed his cousin Saddam Hussein his deputy. Hussein used the Ba'athist security apparatus to increase his power over time, taking complete control of Iraq in 1979.[6]

Under Hussein's rule, Baghdad's story was a tale of two cities. On the surface, Baghdad symbolized the frenetic rush to show modernity and wealth that defined many a developing country. Lucrative oil revenue in the early 1980s sparked a construction revolution that brought office buildings, hotels, shopping centers, highways, and a new airport to the city. City officials designated older neighborhoods for redevelopment and annexed suburbs as Baghdad sprawled. A visitor to the city could not miss Hussein's cult of personality in the form of statues, his image painted on billboards and printed on t-shirts, and his name declared across radio airwaves. But the glare of the desert sun reflecting off the shiny glass of Baghdad's new architecture obscured a sinister subterranean security mechanism responsible for torturing and murdering Hussein's opponents. Agents of Hussein's special police force used electric shock, amputations, sleep deprivation, and other forms of physical and psychological punishment on detainees hidden deep within the heavily guarded presidential compound west of the city center. Death arrived quickly for the luckiest prisoners.[7]

Following the Iran–Iraq War, Hussein set his sights on Kuwait in 1990, and Baghdad suffered international retaliation. Bombs and cruise missiles fell on the city, destroying electrical power stations and communications networks, crippling factories and oil refineries, and damaging roads and bridges. UN postwar sanctions made recovery nearly impossible. Inflation rendered the dinar nearly worthless, and children died of malnutrition. Gangsters and thieves ran the streets of the poorest neighborhoods. Meanwhile, Hussein and his inner circle of family members and close associates enjoyed newly built palaces and yacht cruises on the Tigris and Euphrates. Baghdad had not recovered from the first Gulf War when the second one began in March 2003. When the 3rd ID stormed the city and toppled Hussein for good, the pent-up tension of more than two decades of his rule exploded in looting and petty destruction. Bringing order back to Baghdad was a top priority for the division after combat.

The U.S. had been concerned about Hussein's weapons of mass destruction since the late 1980s. Hussein had used them during the Iran–Iraq War, Iraq's "quagmire" like America's Vietnam and Russia's Afghanistan.[8] The Iran–Iraq War began in September 1980 when Hussein ordered six army divisions into southwestern Iran. Several factors informed Hussein's decision to invade. He believed Iran was weak in the aftermath of the coup that had deposed the Shah and installed the Ayatollah Khomeini. Hussein saw an opportunity to retake a stretch of borderland he had ceded to the Shah in 1975 in exchange for the Shah's promise that he would stop aiding the Kurds. Jordan offered the port of Aqaba as a staging ground, and Saudi Arabia and Kuwait agreed to provide financial support, so Hussein had regional backing.[9] Yet as confident as the Iraqi dictator seemed as he prepared for war, he was also worried. Khomeini's Iran was majority Shia, and Hussein was concerned that Iran's successful Muslim uprising would inspire Iraqi Shiites to fight to transform secular Iraq into an Islamic state. In August 1980, Hussein traveled to Riyadh and told Saudi King Khalid that he intended to wage a "military crusade" against Iran.[10] The combination of bravado and fear caused Hussein to launch his war against Iran with air strikes in September 1980. The UN Security Council called on both sides to cease fighting, but hostilities continued.

Saddam Hussein boasted to an Egyptian journalist that the conflict would be over in three months.[11] Three years later, troops were still fighting in 1983, and Hussein launched a chemical weapons campaign against Iranians. Mustard and nerve gas suffocated, burned, and blinded as many as 50,000 Iranian soldiers and civilians in nearly 200 chemical weapons attacks.[12] Hussein's own people were victims of chemical weapons attacks, too. When Kurds in northern Iraq joined forces with the Iranians in 1986, Hussein retaliated with poison gas attacks that killed an estimated 100,000 Kurds, mostly non-combatants, including women and children. The Kurdish town of Halabja stood as an example of the carnage. In March 1988, a coalition of Kurdish and Iranian forces drove Iraqi troops out of the town, but Hussein responded with a poison gas attack that killed 5,000 inhabitants. Most of the victims were non-combatants.[13]

Fighting continued, with the U.S., the Soviet Union, France, and China all getting involved via talks and weapons agreements. Donald Rumsfeld, President Ronald Reagan's special envoy to the Middle East, traveled to Baghdad three times and met with Hussein to develop diplomatic relations between Iraq and the U.S. American diplomats and Saudi officials also met and agreed to a plan to hit Iran's oil revenues by increasing Saudi oil output. Yet the U.S. also engaged in secret weapons sales to Iran beginning in 1985 in what came to be known as the Iran–Contra affair. Fighting continued, with Iran and Iraq both claiming victories and taking defeats, and the war ground to a stalemate. In July 1988, the Ayatollah Khomeini agreed to accept UN Security Council Resolution 598, which proposed a peace plan to end the war. Hussein eventually accepted the peace plan, and direct negotiations between the two countries began in August in Geneva. On December 29, a joint commission composed of Iraqi and Iranian representatives drew up an agreement to implement a cease-fire.[14]

Iraq emerged from the war deeply in debt. Hussein owed nearly $40 billion to Kuwait and the United Arab Emirates, and he tried to convince the leaders of those nations to cancel Iraq's debts since the fight against Iran was on behalf of regional security. When they refused, Hussein began threatening Kuwait, a rich but militarily weak country. At the same time, Hussein also accused the U.S. of conspiring with Israel to encourage Kuwait to lower oil prices, hurting Iraq's profit margin. President George H.W. Bush initially hoped diplomacy would work to calm relations between the U.S. and Iraq, and he sent Senator Bob Dole and a delegation of American lawmakers to meet with Hussein in April 1990. Later that summer, Bush sent a letter to Hussein affirming his intention to build better relations with Iraq.[15]

Despite those efforts, Iraqi troops invaded Kuwait on August 2. Republican Guard soldiers attacked Kuwait City, and Special Forces units seized Kuwaiti air fields and palaces. Kuwaiti royals escaped to Saudi Arabia as Iraqi forces rolled over Kuwaiti units. At the end of the month, Hussein proclaimed Kuwait a province of his country. In response, the UN issued an embargo and sanctions on Iraq, and Saudi Arabia allowed the U.S. to station troops in the kingdom out of concern that Hussein might come for the Arabian Peninsula next. The Bush administration assembled an international coalition that demanded Iraq's complete and unconditional withdrawal from Kuwait, but Hussein refused to budge.[16]

By the fall of 1990, Bush determined that the U.S. would lead an international coalition to expel Iraq from Kuwait by force if necessary. The UN authorized the use of force if Hussein did not remove his troops in 45 days. When the deadline passed and Iraqi units remained in Kuwait, coalition forces launched air strikes on January 17, 1991, signaling the beginning of the Gulf War. Land forces from more than 30 countries invaded and quickly liberated Kuwait City. On March 2, the UN put forth conditions for a cease-fire, including sanctions and the requirements that Iraq pay war reparations and return stolen property to Kuwait. Iraq also had to submit to weapons inspections.[17] President Bush had not included the removal or assassination of Hussein in his war plans because he assumed Iraqis, emboldened by the swift action of coalition forces, would do the job themselves. By the turn of the century, Hussein was still in power.

After the first Gulf War in 1991, UN weapons inspectors discovered and destroyed biological and chemical weapons caches, but inspectors left Iraq in August 1998 amid arguments between UN officials, the Bush administration, and Iraqis over whether more weapons of mass destruction (WMDs) existed. While the weapons inspectors did their work, the U.S., Britain, and, for a time, France, enforced no-fly zones in Operation *Northern Watch* and Operation *Southern Watch*. *Southern Watch* was planned and controlled by the U.S. Air Force Command Center a couple of blocks from Blount's office in Riyadh. Blount received weekly updates on targeting in Iraq. Both missions were aimed to protect Iraqi citizens from the Hussein regime and limit attacks on humanitarian relief efforts. *Northern Watch* sought to protect Iraqi Kurds, while *Southern Watch* focused on Shia Arabs concentrated in the south of Iraq. At the end of 1998, the U.S. and Britain launched Operation *Desert Fox*, which sought to prevent Iraq from developing or using more weapons of mass destruction.[18]

While the debate over Iraq's weapons raged, two terrorist attacks occurred that foreshadowed what would happen on September 11, 2001. In August 1998, Al-Qaeda operatives bombed the U.S. embassies in Kenya and Tanzania, killing more than 200 people in both cities. Two years later, the terrorist group attacked the USS *Cole* while it was docked at Yemen's Aden harbor to refuel. The attack killed 17 U.S. sailors and injured 37 more in the deadliest attack on a U.S. warship since an Iraqi aircraft bombed the USS *Stark*, a guided missile frigate, in 1987. Although there was no evidence that Saddam Hussein was involved in any of those attacks, U.S. defense authorities considered the Iraqi dictator a security threat in an already volatile region.

For some U.S. policymakers, the 9/11 attacks proved that terrorism was a real risk to American national security and heightened their fears that weapons of mass destruction could fall into terrorists' hands. This concern provided the justification for the Bush Doctrine, which asserted that preemptive action, including war, designed to prevent enemy attacks was defensible even if a clear and concrete threat was not imminent. Bush administration officials hoped that the UN Security Council would authorize Chapter VII action if the Hussein regime did not fully cooperate with UN weapons inspectors. Chapter VII of the UN Charter allowed the Security Council to approve use of force to combat a security threat not resolved by other measures. Bush's demands of Hussein went beyond weapons of mass destruction. He also wanted Hussein to stop supporting terrorists, stop persecuting Iraqi citizens, account for all Gulf War MIAs, and end illegal trade outside the Oil for Food program.[19] Oil for Food was a UN program established in 1995 allowing Iraq to sell oil on the global market in exchange for food, medicines, and other humanitarian aid Iraqi citizens needed.

The UN issued an ultimatum to Hussein in late 2002, threatening action if he did not comply with weapons inspections but stopping short of committing to Chapter VII action. Hussein had allowed weapons inspectors to return in 2002 under the threat of UN action, but the investigations found nothing. Still, for Bush administration hawks, the UN statement was not forceful enough. The president and his advisors decided to not request another UN resolution and instead acted alone. On March 17, 2003, Bush issued a new ultimatum to Hussein: Flee Iraq with your sons in 48 hours, or face U.S. military action.[20]

When planning for Operation *Iraqi Freedom*, U.S. strategists identified combat missions as well as postwar goals for dealing with issues following Hussein's ouster. Bush described America's objectives for an invasion of Iraq in his address to the nation on March 17, 2003. The first goal was to "tear down the apparatus of terror" by removing Hussein and his Ba'ath Party associates for good. After that, the U.S. would remain in Iraq to help local citizens build "a new Iraq that is prosperous and free." It would be a source of stability in the region, not a rogue state that made war with neighbors or harmed its own citizens. U.S. Central Command's Operation *Iraqi Freedom* campaign plan expressed the second goal as the creation of "a stable Iraq, with its territorial integrity intact and a broad-based government that renounces WMD development and use and no longer supports terrorism or threatens its neighbors."[21]

As a military goal, the objective of building a free Iraq would require troops to shift their outlook from combat to stability and support operations once they had fulfilled their combat mission. Military intervention would not end when the war was over as it had after Operation *Desert Storm*. That conflict had liberated Kuwait from Hussein's grip, but it was not a nation-building exercise. President George H.W. Bush had expected Iraqis to topple Hussein themselves and build a new nation on their own. Haunted by America's Vietnam quagmire, the first President Bush aimed to show that the U.S. military could fight quick and decisive wars that achieved clear objectives. Operation *Desert Storm* did that, allowing Bush to announce that the U.S. had "kicked the Vietnam War syndrome" and could still win wars.

While his father sought to not repeat the Vietnam War, George W. Bush's doctrine of preemption and regime change harkened back to U.S. intervention in Vietnam. The Vietnam War was a departure from America's use of the CIA and covert operations to force regime change during the Cold War. In Greece, Turkey, Iran, Guatemala, the Philippines, Cuba, Congo, Chile, and elsewhere, the U.S. had a hand in political upheaval, but in Korea and Vietnam, America fought hot wars with boots on the ground.

Nation building had been central to U.S. foreign policy at least since the late 19th century. After the Spanish–American War, the U.S. took control of the Philippines with the intention of developing democratic political institutions and grooming local leaders to eventually run the country. Filipinos who had fought Spain alongside the Americans had hoped that the U.S. would respect their desire for freedom after the war, but U.S. policymakers argued that Americans had to guide Filipinos to modern democracy. Angry Filipinos tried to resist U.S. intervention and fought a war to secure their independence, but U.S. troops subdued the insurrection, facilitating an occupation that did not end until 1946. Racist beliefs about Filipinos' capability to implement democracy on their own justified U.S. occupation, and U.S. policymakers saw the commercial and military advantage of having outposts in the Pacific en route to markets in Asia, especially China.

Beginning in 1915, the U.S. Marines entered into a nearly 20-year occupation of Haiti on behalf of American business interests there. Political instability, including assassinations and coups, sparked concerns among U.S. banking authorities who had approved loans to Haiti. Meanwhile, U.S. business leaders threatened to stop investing in Haiti if the political chaos did not end. Demonstrations had taken on an anti-American character as Haitians spoke out against U.S. businesses such as the Haitian American Sugar Company. U.S. President Woodrow Wilson authorized the Marines to invade Haiti in 1915, and Congress approved U.S. control of Haiti's government, economy, and military. U.S. occupation ended in 1934 as part of President Franklin D. Roosevelt's "good neighbor" policy toward Latin America.

After World War II, U.S. military forces occupied Japan and Germany with the mission of rebuilding former enemies as democratic capitalist allies. Between 1945 and 1952, General Douglas MacArthur led the U.S. occupying force in enacting sweeping changes to Japan's political system, economy, and military. The new Japanese constitution reduced the role of the emperor to a figurehead with no power, expanded the governing power of parliament, prohibited former military officers from holding political office, and guaranteed more rights for women. Economic restructuring included land redistribution to break up the landholding juggernaut of wealthy landowners and the elimination of business monopolies to integrate Japan's economy into the global capitalist market. Early occupation strategy called for disarming Japan, but by the end of U.S. occupation, concerns about Soviet and Chinese expansion led to remilitarization in 1954. As part of the agreement ending U.S. occupation, the U.S. retained military bases in Okinawa and Japan.

Plans for the postwar occupation of Germany developed out of agreements between the U.S. and the Soviet Union dividing the country into zones of occupation. In 1947, the U.S. government launched the Marshall Plan to pump billions of dollars of aid into Germany's Allied sector as well as Western Europe more broadly. Despite early postwar concerns about the potential security threat a remilitarized and reindustrialized Germany might pose, the U.S. invested in Germany's economy to prevent communism from taking hold as an alternative. The U.S. withdrew its occupying forces from West Germany in 1955 but continued to operate military bases there. Tensions between the U.S. and the Soviet Union ensured that Germany remained divided until the end of the Cold War.

Efforts to maintain a balance of global power between the U.S. and Soviet blocs resulted in the division of Korea and Vietnam as well. In Vietnam, the U.S. entangled itself in a fighting and nation-building combo that revealed the challenges and contradictions in a foreign country's attempt to impose political control in another country through force. After the Geneva Accords partitioned Vietnam into two countries, the Vietnamese on both sides of the 17th parallel struggled to determine Vietnam's postcolonial future. U.S. political and military advisors traveled to Saigon to assess the situation in South Vietnam and figure out how Americans could help the South Vietnamese establish a stable non-communist nation that would be a U.S. ally. Early on, some advisors argued that U.S. intervention was a losing game, and deploying troops would enmesh the U.S. in a quagmire with no clear way of extracting itself on good terms. The conditions in Vietnam were complicated. Southern educated elites who opposed Hanoi-driven communism also bristled at the notion of a foreign occupying force or other outside intervention in Vietnamese affairs. Leaders in Hanoi contributed to the chaos by establishing the National Liberation Front, a communist insurgency in South Vietnam. In the 1950s, after the partition created South Vietnam, U.S. advisors placed their bets on a leader named Ngo Dinh Diem.

Responding to the 1964 Gulf of Tonkin incident, Congress issued what amounted to a blank check to President Lyndon Johnson to use military force in Vietnam. U.S. advisors had already been involved in nation building in Vietnam, supporting Diem as president of South Vietnam from 1956 until his assassination in 1963. Military and diplomatic officers, USAID workers, and NGO personnel attempted to develop South Vietnam's political institutions, modernize its agricultural sector, train its troops, and build public support for a non-communist government in Saigon. U.S. military personnel participated in the nation-building component in various ways. Counterinsurgency in Vietnam included Army and Marine Corps programs aimed at training local security forces at the hamlet or village level while also offering humanitarian assistance, often in the form of medical or engineering work. The Marine Corps Combined Action Program (CAP) assigned U.S. Marines to work with village militias against People's Liberation Armed Forces (PLAF) incursions. CAP fell under the "hearts and minds" umbrella of civic action programs the U.S. military conducted in South Vietnam as part of its counterinsurgency mission. Army medics administered vaccines and provided other forms of healthcare. Engineers built roads, bridges, schools, and hospitals. Military Assistance Command, Vietnam observed and analyzed the political mindsets of students, Buddhists, and activists to determine the potential for widespread support for the Saigon government. U.S. military intervention in Vietnam was all-encompassing and included not only a combat mission but also a nation-building objective.

Operation *Iraqi Freedom* was a throwback to the Vietnam War. Enshrined in the Bush Doctrine was idealism about America's ability to spread democracy that echoed President John F. Kennedy's worldview. Just as a Cold War consensus about the security threat communism posed had led to the Gulf of Tonkin Resolution authorizing military force in Vietnam, the threat of terrorism in the post-9/11 world united Congressmen and women across the aisle to grant Bush the authority to go to war against Iraq. As had been the case during the Vietnam War, State and Defense Department officials lacked clear plans for nation building even as U.S. forces won battles. Insurgencies in both Vietnam and Iraq made it difficult for Americans to maintain control and stability even as U.S. troops tried to win the hearts and minds of locals through civic action and other humanitarian assistance. Operational and political differences distinguished the war in Iraq from the conflict in Vietnam, but the ideology that the U.S. could build a democracy out of the rubble of war inspired action in both places.

Although U.S. forces did not take out Saddam Hussein in Operation *Desert Storm*, U.S. government officials had been plotting regime change in Iraq since the first Gulf War ended in early 1991. In the months following Operation *Desert Storm*, President George H.W. Bush authorized the CIA and Special Forces teams to develop relationships with oppositionists in Iraq and in exile to form a group that would remove Hussein from power. Among the CIA's contacts was Ahmed Chalabi, an Iraqi Shiite Muslim who had been living in exile since 1956. Chalabi was born in 1945 to a wealthy family in northern Baghdad. His family supported the government of King Faisal II, and when Faisal was assassinated on July 14, 1958, the family fled Iraq. Chalabi eventually earned degrees from MIT and the University of Chicago before entering the financial industry and founding Petra Bank in Jordan. Accusations of embezzlement and mishandling of money followed him for much of his adult life, and a Jordanian military court sentenced Chalabi to 22 years in prison for bank fraud, but he had already fled Jordan and never served his sentence.[22]

American policymakers were interested in Chalabi because he was a well-known oppositionist, and CIA agents saw him as a key figure around whom to rally opposition to Hussein and the Ba'athist regime. In June 1992, 200 Iraqi oppositionists met in Vienna and established the Iraqi National Congress (INC). Its mission was to overthrow Saddam Hussein, and the CIA would fund the group. That fall, the group met again, this time in Kurdish-controlled northern Iraq. During that meeting, INC members elected a three-member leadership council and a 25-member executive council. They also appointed Chalabi chairman of the INC and established an office in northern Iraq. Three main goals emerged from the meeting: the removal of the Hussein regime from power, the establishment of democracy in Iraq, and the placing of Hussein and his associates on trial.[23]

Although the INC appeared to be working toward its mission, relations between the CIA and Chalabi were often tense. Some agents accused the INC chairman of being difficult to work with and of not making good on promises to gather intelligence. CIA agents were especially interested in defectors from among Iraq's military officers, and while Chalabi had promised to deliver disaffected officers into the hands of the CIA, agents were disappointed in how few materialized initially. Agents also didn't like how much time Chalabi spent lobbying Congress. For his part, Chalabi refused to be under the thumb of the CIA. He was leading a political process aimed to improve his country; he was not simply a resource for U.S. intelligence agents. Despite the friction between Chalabi and CIA agents in Iraq, the agency's chief of the Iraq Operations Group knew that Chalabi was the best hope for making regime change happen in Iraq. Chalabi proved his diplomatic skills in 1994 when he brokered a cease-fire agreement between two warring Kurdish factions, the Kurdish Democratic Party (KDP) and the Patriotic Union of Kurdistan (PUK), in northern Iraq. Chalabi also worked to deliver more Iraqi officers and soldiers willing to talk to CIA agents.[24]

Relations between the CIA and Chalabi's INC began to deteriorate in December 1994 when the cease-fire between Kurdish parties collapsed and the INC moved on a plan to overthrow Hussein. Intrigue and sleights of hand created a confusing and complicated chain of events involving Americans, Iraqis, Kurds, and Iranians. Focused first on the conflict in northern Iraq, Chalabi tried to bolster the failing cease-fire by telling Kurdish associates that the U.S. supported an Iraqi opposition plan to attack the Hussein regime. Infighting in Kurdistan would interfere with that objective, Chalabi reasoned, and he reminded the Kurds that they all agreed on regime change. Chalabi had not cleared that conversation with his CIA associates, and when they found out, they admonished him for speaking on behalf of the U.S. government. To smooth things over, a State Department official met with KDP and PUK representatives in January 1995 and urged them to maintain the cease-fire. If they did not, the U.S. diplomat warned, the U.S. would stop enforcing the no-fly zone over northern Iraq. KDP and PUK leaders agreed to keep the peace. Not long after the meeting, CIA agents learned of a new INC plot to depose Hussein. An Iraqi intelligence agent outlined a plan for an attack on Hussein's compound in the small village of al-Ujah, just south of Tikrit. The Iraqi agent had heard that Hussein intended to relocate there out of concern for his safety in Baghdad. A military officer in the dictator's security detail had agreed to alert Iraqi intelligence when Hussein was leaving for al-Ujah, likely sometime within the first week of March. The CIA agent told the Iraqi counterpart that the U.S. would neither fund nor participate in any coup or other action against Hussein. U.S. officials held firm to the belief that regime change would be most effective if carried out solely by Iraqis.[25]

Chalabi was involved in the al-Ujah plan, but he did not think it was enough to try to capture Hussein at his residence. He believed the plan required coordinated antigovernment uprisings in Mosul and Kirkuk, as well as in Shia-dominated southern Iraq. Chalabi also wanted to involve Iraq's Shia neighbor, Iran, not least because Iraqi Shia exiles were there. Conditions in northern Iraq worsened in February and March 1995 as Turkish forces moved to the border with Iraq and tensions between the KDP and PUK escalated. CIA agents in the region learned that Turkey was planning counterinsurgency measures against another Kurdish group, the Kurdistan Workers Party, a terrorist organization. Meanwhile, a CIA agent in southern Iraq met with a representative of the Supreme Council for the Islamic Revolution in Iraq (SCIRI) to discuss Shia attitudes towards the al-Ujah plan.[26] SCIRI was founded in 1982 in Iran to counter Iraqi aggression during the Iran–Iraq War.

After the war, the group attracted Iraqi oppositionists seeking to overthrow Saddam Hussein. Funded by Tehran and armed by Iran's Revolutionary Guard, SCIRI had recruited thousands of Iraqi Shia exiles and signed agreements with both the PUK and the KDP to work together against Hussein. The SCIRI representative voiced support for the al-Ujah coup attempt, which was set to launch in early March.

Chalabi also wanted to ensure Iranian government support for the coup. He met with an Iranian intelligence agent on March 3, 1995, and his CIA associate showed up to the building where the meeting took place even though his superiors had denied his request to attend. Iranians saw him and took his presence as a sign of U.S. support for the planned coup. U.S. government officials found out about this from a third-party foreign government official, who said that Iranians believed it was the U.S., not just Chalabi, that sought Iranian support for an uprising against Saddam Hussein. The informant suggested that Chalabi had given a message to the Iranians from the U.S. inviting them to join the operation. On top of that, Chalabi had brought his CIA associate to a meeting with SCIRI leaders who mistook the agent for a member of the U.S. National Security Council (NSC), further bolstering the myth that the U.S. was trying to draw Iran into a coup plot. Somehow the conversation also led the Iranians to believe that the plot might also involve assassination.[27]

When word got back to NSC headquarters, the office erupted into a firestorm as staff members inundated the CIA with phone calls trying to figure out what was going on in Iraq. What was a CIA agent doing meeting with Iranians, posing as a member of the NSC, and advocating for the assassination of Hussein? Agents went into damage control mode. They contacted their associates in Iraq and emphasized that the U.S. did not back an assassination plot and opposed any action that would result in a civil war. Most importantly, U.S. officials contacted Chalabi and other members of the INC and urged them to cancel the coup.[28]

Chalabi's CIA contact told him the decision was his. By that point, it was too late to stop what had already been put in motion.

INC members were already in position and unable to be reached, so Chalabi decided to go ahead as planned. The mission failed. INC forces captured some Iraqi military equipment and POWs, but they did not reach Hussein. Communities did not rise up in revolt as Chalabi had hoped. Iraqi troops eventually subdued the rebellion. Meanwhile, the CIA began rethinking its relationship with Chalabi and the INC while searching for new contacts among Iraqi expats and oppositionists.[29]

Fighting between Kurdish factions continued into the summer of 1996, and in August, Saddam Hussein sent his forces into northern Iraq, executed 100 INC members, and evacuated the rest. Relations between the CIA and INC deteriorated further in the wake of the incident, and the CIA ended its relationship with the organization in February 1997. Yet it was not the end of the INC. In 1998, Congress passed the Iraq Liberation Act, which authorized the U.S. to aid democracy building in Iraq. The law required the president to designate Iraqi opposition organizations to receive U.S. funds, and President Bill Clinton selected the INC. Beginning in March 2000, the State Department funneled nearly $33 million into Iraq through the INC to fund projects including a weekly newspaper, radio and television broadcasts, a public information campaign, and efforts to gather evidence proving that the Hussein regime was guilty of war crimes and crimes against humanity.[30]

Tensions between State Department representatives and INC officials never dissolved during the period in which the U.S. funded the Iraqi group. Concerns about Iranian influence in the INC, as well as suspected infiltration by intelligence agents from other nations, eroded State Department trust in the INC. In September 2002, the State Department terminated its relationship with the INC, but Defense Department authorities believed that the INC could still be useful to the U.S. The Defense Intelligence Agency entered into an agreement with the INC in October with the goal of using the INC to gather intelligence from Iraqis throughout the world about the Hussein regime. According to the agreement, INC members promised to keep secret any information-gathering efforts and cancel the publicity programs the State Department had funded. As the DIA assumed responsibility for the INC, CIA agents familiar with the Iraqi group warned their Defense counterparts of suspected infiltration by Iraqi national intelligence agents and Iranians. Despite the warnings, the DIA remained connected to the INC until 2004, assuming that at least some members of the INC would go on to staff a new Iraqi government.[31]

Despite the strain Chalabi's actions in the 1990s placed on his relationship with his American associates, Chalabi continued to influence U.S. policymaking in the lead-up to the 2003 invasion. Chalabi and other members of the INC insisted that Iraqis would greet U.S. troops as liberators when they arrived in Baghdad. INC members held media events in Washington, DC, where they emphasized the theme of liberation. The INC also remained a primary source of information about the alleged existence of WMDs in Iraq. In February 2003, Secretary of State Colin Powell gave a speech to the UN in which he argued, using evidence from Chalabi and other INC members, that Hussein had stockpiled weapons of mass destruction.[32] Chalabi and U.S. officials would continue their on-again, off-again relationship for several years after the invasion.

Planning for Operation *Iraqi Freedom* began two months after the September 11 attacks. In late November 2001, President Bush asked Secretary of Defense Donald Rumsfeld to develop a plan for regime change in Iraq. Rumsfeld then turned to CENTCOM commander General Tommy Franks and put him in charge of the president's directive. Building blocks were already in place. In the 1990s, the Pentagon had developed a war plan for Iraq called 1003-98. The proposal called for as many as 500,000 U.S. troops and long timelines for buildup and deployment. Franks briefed Rumsfeld on 1003-98, but the defense secretary wanted a smaller force and a shorter timeline. Franks went back to his team and worked on a revised plan, which he presented to Rumsfeld in early 2002. The new plan had CIA agents engaging first to gather intelligence and build relationships. Following the CIA, Special Operations teams would infiltrate northern Iraq and Al Anbar Province in the west.

Third in line were conventional forces, which would launch joint air and ground attacks. The revised plan cut the number of troops in Iraq nearly in half, down to about 275,000.[33]

Lieutenant General William Scott Wallace was commander of V Corps, the unit designated to command and oversee U.S. Army forces in Iraq. The smaller number of troops initially made Wallace uneasy, but he was satisfied with the level of specialized training the Army troops had been conducting, and he also appreciated the joint nature of the proposed operation. The Air Force, the Marine air wing, and Navy aviation complemented the ground component well. Although the Pentagon had committed more troops to Operation *Desert Storm* than were in the plan for what came to be known as Operation *Iraqi Freedom*, Wallace saw synergy between the forces in the new plan that had not existed in 1991. Wallace also saw the importance of new intelligence technology, particularly unmanned aerial vehicles, in showing U.S. forces where the enemy was not, so the Americans could focus on finding where the enemy was.[34]

Wallace knew there would be difficulties: how to move a large land force through complex terrain, Iraqis' ability to counter American technology. Southern Iraq had a vast desert, but it also had canals, farmland, palm trees, and, most concerning to military planners, cities. It would be challenging to move a large armored formation through an urban area without rear supply units getting cut off from the forward combat units. As for technology, what the U.S. military had was advanced, but Iraqis also knew how to negate America's technological advantage to a certain degree. Radar picked up movement, so if Iraqi troops hid in their fighting positions and remained still, radar might not pick up their locations. If Iraqis burned a piece of metal as a decoy, they could throw off thermal sensory systems. Hiding vehicles in lush palm groves would make it difficult for the Americans to spot Iraqi equipment.[35]

During the war-planning stage, CENTCOM defined the Operation *Iraqi Freedom* military objectives as: overthrow the Hussein regime; provide support to a new government; destroy Iraq's weapons of mass destruction and capability for building them;

protect allies from Iraqi terrorism; destroy terrorist networks in Iraq; gain intelligence about terrorist connections and people detained under the Hussein regime; support international efforts to build stability in Iraq. It was an ambitious and not totally concrete set of objectives. Debates during the combat planning phase for Operation *Iraqi Freedom* centered on the size of the force, the timeline for action, and the coordination of air and ground forces. Rumsfeld was closely involved in the discussions and pushed for a quick timeline. He approached the planning as a chance to modify the U.S. military at large and transform it from its Cold War state, in which it was designed to fight large armies, to a leaner and more flexible force. In Rumsfeld's mind, the military that took stage in the Iraqi theater of war would represent America's 21st-century fighting force.[36]

CENTCOM's air component urged war planners to open with up to two weeks of air strikes aimed at Iraq's missile, radar, and command and control locations, but other strategists contended that deploying ground forces early would surprise the Iraqis. Still others countered with the possibility that Hussein could start the war by using weapons of mass destruction, rendering irrelevant any proposed U.S. launch date. Such a scenario required the U.S. to have prepared a smaller force on a faster timeline to get in and get the job done. In January 2003, CENTCOM commanders met in Tampa and decided on a plan that would begin with a brief air campaign of a few days followed by a combined ground campaign led by the Army's V Corps and the Marines' 1st Expeditionary Force crossing into Iraq from Kuwait, while the Army's 4th Infantry Division would open a northern front invading Iraq from Turkey. By the end of January, the plan called for two Army divisions, the 3rd and 4th Infantry divisions, which leaders including V Corps commander Lieutenant General William Scott Wallace worried were not enough.[37] The Turkish government opposed the plan for the 4th Infantry, concerned that if Iraqi Kurds were successful in creating a separatist state, it would inspire Turkey's Kurds to do the same.

Even before combat began, strategists recognized that the real war in Iraq would be nation building post hostilities. Iraq had already fought colonialism and had been a stable, if authoritarian, nation.

To suddenly be under American control, even if temporarily, would not be acceptable to many Iraqis. In addition to that, ancient tribal divisions and deeply rooted religious divides among Sunni and Shia Muslims also made nation building in Iraq a daunting task. The Bush administration formed an Executive Steering Committee to develop a nation-building plan, while the Pentagon took control of war planning. Seeking guidance from history, war planners studied reports from the U.S. occupations of Germany and Japan after World War II.

Pentagon officials had envisioned some sort of U.S.-led transitional authority at least since the summer of 2002. Assistant Secretary of Defense Peter Rodman warned Rumsfeld that a prolonged U.S. occupation would only mobilize anti-U.S. insurgencies and result in the wrong person filling the power vacuum in Baghdad. Defense analysts had been making all sorts of comparisons with Germany and Japan after World War II, but Rodman argued that the analogies were inaccurate. He doubted that the U.S. would have control of Iraq like the Americans had over the vanquished Axis powers in 1945. The Japan analogy also didn't work because it failed to take into account the specific sectarian conflicts and terrorist infiltration that made Iraq different from Japan. In 1945, Japanese society was homogenous and mostly unified. When Emperor Hirohito surrendered to the Allies, the Japanese citizenry acquiesced to U.S. occupation. Iraq's deeply rooted animosities between Sunni and Shia Muslims and the activities of regional terrorist groups within and around Iraq's borders assured that no such submission to an occupying authority would be possible, Rodman contended. Yet even with Japan's compliance, the U.S. still occupied the country for nearly seven years. That history offered a warning about the difficulty of postwar occupation, but war planners either missed or ignored it during the strategizing for the 2003 invasion of Iraq.

Of the post-World War II analogies, Rodman preferred France. Franklin D. Roosevelt and Winston Churchill initially didn't take Charles de Gaulle seriously as the true representative of Free France, and they had planned to establish a provisional government in

France similar to the one the Allies established in Germany. Yet when de Gaulle returned to Paris after D-Day and millions of adoring French citizens turned out to cheer him on, the Anglo-American allies changed their minds on the Frenchman. Had Roosevelt and Churchill gone forward with their plan to impose an occupation government rather than support de Gaulle, French communists would have risen up in opposition to the Allied presence. Rodman worried that if the U.S. appeared to occupy Iraq, it would embolden terrorist groups and others that posed a threat to local and regional security.[38]

The nation-building plan included three stages – first would be a military occupation involving humanitarian relief, stability, and security and headed by an American general. The second stage would involve a diminished U.S. role in Iraq, as Iraqis took more control of their country, especially their political institutions. Optimistic planners hoped stage one would last six months to a year, and that a new government would be in place in Baghdad in about two years. The final stage would feature elections for a representative government in Iraq. But there were problems from the start. U.S. planners lacked information about Iraq that would have helped with the planning. The Iraqi government had not conducted a census in years, so without concrete statistics Americans made their plans based on estimates and guesses. The question of how long the rebuilding would take was unanswered. Some U.S. analysts predicted a ten-year troop presence to build up a strong enough Iraqi military.[39]

Central to the discussions about postwar Iraq was who would be in charge and how the transition would occur. Military leaders believed much of the postwar mission would fall to troops, especially any unplanned-for tasks. Iraq from the mid-20th century onward had produced an educated citizenry that hoped to be the ones to craft a post-Hussein future. They would not look kindly on American meddling. Some Iraqis were suspicious of Americans due in part to sanctions that had been in place since the end of *Desert Storm*. In a village east of Hussein's hometown of Tikrit, farmers watched helplessly as their citrus crops died of disease. Sanctions prevented them from getting the insecticide that would prevent infestation, and so their unripe limes, oranges, and grapefruits developed black spots before dying. Sheep herders blamed birth defects and illnesses in their livestock on depleted uranium from U.S. missiles used in Operation *Desert Storm*.[40] For some U.S. policymakers, the ideal approach was to identify Iraqi oppositionists, including Iraqi Kurds and those in exile; to that end, a series of conferences hosted by the U.S. and Great Britain were held in London and Iraq in late 2002 and early 2003.

The State Department established a "Future of Iraq" program in 2002 that brought together Iraqi oppositionists and regional experts to analyze potential postwar scenarios in Iraq.[41] Central to the Future of Iraq program were Iraqi expats in the U.S. and Europe, as well as opposition Iraqis, primarily in the northern regions of the country. They were educated professionals – doctors, lawyers, engineers – who could speak to Iraq's problems and offer potential solutions. Diplomats also hoped that working with Iraqis and Iraqi expats would allow the State Department to identify leaders for postwar Iraq and would show real Iraqi involvement in rebuilding their nation.[42]

Under the umbrella of "Future of Iraq" were 16 working groups, each focused on an aspect of postwar development. The working groups consisted of Iraqis and international experts on the topics at hand. Groups covered issues such as democratic principles, local government, civil society, finance and economic development, public health, water and other environmental concerns, energy, education, refugees, and foreign policy. State Department authorities emphasized that the purpose of the working groups was not to create a government in exile, but rather to give Iraqi expats a chance to offer guidance on what Iraqis would need from a new government. It seemed a given that Saddam Hussein would fall from power, but State Department officials appeared to understand that the hard part would be the postwar nation building. Although the working groups discussed the issues that would likely be most pressing after Hussein was out, they did not outline specific plans for how to address the various concerns. U.S. diplomats hoped that other countries and international institutions would assist, but few concrete plans existed beyond the Future of Iraq project.[43]

In October 2002, Congress authorized the use of American force against Iraq for the purpose of protecting U.S. national security if Hussein refused to abide by UN resolutions prohibiting him from having or developing WMDs.[44] The Congressional resolution required President Bush to notify Congress within 48 hours of military action and to report to Congress on the progress of a war with Iraq every 60 days. War planners cited numerous threats that they believed Iraq posed to the U.S. – not just weapons of mass destruction but also that Iraq could harbor terrorists and spread instability throughout the region if internal conflicts such as tensions between Sunni and Shia Muslims bled out across Iraq's borders. If Iran were to get involved, it could incite major regional strife. Hussein continued to deny that he harbored any WMDs.

General Franks and his team sought confirmation from the Bush administration about its plans for the development of a provisional government in Baghdad. Receiving no clear direction, Franks assumed that the State Department would be in charge of the political issues. By the end of 2002, Franks and other Pentagon officials set initial military plans in motion. CENTCOM established Task Force IV, a committee responsible for drawing up the blueprints for America's postwar actions in Iraq. The committee received little formal guidance, so members went by the general objectives that the Defense Department submitted to the Senate Foreign Relations Committee, which included the elimination of Iraq's biological and chemical weapons capabilities and terrorist infrastructure. Of primary importance to U.S. policymakers was that Americans convince Iraqis that U.S. forces intended to liberate Iraq, not occupy it.[45]

In January 2003, the Bush administration settled on a vague plan that had Americans assisting Iraqis in the postwar nation-building process. Americans would guide Iraqis through a deliberate process of establishing political stability in the country. Tasks would include conducting a census, holding elections from the municipal level on up, forming a committee to draft a constitution, and creating an

Iraqi judicial council. Only after all of these goals were achieved would an election be held to determine a new Iraqi president. Bush's advisors envisioned the nation-building process to take years and to require close involvement by U.S. and coalition personnel.[46]

Bush's plan included the creation of the Office of Reconstruction and Humanitarian Assistance (ORHA). Reporting to the Pentagon, ORHA would be responsible for postwar Iraq. The Defense Department appointed retired Army Lieutenant General Jay Garner to head ORHA. Garner was experienced in the type of work ORHA would do, having led Operation *Provide Comfort* in northern Iraq after *Desert Storm*. Garner's team consisted of other retired Army officers and one State Department representative, Barbara Bodine. Bodine had served as deputy chief of mission in Kuwait during the first Gulf War and was U.S. ambassador to Yemen at the time of the USS *Cole* bombing. But ORHA faced a problem from the beginning. The Bush administration had taken so long to create ORHA that there was not enough time to build up its personnel and resources before the start of major combat operations. When ORHA finally left the U.S. for Kuwait, it was a skeleton crew that set up at the Kuwait Hilton.

From the perspective of the State Department, the military's objectives needed to extend past the combat mission. Post-conflict security and humanitarian aid would require the assistance of U.S. troops, diplomats argued. In early 2003, Paul Simons, acting assistant secretary of the Bureau for International Narcotics and Law Enforcement Affairs; Lorne W. Craner, assistant secretary for the Bureau of Democracy, Human Rights, and Labor; and Arthur Dewey, assistant secretary for Population, Refugees, and Migration for the State Department met to discuss joint contingency planning for Iraq. Meanwhile, Under Secretary of State Paula Dobriansky visited CENTCOM and ORHA director Jay Garner to discuss postwar planning. Simons, Craner, and Dewey submitted a joint bureau report to Dobriansky in February concluding that the military had to take charge of these tasks until an international security force could step in. The problem was that neither State Department officials nor Pentagon war planners had determined what international body would do that.[47] Meanwhile, Blount and his 3rd ID soldiers had no insight into what was being discussed or planned in Washington.

Before the ground invasion of Iraq occurred, CIA agents infiltrated provinces in northern and southern Iraq to gather intelligence and develop relationships with locals. Their work created the foundation for the Special Operations units that followed. Special Ops secured bases in Iraq's western Al Anbar Province and worked with the peshmerga, Iraqi Kurdish forces in northern Iraq, to attack a terrorist organization known as Ansar al-Islam. Founded in December 2001, the group consisted of mostly Kurdish Salafist extremists in Iraqi Kurdistan and had ties to Osama bin Laden and Al-Qaeda. Secretary Powell warned the UN Security Council about Ansar al-Islam in his address regarding America's proposed invasion of Iraq. Powell told of Baghdad officials who had ties to high-ranking Ansar al-Islam operatives and who offered Al-Qaeda sanctuary in Kurdistan. Powell argued that Al-Qaeda members who fled Afghanistan in the wake of the U.S. invasion had accepted the offer and were hiding out in northern Iraq. This was part of the justification for America's proposed incursion into Iraq.[48]

CIA agents worked their connections inside Iraq to assess the WMD situation. Part of the problem from an intelligence standpoint was that the CIA did not prioritize information that might have helped analysts estimate what conditions in postwar Iraq would be like. CIA efforts focused primarily on WMDs, Hussein's connections to terrorist organizations, and the capabilities of the Iraqi military. From the CIA's perspective, prewar intelligence was limited in its use for making projections about postwar conditions. Experts on local and regional issues could look at historical trends to envision potential postwar situations, a more useful type of speculation. Ultimately, analysts understood that so much of postwar Iraq depended on how Hussein's ouster occurred, including the duration of the war, ensuing damage, and the presence of coalition forces after the fighting was over. All the variables limited the effectiveness of predictions of any kind, whether from intelligence gathering or from expert analysis.[49]

Yet the U.S. intelligence community offered opinions about various factors related to nation building in postwar Iraq. In January 2003, just two months before the 3rd Infantry Division led the charge to Baghdad, the National Intelligence Council (NIC) concluded that establishing a stable democratic government in Iraq would be a lengthy and difficult challenge. Iraq had no tradition of democracy, and while the concept would likely be popular among much of the population, its implementation would take time and patience. Agents acknowledged Iraq's potential for sustaining democratic political institutions, especially with the involvement of educated Iraqi exiles as well as middle-class Iraqis who remained in the country. But none of the opposition groups had the popular support, political power, or military strength to run the country without significant foreign assistance.[50] If the Bush administration was committed to regime change actually occurring, the president and his advisors had to accept a protracted U.S. engagement in Iraq.

As for terrorism, prewar intelligence assessments concluded that a war likely would increase the possibility that Al-Qaeda would move into Iraq, but analysts also projected that terrorist activity would slow down three to five years after the war. More concerning than terrorism was the possibility that internal factional strife would disrupt postwar Iraq. Intelligence analysts asserted that sectarian violence would erupt unless an occupying power remained on hand to deter it. After decades of oppression under the Ba'athist regime, Shia could rise up and target Sunnis, who would no longer enjoy Hussein's favor. Agents in Iraq had learned that Shia would seek power while Sunnis would try desperately to keep it, and the tension would make it difficult for democracy to take hold. In the north, agents believed that Kurds might take advantage of Hussein's departure and seize regional oil fields.[51]

Beyond Iraq's borders, neighboring countries could also attempt to dictate the terms of Iraq's postwar future, intelligence revealed. Influence could come in the form of humanitarian assistance or the fomenting of violence. Iran in particular would be a regional leader regarding the future of Iraq. Intelligence agents determined that Iran's response to the situation in Iraq would depend on Tehran's assessment of whether U.S. involvement in Iraq was a threat to Iran's interests. Iran had contacts among Iraq's Shia population, as well as among the Kurds, and could use those connections to undermine U.S. efforts to build a friendly government in Baghdad. U.S. intelligence emphasized that including Iranians in Iraq's postwar development would reduce the threat that Iran would take an adversarial approach to U.S. intervention in Iraq.[52] All of the variables made advance planning of postwar strategies difficult, and given the uncertainty within the State Department regarding who would be in charge of nation building, the U.S. faced a murky future as it prepared to invade Iraq.

Humanitarian, security, and infrastructure issues would be the concerns Americans would face immediately in a postwar occupation. The January 2003 report from the National Intelligence Council concluded that Iraq's survival would depend on massive humanitarian assistance, and food distribution and healthcare would need to be a primary priority of an occupying force. Before the war, only about half of Iraq's population had reliable access to basic services like water and electricity, intelligence agents reported. War would only exacerbate that problem, and so infrastructure repair would be of prime importance in the immediate aftermath of the war. Resumption of public utilities, along with food distribution and local security, were foundational to building stability in post-Hussein Iraq.

Iraqis under Hussein relied on the government's rationing program for their food, and so Americans and their coalition partners would have to find and secure the government food warehouses to prevent looting. The occupiers would then develop a nationwide food distribution program in order to prevent widespread hunger, intelligence agents asserted. If Iraq's oil industry escaped the war mostly unscathed, oil revenues could fund some of the country's reconstruction, but intelligence analysts suggested that Iraq would require a foreign aid package along the lines of the Marshall Plan to bring economic stability. To ensure local and national security, some elements of the Iraqi regular army could be retained if Americans believed soldiers were not loyal to the Ba'ath

Party or Hussein. If not, the U.S. and coalition partners would remain in-country longer than their constituents would accept. Even if some Iraqi regulars remained in security positions, Iraq faced a long-term process of building a permanent police force.[53]

Also in January 2003, a State Department and intelligence analysis outlined four assumptions meant to guide U.S. policy toward Iraq. First, a UN-backed coalition force led by the U.S. would remove Hussein and the Ba'ath Party from power and destroy WMDs. Analysts urged that Israeli forces not be included in the coalition. Once the U.S. and its partners achieved the first objective, the next step was to shore up Iraq's defenses against its neighbors. A U.S. military occupation would provide security in the initial phase until Iraq rebuilt a conventional force. The report projected a five-year process to establish a stable government in Baghdad, the third goal of U.S. intervention. A U.S. military occupation for at least a year would begin the process, and then American troops would gradually withdraw, although some would stay long-term to ensure stability, provide humanitarian assistance, and help establish political institutions. Finally, the report assumed that the UN would lift sanctions against Iraq. Analysts worried about regional and international public opinion and believed that if it looked like the U.S. imposed a political transformation on Iraq, regional observers might not view it as positive change.[54]

Nothing from the intelligence reports of January 2003 predicted that regime change in Iraq would lead to the development of stable democracy or bolster regional security. At best, the reports outlined a lengthy and challenging U.S. occupation that had some potential to result in a stable, pro-U.S. government, but only if internal adversaries played it cool and terrorist organizations didn't manage to gain footholds in Iraq. While working to build Iraq's political institutions and meet the daily needs of the population, Americans would have to remain vigilant to security threats from neighboring countries while also managing regional concerns about what a U.S. occupation of Iraq might mean for the Middle East broadly. Would Iranian spies try to foment an Iraqi Shia uprising against their Sunni brethren? Would Bashar al-Assad worry that a democratic Iraq could threaten his authoritarian regime in Syria? Would Arabs assume that American occupation of Iraq was a step toward intervention in the Israeli–Palestinian crisis? Would the image of foreign control overshadow the local and regional benefits of Hussein's ouster? The NIC's reports raised these concerns and made clear the difficulty the U.S. would have in establishing a stable democracy in a country that had not experimented with representative government of any kind since the 1950s. A true and lasting political transformation could take a generation to be fully realized, intelligence agents warned.

A flashback to the Vietnam War might have offered policymakers a cautionary tale. U.S. nation-building efforts in South Vietnam failed. Neither the Americans nor the Vietnamese resolved the tensions in nation building. U.S. advisors wanted an independent South Vietnam that would be on their side, but they were not able to let go and hand control over to their Vietnamese counterparts. Identifying leaders was difficult in part because National Liberation Front (NLF) cadres had infiltrated South Vietnam's political organizations. As U.S. intervention and the war continued on with no clear goal or end in sight, some Vietnamese who had supported an independent South Vietnam joined the reconciliation and reunification camp even if it meant ceding power to Hanoi. The U.S. fought two wars, one against NLF guerrillas and the other against North Vietnam's regular forces. American troops and the U.S. public grew weary of the war, and both the New Left and the Silent Majority hoped it would end. Escalation brought down the presidency of Lyndon Johnson, while a promise of "peace with honor" elevated Richard Nixon to America's top political office. U.S. forces eventually withdrew from Vietnam, and Saigon fell on April 30, 1975.

The issues and conditions in Iraq in 2003 were different than the ones in Vietnam between 1954 and 1975. America's plan for Iraq was regime change, whereas in South Vietnam, Americans had worked to bolster a non-communist, pro-U.S. government in a new country created out of decolonization. Yet similar ideas informed U.S. policymakers' approaches to both countries. At the center was the search for a local leader who would tow the American line while also maintaining some degree of popularity with the masses. In both Vietnam and Iraq, Americans struggled to let go and hand control over to the local partners. Americans wanted to build stable nations in both places, but in neither did they ever fully trust local politicians and activists to do the job on their own. That doubt motivated Americans to remain in-country for years, fueling the frustration of locals who initially appreciated U.S. support but grew aggravated as U.S. occupation continued without an end in sight. Military forces would be the predominant representative of the U.S. in the immediate aftermath of the war.

4

Preparations in Kuwait

In June 2001, Colonel David Perkins took command of 2nd Brigade, 3rd Infantry Division, and he was at Fort Stewart with the division on September 11. In the days and weeks that followed, Perkins and his commanders within the brigade discussed the possibilities for what the aftermath of 9/11 might mean for 2nd Brigade. Would brigade units deploy to Afghanistan? Elsewhere in the Middle East? Perkins was certain they'd be going somewhere in the Middle East, and about a year after the 9/11 attacks, 2nd Brigade deployed to Kuwait. For months, it was the only American military unit at Camp Udairi in the Kuwaiti desert, and while they didn't yet know that they would be going to Iraq, Perkins and his commanders used the time and space to think about how they would get to Baghdad if given the mission. How would a heavy armored division make the trek from Kuwait to Baghdad and fight an urban war once the soldiers got there?[1]

Perkins and his commanders also began thinking about logistics, and fuel was at the top of their list. An M1 Abrams tank consumed 57 gallons of fuel per hour whether moving or idle, and so tank commanders measured their fuel consumption in hours rather than miles. Heavy expanded mobility tactical tankers (HEMTTs) carried about 10,000 gallons for resupply, and keeping the lines open between the forward combat units and the supply units following them would be critical if the division was going to make it to Baghdad. Perkins remembered that General George Patton's Third Army had run out of fuel in September 1944 as his tanks pursued the retreating German Army. Running out of gas ground Patton's forces to a halt in the Lorraine region of northeast France bordering Germany. As Perkins and his commanders discussed the possibilities for an invasion of Iraq, they understood that logistics, especially fuel, would be key to whether the 3rd ID succeeded or failed. Though he came from the tactical side of the Army, Perkins didn't hesitate to quote a quip he had once heard: "Tactics are for amateurs. Logistics are for professionals."[2]

Since the end of the first Gulf War, the U.S. Army had kept part of a brigade in Kuwait as a deterrent to Hussein. Brigades embarked on six-month rotations in Kuwait for training and to show the Kuwaitis and the Saudis that the U.S. was committed to defending regional allies against Hussein's aggression. Brigades rotated through deployments, where training ensured that troops were always ready should war begin. Training exercises included the maintenance and use of brigade-level combat equipment that the Army had pre-positioned in Kuwait and on the island of Diego Garcia in the Indian Ocean. Contractors controlled and managed the equipment until the Army needed it. Operating the equipment during training ensured it was combat ready should war begin. Rotations and staging in Kuwait, as well as rotations at the National Training Center at Fort Irwin in the Mojave Desert, over the course of more than a decade, prepared the 3rd Infantry Division well for war in southern Iraq.[3]

The 3rd Infantry Division consisted of seven brigades plus additional support groups on loan from V Corps. Blount was at the helm, followed by two assistant division commanders. Brigadier General Lloyd Austin was the assistant division commander for maneuver, and Brigadier General Bill Weber commanded the support units, which included an engineer brigade and an aviation brigade, division support command, and the V Corps support units. Weber was responsible for all the logistics and supply support for the maneuver forces Austin commanded.[4]

During the Cold War, the U.S. Army kept pre-positioned stocks in Europe to be prepared for war with the Soviet Union. Moving thousands of vehicles and heavy equipment from the U.S. to overseas locations was cumbersome and time-consuming, and if the Russians attacked unexpectedly, U.S. forces deploying by air to Germany would be without the equipment they needed to fight. By pre-positioning equipment near potential conflict zones, units would be able to show up and use it. As war with the Soviet Union did not materialize, the Army took to sending a division out once a year to take the pre-positioned equipment out of storage, shoot it, maneuver it, and then put it back in storage after about a month's exercise. When the Cold War ended, the pre-positioning process the Army used in Europe served as a model for doing the same thing in the Middle East. War planners also realized the need for Arabic linguists and others with regional expertise. By the time Blount took command of the 3rd ID, the division had intelligence personnel who spoke Arabic and Farsi.

Blount had not served in Operation *Desert Storm*. During that conflict, he was the commander of 3-64 Armor Battalion in Germany. But he had proven Middle East experience. Blount's tours of duty in Saudi Arabia had put him on Shinseki's radar, and he had also taken a brigade to Kuwait for training when he was a colonel with the 24th Infantry Division. The exercise had required him to draw pre-positioned equipment and execute other procedures for operations in Kuwait. Since the days in Riyadh when Blount stared at the map on his office wall and imagined leading a tank division through the desert to attack Baghdad, Blount had been training for the invasion of Iraq. In Blount's mind, Hussein was a singular threat to regional security and U.S. interests in the Middle East. It wasn't Iraq or Iraqis. He believed that most Iraqis would be relieved if not thrilled to see Hussein gone.

When Blount took command of the 3rd ID in October 2001, Army Chief of Staff Eric Shinseki told him to get the division ready to go to war. Blount didn't know where or when his division would go, but he had clear orders to get ready. Blount kept Shinseki's words to himself and moved forward as the division would normally, training, planning, wargaming. At that time, the 3rd ID had brigades stationed in Bosnia and Kosovo, but they were in the process of being replaced by other units at the end of 2001. The troops in those brigades had to go through a rotation at the National Training Center (NTC) at Fort Irwin in California's Mojave Desert to be trained for the Middle East environment before deploying to Kuwait. Brigadier General Lloyd Austin was Blount's second in command and offered a calming presence in chaotic moments. Brigade commanders included Colonel William Grimsley leading 1st Brigade, Perkins at the helm of 2nd Brigade, and Colonel Dan Allyn commanding 3rd Brigade. In addition to the division's three heavy combat brigades, Blount also had command of an aviation brigade of attack helicopters commanded by Colonel Curtis Potts, an artillery brigade commanded by Colonel Tom Torrance, a cavalry squad commanded by Lieutenant Colonel Terry Ferrell, and a logistics brigade commanded by Colonel Jim Hodge. Blount had a lot to work with, and he would need all the various units.

Some of the training for the war took place with the aid of computer simulations. Commanders prepared battlefield plans and gave orders, and units fought battles on computer screens. Other units played the enemy, also fighting on computer screens. Once the battle simulations began, they played out organically as they would in real fighting. Unit commanders worked in real or replicas of command centers and received radio calls and reports as they would during battle. They practiced planning on the fly as conditions changed due to the fighting. Then they assessed strengths and weaknesses, and the assessments guided the development of subsequent training operations.

Another facet of training involved brigade rotations at the National Training Center. Three-week sessions at NTC replicated the conditions of desert warfare as closely as possible in the U.S. At NTC, a sprawling complex of about 1,000 square miles, units rehearsed real-life urban battle situations in replicas of Iraqi villages. They practiced moving in and out of buildings while avoiding sniper fire. Dummies positioned inside buildings forced soldiers to think about how to avoid civilian casualties while eliminating enemy troops. The Army hired ethnic Arabs to act as locals, including insurgents and enemy troops, in the villages. Some of the training events used live fire.

Rotations at NTC were important for the 3rd ID because the conditions and terrain at Fort Stewart, the 3rd ID's home base, were nothing like the desert. Tall pines hid Fort Stewart from view, and the humidity of southeast Georgia was more like the tropics. For tanks, the expansive desert was ideal. They travel and shoot long distances, neither of which they could do at Fort Stewart. When the tank crews arrived in Kuwait and began working with their equipment, they saw what their tanks could do in the wide open desert.

One of Blount's closest staff members was Captain Erik Berdy, his aide-de-camp. Berdy had done rotations in Haiti and Bosnia, and his Haiti tour especially had exposed him to stability and support operations (SASO) such as bilateral agreements with local leaders, neighborhood patrols, and police training. The knowledge he gained from those deployments would prove useful in the days, weeks, and months after the 3rd ID took Baghdad. He got the job of aide-de-camp in June 2002 after interviewing with Brigadier General Lloyd Austin, assistant division commander, who was building the personal support staff for division leadership and was looking for officers who had infantry experience and had been deployed. Soon after Berdy accepted the position, he traveled with Blount to Kuwait to visit with 3rd Brigade, which was deployed as the reaction force for CENTCOM. Berdy and Blount made monthly trips to Kuwait and also traveled to Heidelberg, Germany, to meet with leaders at V Corps headquarters. By November 2002, most of Blount's staff had deployed to Kuwait.[5]

As Blount's aide, Berdy handled his personal needs, controlled his calendar, ensured his living quarters were suitable, arranged for his security detail, provided preparation materials for briefings and meetings, and acted as gatekeeper, filtering those materials Blount needed to see from those he didn't. This kind of close engagement with Blount's daily life in Kuwait allowed Berdy to be privy to most of Blount's meetings; he had a top-secret security clearance. Working so closely with Blount, Berdy observed that his leadership style was quiet and "cerebral," and that his personality was not a "gregarious, warm, slap-people-on-the-back kind." But Blount impressed Berdy with his patience and his dispassionate approach to problem solving. Berdy never saw Blount make emotional decisions, and he rarely saw Blount get flustered. Sometimes Berdy wondered why Blount didn't push his ideas more forcefully at meetings with V Corps leaders, but he soon realized that Blount was usually biding his time until the moment when approval of his ideas was without question.[6]

One of the earliest debates Berdy observed was over the plan for advancing from the border to Baghdad. Beginning in June 2002, Blount argued against V Corps' plan to attack along Highway 1 and Highway 8 through the center of Iraq. He wanted to maneuver west into the desert, where he could take advantage of speed capability and spread his formations out rather than advancing up a highway in one column. The debate remained unresolved until Victory Scrimmage in Germany in January 2003, when Blount's plan was solidified.[7] Another disagreement between Blount and V Corps was over the timetable and what the division would do when it got close to Baghdad. V Corps planners estimated that it would take more than 100 days to get from Kuwait to the capital city, and once there, Corps proposed the establishment of several forward operating bases from which 3rd ID troops would conduct raids into the city. 3rd ID planners saw a much shorter trek to Baghdad, estimating that division forces could get there in three weeks. Blount envisioned a drive into the heart of the city. Logistics, especially the fuel needs of an armor division, were a concern across leadership.

Colonel Roberta A. Woods, commander of the 24th Corps Support Group (CSG), played a key role in preparing to provide fuel for the 3rd ID. She deployed to Kuwait in January 2003, but in October and November 2002, Blount had invited Woods, her deputy commander, Lieutenant Colonel Pat Voller, and other key 24th CSG staff to help develop a plan for providing fuel to a fast-moving division. Voller had been the executive officer for the 24th CSG's fuel battalion before becoming Woods' deputy commander, and he suggested the idea of positioning fuel bags – huge bladders that held thousands of gallons of fuel and included hook-up valves for fueling – on the ground in "fuel farms" for conducting fuel operations. When Blount moved 3rd ID headquarters to Kuwait in late November 2002, Woods sent two of her CSG planners with division HQ staff so that they could keep up with the division's plans and report back to Woods. After 24th CSG deployed to Kuwait, Woods and her soldiers and staff rehearsed fuel resupply with 3rd ID combat forces. Division leaders placed more emphasis on fuel than on any other supply need.[8]

To prepare the supplies the division would need, Weber took a look at every class of supplies and thought through how to provision each unit. When it came to food and water, the Army's general rule is to provide soldiers with enough sustenance to last three days. But resupplying after three days meant stopping every three days, slowing the division's progress. To keep the columns moving, Weber decided to give each unit enough food and water for five days. That way, Weber would have two extra days to move forward the rations resupply, and the division would get to Baghdad more quickly. Anytime the division stopped, it allowed the enemy to regroup, make adjustments, and plan defensive moves based on the tenor of the attack. Weber did not want logistics to define or restrict the operational tempo of the 3rd ID's attack.[9]

When planning for food, Weber ensured that each commander had a day's worth of hot rations so that soldiers could eat a hot meal every once in a while during the fight to Baghdad. It was another learning experience from *Desert Storm*, where he had gone 36 days without a hot meal. As part of his rations plan for Operation *Iraqi Freedom*, Weber ordered rations that could be heated with water, the best he could do for the soldiers while the division was on the move. Weber understood that hot rations were not a high priority item during a war, but he also knew that it meant a lot to soldiers to eat a hot meal after they had been fighting for days or weeks. Hot rations were good for morale.[10]

As he planned for ammunition, Weber drew on his experience as a major in Operation *Desert Storm*. U.S. forces had destroyed many of Iraq's armored units, so this time around soldiers would need fewer tank-killing ammunition. Based on that knowledge,

Weber changed the ammunition issue for tanks and Bradleys and ordered less tank-killing ammunition and more high-explosive ammunition that could destroy buildings, trucks, and lightly armored vehicles. Weber also doubled the machine-gun ammunition issue for every vehicle that had a machine gun. Weber, like other commanders, figured the primary threat to American troops in Operation *Iraqi Freedom* would appear in the urban environment rather than out in the open desert.[11] Along with changing the ammunition issue, Weber also doubled the amount of ammunition each vehicle carried. Instead of having to resupply after three days, Weber issued six days of ammo to each vehicle. Doubling the amount of ammo meant that soldiers had to figure out where to put it all. They found that the best option was strapping it to the outside of the tank.[12]

Weber also considered decreasing the resupply frequency of sundry packs, boxes of personal hygiene products like toothpaste and deodorant. Each sundry pack included 30 days' worth of products for ten soldiers. To resupply a division of 20,000 soldiers required about 2,000 sundry packs to be brought forward on supply trucks, a big job. In talking with some of his officers, Weber wondered if the boxes could be brought up less frequently than every 30 days. The female officers in the group asked Weber if he knew exactly what was in the packs. In addition to the toothbrushes and toothpaste, the sundry packs also carried feminine hygiene products. Servicewomen made up about 15 percent of the division, and Weber realized how critical the sundry packs were for that segment of his soldiers. Women were medics, truck drivers and MPs, and if they didn't have an adequate supply of tampons, sanitary pads, and other products they needed each month, this might affect their ability to do their jobs. As Weber saw it, that was 15 percent of his combat power, and he wasn't going to write that off. Weber made sure sundry packs were delivered to the forward units every 30 days.[13]

When it came time to mobilize for the invasion, the scale of machines and people that had to move was staggering. In Kuwait, Blount worked out plans for driving the 10,000 vehicles under his command through the desert. About 8,000 of them were the 3rd ID's, while the remaining 2,000 were from V Corps, including vehicles of the 101st and 82nd. Blount had to move even more humans. Under his command were 20,000 3rd ID soldiers plus another 5,000 from other Army units. Before the invasion began, the general knew that the division's fuel usage would run into the millions of gallons. An Abrams tank alone used 500 gallons a day, even when idling. In September 2002, 2nd Brigade, 3rd Infantry Division, arrived in Kuwait. Commanders prepared their soldiers to go to war in about two months, and a sense of urgency pushed them as December approached. Captain Andrew Hilms, commander of Alpha Company, 1st Battalion, 64th Armor Regiment (1-64 Armor), 2nd Brigade, worked his soldiers two tanks at a time, training them how to maneuver in a wing-man concept in all types of conditions, day and night, under attack and on the offensive. Alpha Company was the "Wild Bunch" – 100 soldiers, two tank platoons, four tanks each, an infantry rifle platoon, and four Bradley fighting vehicles. Alpha Company was the lead company in 1-64 Armor, something of which the Wild Bunch was very proud. Given concerns about chemical warfare, A Company and other units of 1-64 Armor also focused on training in a chemically contaminated environment. By December 2002, the troops were conducting brigade-level, live-fire exercises involving all of 2nd Brigade's 2,500 vehicles.[14]

The first time Captain Alexis Perez-Cruz climbed into a tank, he was in second grade. His father was career military and had been in the 3rd ID, so Perez-Cruz spent several years of his childhood at Fort Stewart. Born in Aguadilla, Puerto Rico, Perez-Cruz grew up in El Paso, Texas and elsewhere as an Army brat. He enjoyed the military life and enlisted in the Army as a private first class right out of high school in 1994. After ten months on active duty, Perez-Cruz went to college, starting at the University of Texas-El Paso and graduating from Stephen F. Austin State University. After college, Perez-Cruz was commissioned an armor officer and assigned to 2nd Battalion, 69th Armor Regiment (2-69 Armor), 2nd Brigade, 3rd ID. He was the executive officer of Charlie Company when his unit deployed to Kuwait. The soldiers did seven months of training in the desert, got a two-month trip back home, and then returned to Kuwait to prepare for the invasion of Iraq.[15]

December 2002 came and went, as did January 2003, but 2nd Brigade remained in Kuwait. A rumor began circulating among the soldiers that the invasion would happen on Valentine's Day. Hilms knew that the uncertainty could take a toll on his soldiers mentally. They had a well-developed base camp and decent food, but there was limited internet access, so the soldiers were disconnected from their families back home, and that added to the anxiety many of them already felt waiting for the order to invade and worrying about the possibility that Hussein would unleash weapons of mass destruction on them. Hilms and his first sergeant made regular rounds, walking through the tents where his soldiers lived and visiting them in their fighting positions out in the field. They'd talk to the soldiers one-on-one to get a sense of how they felt about the mission. It was likely that they'd see combat, and Hilms reminded his soldiers that the Wild Bunch was a team. They would fight as a team and move as a team, and they would leave no one behind no matter what they encountered. For as long as they had been in Kuwait together by that point, the bonds they had developed with one another were familial.[16]

That is what happens when soldiers live together halfway around the world and train together for a shared mission. The Wild Bunch was close-knit, and Hilms reinforced that kinship when he talked to his soldiers. Looking out for each other was to be their focus. Not the news reports, not the political rhetoric – none of it mattered. Taking care of each other is what would get them through, and hopefully get them home. When they weren't talking, they were working. Hilms had his soldiers maintaining their tanks and vehicles so they would be in the best possible shape for the long drive to Baghdad. The dusty desert terrain made maintenance challenging but also essential. Soldiers had to be careful about sealing up openings to engines and sealing open compartments so dirt and sand didn't get in. Because of the sand, conducting regular proactive maintenance was vital.

Mental preparation for war was as important as physical training. Perez-Cruz took an officer development program that had participants study battle history and theories of leadership. Looking to learn from the past, they read Anton Myrer's *Once an Eagle*, T.R. Fehrenbach's *This Kind of War*, and Joseph Galloway's *We Were Soldiers Once ... and Young*. There was so much for officers to consider, from training their soldiers' bodies and minds to figuring out the enemy's strengths and weaknesses. They had to know how to maintain equipment and save lives, and they had to know how to do those things as the enemy tried to kill them.[17]

As for knowing the enemy, Perez-Cruz learned that Iraqi troops had Russian tanks and infantry fighting vehicles. He and his fellow officers knew that in Operation *Desert Storm*, the 24th Infantry Division and the 3rd Infantry Division easily defeated the Iraqis, but this time could be different. Global terrorism made it challenging for military leaders to know who might have infiltrated or be assisting the Iraqi Army. The best course of action for the Americans was to assume the enemy was going to be prepared, disciplined, and determined to fight. Perez-Cruz told his soldiers to never assume a paper tiger and never go into battle overconfident.[18]

Staff Sergeant Jabari Williams *owned* the tank gunnery. He had impressed his superiors in training exercises in South Korea, where he had been stationed with 4th Squadron, 7th Cavalry Regiment before being reassigned to Charlie Company, 1-64 Armor at Fort Stewart. The Army sent Williams to master gunner school, so by the time he got to Kuwait in September 2002, he had earned a reputation for being a sharpshooter. Because of that, his commanders tasked him with setting up the range course and targets in the desert for the battalion's tank training exercises. Williams believed that the 3rd ID, especially 2nd Brigade, conducted some of the most effective training in the Army. 1-64 Armor staged what the troops called "cage matches," in which they created a boxed-in area of about a third of a square mile and put tanks in to maneuver against one another to see who had the best fire control systems and the most prepared crew. By the end of it, soldiers knew the M1A1 tank inside and out, and they operated it confidently and proficiently. To Williams, it was as though he and his comrades knew whether something was wrong with their tank simply by listening to it. Charlie Company was a team of teams that had trained hard together for five months and was a family because of it.[19]

The soldiers needed each other because they had limited contact with family and loved ones back home. There was no Facetime then; the best they had was Yahoo Messenger. On base was a voiceover phone that soldiers could use from time to time, but mostly they talked to each other about the ones they missed, sometimes pulling a picture out of a wallet or a pocket. The soldiers were close enough to ask about relatives by name, to know what the family concerns were. Williams missed his two-year-old daughter, his first child. Williams likened 2nd Brigade's barracks to ancient Sparta. The entire brigade was inside a compound in the middle of the desert, alone but unafraid.[20]

As the political situation developed throughout 2002 and into January 2003, it looked more and more like President George W. Bush was going to demand that Saddam open Iraq up for more weapons inspections. Blount started moving more 3rd ID resources, including his assault command post and one of his command vehicles, over to Kuwait. It wasn't on orders; Blount sensed where things were going and started moving as many assets as he could to Kuwait because he believed it was the smart thing to do. Central to his leadership style was anticipating next steps and making decisions based on his knowledge of the situation at hand, sometimes without waiting for higher approval.

As CENTCOM war planners got to the specifics of operational planning, they established the Coalition Forces Land Component Command, commanded by Lieutenant General David McKiernan. Two corps-level formations – the Army's V Corps, commanded by Lieutenant General William Scott Wallace, and I Marine Expeditionary Force, commanded by General James Terry Conway – fell under CFLCC control. All three of the 3rd ID's brigades were included in the war plans, along with brigades of the 101st Airborne, 82nd Airborne, and 4th Infantry divisions, all under the command of V Corps. Corps assets – hospital, engineering, field artillery, military police, intelligence – also came under V Corps in the order of battle. Commanders at the division level along with Blount included General David Petraeus commanding the 101st Airborne, General Charles Swannack commanding the 82nd Airborne, and General Raymond Odierno commanding the 4th Infantry Division.

Orders came down at the end of 2002, and Blount and his staff flew from Kuwait to Germany in January, trading sand for snow. They made for an incongruous picture when they reported for training in Germany's winter in their desert uniforms. V Corps commanders met in Grafenwöhr, Germany, in January 2003 to conduct a command post exercise, called the Victory Scrimmage, which brought together unit commanders to plan and practice coordination and communication as might be needed during wartime. General David Petraeus and his 101st Airborne Division were there, along with the commanders of the Army's other divisions that were part of Operation *Iraqi Freedom*. For about two weeks, Army commanders and staff simulated the fighting on computers, and they formulated the final battle plans for the mission. Blount and the 3rd ID learned that they would focus on Iraq's 11th Infantry Division and the Medina Division, one of Hussein's elite units. Once the 3rd ID defeated the Iraqi forces, and the assumption in the room was that the division *would* defeat the Iraqis, the soldiers were to establish a forward operating base south and west of Baghdad as part of the Army's efforts to unseat Hussein. The plan formulated in Germany did not have the 3rd ID going into Baghdad. Capturing Tikrit, Hussein's hometown, was Blount's original mission. According to the plans outlined in Germany, the 101st and 82nd would take the capital city.

Initial plans had the 3rd ID fighting between the Tigris and Euphrates rivers straight up to Baghdad while the Marines took a route east of the Tigris. But Blount had wargamed an advance to Baghdad in his office in Riyadh many times, and he knew that his tanks would move more quickly in the desert west of the Euphrates. Going between the rivers, the division would encounter canals, irrigation systems, and farmers' villages, all of which would slow the formations down. Blount explained his vision to his colleagues, and when a computer simulation of the route between the rivers showed slow progress and heavy casualties, they came around to his plan. V Corps commander Wallace gave Blount his blessing. General Tommy Franks, commander of CENTCOM, also approved Blount's plan. The 3rd ID would approach Baghdad from the western desert; war planners in Germany revised their blueprints and plotted objectives according to Blount's course of action.

Other plans included sending 25,000 British troops to take Basra, while I Marine Expeditionary Force ran a parallel course to the 3rd ID, attacking the more heavily populated cities in the Tigris River Valley. Marines and British forces also worked to secure Iraq's southern oil fields. The U.S. Special Forces units working with the Kurds in northern Iraq had found that Hussein's military was about one-third the size of his *Desert Storm*-era force. The U.S. embargo had hurt Saddam's arsenal, but Iraq still had managed to obtain some defense systems, and most of his soldiers had combat experience. U.S. mobilization was a joint effort across the forces, with the 3rd Infantry Division leading while other units readied for war. The 3rd ID's tanks and other armored fighting vehicles were the tip of the spear. V Corps, based in Germany, provided command, intelligence, and military police. XVIII Airborne Corps provided fuel, medical, and Army aviation units. The Marines sent the 1st and 2nd Expeditionary Forces. The Navy's carriers included the USS *Abraham Lincoln* and the USS *Theodore Roosevelt*, and the Navy also sent amphibious task forces that transported thousands of Marines to the Persian Gulf region. Representing the Air Force were the 28th Bomb Wing, 116th Air Control Wing, 16th Special Ops Wing, 57th Operations Wing, and the 49th Fighter Wing. In total, the U.S. was sending more than 200,000 troops, 900 aircraft, more than 100 ships, and more than 1,500 tanks and other armored vehicles. The sheer mass of American force would seem to be unstoppable. As the planning and time progressed, it was determined that V Corps would deploy to Kuwait to take command of the Army units. V Corps would conduct a war-fighter exercise in Germany in January similar to the one the 3rd ID had done at Fort Stewart.

By the end of January 2003, the remaining 3rd ID units still in Fort Stewart had arrived in Kuwait. Division equipment that had not been pre-positioned – mostly aviation, logistics, and command and control vehicles and equipment – was loaded onto several ships docked in Savannah, Georgia. When the loading was complete, the ships set sail for the Middle East. Once in Kuwait, brigade units trained in the Udari Desert in preparation for large-scale conventional ground combat operations against the forces of Saddam Hussein. For four months, 3rd ID soldiers trained daily using battle-ready equipment that was immediately available to them due to the lengthy military buildup before the war.[21] Captain Charles O'Brien was the commander of Alpha Company, 3-69 Armor Battalion, 1st Brigade, and he had been commander of the tank company for about a year. Before that, he had been a Headquarters and Headquarters Company commander. At the platoon and company levels, O'Brien led his soldiers through live fire, maneuver, and nuclear, biological, and chemical warfare training, with the latter including training on how to use chemical suits. After completing basic skills training, O'Brien's company rehearsed actual missions, and rehearsed and rehearsed until O'Brien was sure his soldiers understood the conditions, the environment, and the plans and their intent. Equipment maintenance took up a good portion of Alpha Company's days. Soldiers also had to go through health and welfare procedures, including getting immunizations. When there was down time, Alpha Company played football and soccer as a break from preparing for war.[22]

The 3rd Infantry Division established its main headquarters in Kuwait under the direction of Colonel Jack Sterling, division chief of staff. Headquarters consisted of four high-tech tents connected to each other, and generators powered the lights, computer systems, and air conditioning units. Off to the side was Blount's office with a private entrance. It was where he held meetings, and sometimes he went there to be alone and think about what was coming next, how to handle the training issues at hand. The general's tent office was an oasis in a wartime desert, and stepping through the entrance flap brought him from chaos to quiet. He had two command vehicles, one which was an M113 he used when the division was moving, and a new large prototype tracked vehicle named Zeus. Blount's wife, Anita, fussed at him when she saw a photograph of the M113 with "Zeus" painted clearly on it. Now the Iraqis would know which vehicle to target, she admonished him. At night, Blount slept in a van that had been converted into sleeping quarters.

While the division's brigades were training in Kuwait, Blount and Colonel Mike Birmingham, the 3rd ID's public affairs officer, began bringing in the journalists and photographers who would embed with the three brigades. Pentagon officials had committed to getting more news coverage of the war than had occurred during Operation *Desert Storm*, when only one reporter, Joe Galloway, was embedded with the 24th Infantry Division. Under the leadership of General Barry McCaffrey, the 24th ID had fought one of the largest tank battles since World War II and won a decisive victory for coalition forces, but the battle received little media coverage. Birmingham believed it was possible for the Army to do better. Before Birmingham deployed to Kuwait, Blount called him into his office and laid a copy of *Army Times* on his desk. On the front page was a photograph of a division brigade conducting a training exercise. Blount told Birmingham he wanted the 3rd ID to be as well-known as the 82nd Airborne, the 101st Airborne, and the 10th Mountain divisions. Birmingham recognized the magnitude of Blount's order, and he pledged to make it happen.[23]

Birmingham's route to public affairs wasn't direct, but it was informed by his growing up in working-class Baltimore with parents who subscribed to five daily newspapers and who watched all three network nightly news broadcasts plus *60 Minutes* on Sundays. His father was a Navy veteran who had served on the USS *Nevada* at Iwo Jima, and Birmingham carried on the family's military legacy through ROTC at what was then Western Maryland College. After he was commissioned, Birmingham worked in field artillery and military police in the late 1980s as the Cold War was coming to an end, but in 1991, after Operation *Desert Storm*, he found himself drawn to public affairs, in part because of what he believed to be a lack of media attention to what coalition troops had accomplished in the Gulf War. It took six years and a few more MP assignments, but in 1997 Birmingham received the public affairs officer assignment at North American Aerospace Defense (NORAD) and U.S. Space Command in Colorado Springs. As a joint command, Space Com offered Birmingham the opportunity to work with Air Force, Navy, and Canadian officers as well as Army personnel, and his three years there were crucial to his development as a public affairs officer. It coincided with Y2K, when several dozen reporters were embedded at Space Command to cover the computer crisis some thought would happen when the date rolled over to 2000. His assignment also overlapped with Operation *Desert Fox*, the Clinton administration's bombing of Iraq in 1998 after Hussein failed to comply with UN weapons inspections.[24]

In 2000, Birmingham's assignment at Space Com was up, and he was looking to join an infantry division where he could be the senior public affairs officer. It turned out that the 3rd ID's position was open, and Birmingham took it. The division was deployed to Bosnia, and that was Birmingham's first chance to bring reporters overseas, which involved working through bureaucratic red tape to get reporters on military flights over. He authorized reporters from various media outlets in the Savannah, Georgia, area, which was the location of Fort Stewart, the division's home. When Tennessee National Guard units arrived in Bosnia, Birmingham brought Tennessee reporters over. He saw what was possible when the Army cooperated with the media, not in terms of dictating coverage but of ensuring that reporters knew whom to talk to and understood military operations. It was a complex world for anyone who hadn't been there, and Birmingham believed that if the Army could help civilian reporters understand it, the reporters would be better equipped to cover operations accurately.[25]

Kuwait turned out to be a training ground not just for the 3rd ID, but for the more than 80 reporters and photographers from U.S. and international media who embedded with the division. Birmingham proposed to his superiors at U.S. Army Central (ARCENT) that the division embed journalists for the training period in Kuwait, including the three-day, two-night breaching exercise that every battalion was scheduled to conduct. ARCENT took it to McKiernan at CFLCC and got the green light. During about 90 days of training exercises, journalists learned firsthand what the division was going to do once the invasion began, and Birmingham and his staff briefed them about what to wear, what to bring, and other logistics. There wouldn't be time for hand-holding once the war began. Blount also decided to bring journalists inside the wire – onto the base. They were dropped off with the units they would embed with, and they figured out with the unit commanders where they would go, whom they would ride with, and what the unit was going to do. As the division got closer to "go time," Blount brought all the journalists in and walked them through the division's war plan. It was all off the record, and no cameras or recorders were allowed, but Blount showed them a large map illustrating the drive from Kuwait to Baghdad. He didn't include all the details, but it was enough for the reporters to get a decent sense of what was coming.[26]

Not all officers bought into Birmingham's plan initially, and he knew that some out in the world would accuse the division of trying to propagandize the media. But he was confident that the process would give journalists more confidence to do their jobs, resulting in more precise coverage of 3rd ID operations. Each of the three major U.S. television networks – ABC, NBC, and CBS – sent journalists to embed with the division, as did AP and Reuters, the major newspaper companies such as Gannett and McClatchy, and international news outlets including the BBC, Agence France-Presse, and Sky News. Some came with large crews and elaborate equipment, while others showed up with a backpack and a recorder. As part of the training, Birmingham laid four ground rules for reporters: don't say where division forces are located unless already in contact with the enemy; don't say where troops are going; focus tightly on live shots to avoid giving clues to location; and no footage or photos of dead or dying soldiers. Breaking the last rule was cause for dismissal.[27]

Blount and V Corps leaders had conducted extensive analysis on Iraq's regular army and Republican Guard units. They knew the names of division commanders, where they lived, and how many soldiers were under their command. Intelligence indicated that soldiers in the regular army likely wouldn't fight hard because they felt no loyalty to Hussein. Many of the soldiers had taken a beating in the first Gulf War and believed Hussein had abandoned them. Americans had tried to capitalize on their disaffection by waging psychological warfare prior to the invasion, dropping leaflets encouraging them to go home. Blount estimated that half or more might lay down their arms once the fighting intensified. The Republican Guard was a different story. U.S. Army leaders expected them to fight. Their mission was to protect Hussein and his rule. The X factor was the Fedayeen, civilian militias. The Americans were aware of paramilitary units but didn't know much about them. Intelligence reports stating that most Iraqis would surrender in the face of U.S. forces led Blount and others to believe that included the militia.

CENTCOM planners knew they had to strategize for urban warfare. Perkins and his commanders often discussed the risks involved in an urban fight. The thought of urban warfare conjured images of the 1993 fighting in Mogadishu, Somalia, during which soldiers of Task Force Ranger and the 10th Mountain Division battled the Somali National Alliance and Somali irregulars. During the fighting, Somali forces shot down three U.S. Blackhawk helicopters, and a mob of Somali civilians and irregulars dragged the bodies of dead U.S. soldiers through the streets of Mogadishu. The memory of Mogadishu weighed on Perkins as he thought about leading an armored brigade into another capital city. Baghdad's population numbered around six million, and it had been one of the most heavily armed cities since Operation *Desert Storm*. Alleys, doorways, and rooftops provided fighting positions that would give the Iraqis an advantage in an urban battle.[28]

Saddam's regime was headquartered in Baghdad, and there were at least 40 other cities that planners expected could factor into a campaign. Army leaders remembered Stalingrad and Berlin in World War II, Hue in the Vietnam War, and Russia's experience in Grozny in the Chechen War. Urban warfare involved house-to-house combat, civilian casualties, and massive destruction of buildings and homes. Major Louis Rago led the Army's planning effort for urban warfare in Iraq. Rago saw how Saddam used municipal services and city organization to control his population. Saddam poured money into neighborhoods that supported his regime and neglected the areas that didn't.[29]

Rago sketched out a six-pronged urban organization system to illustrate how Saddam used city operations to control Iraqis. The economic system included oil and gasoline, banking, trade, and industry. Ethnic and tribal divisions, religion, culture, and education fell under the human system. Political parties, local and national government, and information were part of the political system. Under infrastructure were telecommunications, media, transportation, power, water, food, and medical services. The military system included regular and elite forces, as well as militias and paramilitary groups. Internal security and intelligence included the executive office and cabinet, counterintelligence and foreign intelligence agencies, executive personal security forces, local and national police, and weapons of mass destruction.[30] Rago posited that if U.S. forces could attack the systems Saddam most relied upon to control the population, Americans could avoid the kind of urban combat that resulted in massive death and destruction. As U.S. policymakers intended the war to be one of liberation, Rago and other strategists sought ways to minimize civilian casualties.[31] Based on Rago's analysis and proposals, McKiernan and Wallace, along with the Marine Corps' Conway, planned raids, air strikes, ground attacks, and psychological operations designed to break the Ba'ath regime's control of Baghdad.

What the division would do once it got to Baghdad was on the minds of commanders across the ranks. Colonel William Grimsley, commander of 1st Brigade, was among the leaders who assembled in an auditorium at Camp Udairi the Sunday before the invasion for a briefing on the Army's war plans. As the commanders sat in theater seats, V Corps planners filed in and presented what they had wargamed in Germany. From crossing the Iraq border to reaching Baghdad, the blueprint was detailed down to brigade level. Who, what, when, where, and why. But the plans grew foggy once U.S. forces arrived in Baghdad. The planners envisioned units embarking on a series of raids into the city to capture or kill regime targets and then coming back out. Grimsley wondered about the logic in the idea. It seemed that V Corps planners were imagining Paris in 1848, where citizens stormed the Champs-Elysées in protest and King Louis Philippe abdicated the throne. Did the planners think U.S. troops would march up Baghdad's version of the Arc de Triomphe and citizens would shower them with roses? Grimsley knew what his brigade had to do to get to Baghdad, but he wasn't sure what would happen once his soldiers got there.[32]

Back at Camp Udairi, food for U.S. troops consisted of hot meals during training, but once the division received orders to tear down and prepare to attack in the weeks leading up to the invasion, Blount had his soldiers shift over to MREs – meals ready-to-eat. He hoped it would prepare them for what they would eat over the next several weeks, if not months. Soldiers couldn't tell their families and friends back home about the food, though, because they didn't have much chance to call home. There were no cell phone towers out in the desert, so the best they could do was go to a small internet café set up in the camp and send e-mails. The lack of communication was stressful on the families, not because they wanted to know what their men and women were eating, but because they paid attention to the news. Secretary of State Colin Powell had addressed the UN on the problem of Saddam Hussein. President Bush talked about ultimatums. Hussein refused to cooperate with weapons inspectors. From what television and newspapers told the families back home, it seemed that war was imminent.

Managing soldiers' and their families' needs made Blount feel like a corporate CEO. As a division commander, he was responsible for some 20,000 soldiers, many of whom had young families. His service in previous ranks had gradually prepared him for managing people on a large scale. When he was an installation commander, he was responsible for the day-to-day lives of his soldiers. Fort Stewart had family housing, two elementary schools, a hospital, and thousands of acres of land, and the installation commander was the point person for all of it. Blount relied on the assistance of his garrison commander, Colonel Gerry Poltorak, to help soldiers and their families with day-to-day problems, from a broken dishwasher in someone's house to reports of mold in the air conditioning unit at the elementary school on post. Blount had to remember that most of the newly enlisted soldiers were still teenagers. Some married young, but others were there completely on their own. Blount had to be a father to some of them, teaching them how to manage their first checking account, or encouraging them to go to parent-teacher conferences if they had children in school.

Reaching soldiers on such a deeply personal level required earning their trust, which Blount strove to achieve. A naturally reserved man, Blount realized the importance of sitting down and talking with people in their own environments, whether in the Saudi desert or in a mess hall on a U.S. military base. At Fort Stewart, Blount ate in the dining hall with the soldiers. He'd walked up to a table and ask to join those sitting at it. He was the division commander, but he was also a person who had wanted to be a soldier since he was a child. Although it became more difficult as he progressed in rank, Blount tried to be a father figure to the young soldiers, encouraging them to open up and unload their feelings and opinions. Beyond instruction, cajoling, and punishment, Blount wanted to be there for his soldiers.

Blount would also go out and observe training exercises between meetings as a way to connect with the division's soldiers. About once a week, he observed night gunnery training in addition to supervising his staff who were involved in personnel management, logistics, intelligence, linguistics, war planning, training exercises, and everything else that went into running an Army division. Learning to manage people went back even further than Blount's days as installation commander. As a second lieutenant, he was responsible for 15 soldiers. Then he moved up the ranks to captain, and then to company commander, where he supervised about 150 troops. At every level, the Army trained the officers on what would be new in their new roles, what to do if a soldier broke the law, how to talk to the media, and other issues. As Blount rose higher on the promotion ladder, he thought of ways to delegate some of the managerial responsibilities to those below him so that he could focus on war planning. When Blount took command of the 3rd ID, he found a colonel he trusted and assigned him to deal with the schools, and housing and family issues. Doing so gave Blount the freedom to strategize and come up with battle plans.

As division commander, Blount had court-martial authority and had to handle accidents, incidents of fraternization, AWOL incidents, DUIs, and other cases that required judicial handling. Suicide, attempted suicide, a missing weapon, and personal issues such as divorce also required reporting. On these types of issues, Blount saw himself responsible for unit morale and keeping track of his soldiers' mental health in order to prevent suicide or accidents related to mental health. Every week, Blount sat down for an hour with the division's staff judge advocate, Colonel Lyle Cayce, to discuss legal issues and make sure he had a clear sense of military crime and punishment, what required a lawyer, what required a judge, and what didn't. Cayce also helped soldiers prepare to deploy by working with them to ensure they had their legal affairs in order. Up to that point in their military careers, most young soldiers had not thought about designating power of attorney or writing a will, but both were necessary tasks to complete before entering a war zone. As word came down that the division would be deployed in the spring, soldiers also had to make sure someone filed their taxes for them.[33]

In Kuwait, and later in Iraq, Cayce's primary responsibility was offering commanders legal advice on the rules of engagement. Cayce had deployed to Kuwait in January 2003 and was stationed at the Division Tactical Command Post (DTAC), serving as legal advisor to Blount and Brigadier General Lloyd Austin. Normally, the staff judge advocate stays at Division Main headquarters with the commanding general, but because the 3rd ID's goal was to get to Baghdad quickly, Cayce asked for permission to ride with Austin, who would be closest to the front-line battles. As battle captain, Austin would be advising the lead elements of the battalions and brigades whose soldiers would likely be the ones engaging most closely with the enemy. Cayce figured this would be where knowledge of the rules of engagement would be most needed. He did not make orders or decisions; he provided legal analysis that commanders then used to give orders. What collateral damage might occur if the unit fires on the target? What weapons systems are available to handle the target? As commanders attempted to answer such questions, Cayce gave his legal opinions about whether proposed plans of action violated the rules of war.

Soldiers had received some training on the rules of engagement while at Fort Stewart, but the bulk of the training occurred in Kuwait. Division legal experts trained soldiers on topics such as employing force lawfully, self-defense, unnecessary civilian suffering, collateral damage, and engaging with noncombatants. The rules of engagement were based on the international standards enshrined in the Hague and Geneva Conventions. About 70 paralegals and lawyers, including some civilians, worked for Cayce in Kuwait. Among the rules that soldiers needed to know was a directive from CFLCC that U.S. troops should not fire at mosques, schools, or populations centers.[34]

On March 17, Bush gave Hussein his ultimatum – 48 hours to leave Iraq. While Hussein mulled it over, or didn't, 250,000 troops, 1,000 combat aircraft, and a naval fleet were on the ready in the Persian Gulf region to attack Iraq at Bush's command. Thirty U.S. Navy ships and submarines were poised to launch hundreds of Tomahawk missiles on Iraqi targets. The Navy had also mobilized five aircraft carriers – three in the Persian Gulf and two in the eastern Mediterranean Sea. Each aircraft carrier featured about 50 strike planes. F/A-18 Hornets and F-14 Tomcats were ready for the air war.[35] Hussein scoffed at the Americans, saying that Iraqis lay in wait to become martyrs for their nation. He also continued to deny having weapons of mass destruction while admitting that he once possessed them. Australia, Poland, and Britain promised to commit troops, while Canada, France, and Russia questioned and criticized U.S. plans. Rumsfeld and Bush dismissed European criticism of their war plans, but Bush took seriously Britain's opinion, and Tony Blair came through for him. Other European allies wanted to continue UN weapons inspections, but State and Defense officials argued that Hussein was pulling the wool over inspectors' eyes.[36]

In the U.S., an antiwar movement attempted to mobilize before the war started, running ads on television and organizing protests in Washington, DC. Polls indicated that American public opinion on a war in Iraq was lukewarm. According to a *Newsweek* poll, about 53 percent agreed with Bush's position on Iraq, but two-thirds of Americans wanted the president to be more patient with the weapons inspection and disarmament process before going to war. Some Americans disapproved of the U.S. going it alone or with just one or two allies rather than UN support. Cheney and Rumsfeld, the most hawkish of Bush's advisors, argued that pre-emptive war was morally justified in the post-9/11 world. The Bush administration also asserted that invading Iraq was morally justified because the U.S. should use its power for good by bringing freedom and democracy to those who don't have it. "This nation never conquers, but we liberate," Bush once said. Colin Powell, more moderate than Cheney or Rumsfeld, compared a possible invasion of Iraq to U.S. intervention in Panama in 1989. The removal of Manuel Noriega led to the country's democratization.

Some U.S. allies objected to what they saw as the start of a 21st-century American empire, in which the U.S. would set the world order, through war or other means, on its own without the input of allies or the UN. Britain, Spain, and Bulgaria offered support to Bush's move to war, but most UN members, including those on the Security Council, wanted to wait and allow inspections to go on longer. France and Germany were particularly vocal about their opposition to war in Iraq. Part of what bothered the skeptics was Bush's personality. Some allies saw him as a cowboy with his hand always ready to draw his pistol from its holster and shoot first, ask questions later. Bush tried to downplay that, telling Czech president Vaclav Havel, "I know some in Europe see me as a Texas cowboy with six-shooters at my side. But the truth is I prefer to work with a posse."[37] But even his folksy statements reflected the cowboy image that concerned some in the UN.

Among those who cautioned against war were Arab intelligence contacts who warned that it would give Osama bin Laden another reason to attack the U.S. again. Since Al-Qaeda's attacks on the U.S. embassies in Kenya and Tanzania in 1998, Bin Laden had asserted that America's support for Israel against Arab states was a primary reason for targeting the U.S. If the U.S. military were to roll into Iraq, it would confirm Bin Laden's accusation that U.S. policy in the Middle East meant harm to the Arab world. Some regional observers feared a domino effect if war broke out in Iraq. It could embolden Arab states and supporting non-state actors to attack Israel in retaliation, and if that happened, it could give Israel reason to expel Palestinians from the West Bank and Gaza. The chaos could destabilize the region for years. Skepticism about America's ability to build a viable democracy in Iraq after a war marked reports about postwar plans. A refugee crisis, corruption, and weapons falling into unknown hands were just some of the ominous scenarios analysts predicted.[38]

Iraq could not compete with the U.S. militarily. The sheer size and strength of America's armed forces, as well as its technologically advanced military, would have little problem crushing even Iraq's most elite Republican Guard units. It was the aftermath that worried observers. Iraqis might welcome U.S. forces initially and embrace humanitarian aid in the wake of Hussein's removal, but the good feelings might likely be temporary, and when resentment at U.S. occupation set in, terrorism worse than before would strike. Iraqis would no longer embrace U.S. soldiers and the items they handed out. The U.S. would be seen as another colonizer, and any person who took power in the wake of U.S. occupation would appear to be a puppet of America. Regardless of how much Iraqis wanted democracy and freedom, how much they wanted an end to Hussein's tyranny, they would not be happy with anything that looked like American imperialism.

Writing for *Newsweek*, journalist Christopher Dickey summed up the international concern: "No one doubts that America will win a war with Iraq. But many wonder if it will win the peace." In the lead-up to the war, Bush showed his idealism in speeches and comments that seemed committed to the notion of America's destiny to spread freedom and order in the world. He expressed an intractable, almost naïve, belief in America's responsibility to remove evil governments through military force for the good of those who couldn't. Bush seemed to be a true believer in the notion that war in Iraq would lead to peace in the Middle East. Such an attitude showed Bush to be out of touch with the history of the region, where widespread peace had not been a reality in the 20th century. The status quo held on at the turn of the 21st. Naivete or hubris or both caused Bush to believe that U.S. military intervention could finally be the thing that brought peace to the Middle East.[39]

The night before the invasion, Blount and his team of commanders sat down to dinner together. It was their last meal before the war, and the last hot meal any of them would have for nearly a month. It had the feeling of a last supper, and Blount called it such as he presided over the meal with his most trusted colleagues to his right and his left. Brigadier General Lloyd Austin was his assistant division commander for maneuver, also known as Blount's right-hand man. Command Sergeant Major Julian Kellerman, the senior enlisted soldier in the division, Brigadier General Bill Weber, all three brigade commanders, the logistics team, and the division's lawyer, among others, were there. Colonel Roberta A. Woods, commander of the 24th Corps Support Group, literally kept the division running as its fuel supplier. The division's vehicles needed about 600,000 gallons of fuel per day. Blount had worked with Woods at Fort Stewart, and when he got word that V Corps wanted to use her fuel trucks to build fuel farms near Tallil and other air bases, Blount jokingly told her that she should remember who she worked for. He made his case to Wallace that the division needed Woods' fuel trucks to keep moving, and Wallace agreed. As they ate, they discussed battle plans and contingencies in the matter-of-fact way of those who have prepared for a job and understand that whatever is ahead is simply part of that job.

The troops of the 3rd Infantry Division waited in northern Kuwait a few miles from the Iraq border for the green light to roll. Soldiers knew their Bradley fighting vehicles and M1 Abrams tanks, which they had been training on for months. They were to lead the U.S. invasion, and they were trained as a rapid-reaction armor and infantry force that could go anywhere on short notice. The 3rd Infantry Division was a combination of what made the U.S. military the deadliest fighting force in the world: America's technologically advanced weaponry and its well-trained soldiers. One tank read "All the way to Baghdad." Many of the soldiers in Kuwait had not seen combat before.[40]

"Go time" approached, and soldiers and tank crews were sleeping on their vehicles. They were loaded up and ready to go. UN representatives traveled to Kuwait to observe the American troops as they corralled near the berm. All of the leaders high up on the chain of command were being briefed on war plans, so Jabari Williams, the senior staff sergeant in Charlie Company, represented the 3rd ID as the liaison to the UN team. Williams articulated the division's task and purpose to the diplomats, and as he reflected later on the meeting, he recognized the impact of his mentors on his ability to speak confidently for the division. Mentorship had been part of the training that prepared the soldiers of the 3rd ID for what was ahead.[41]

As the soldiers of the 3rd ID got ready for the invasion, they kept in mind a mantra: "Your ticket home is Baghdad." Their mission was to get to the capital city and depose Hussein, and if they completed the mission, they could go home. Even the most gung-ho soldier longed for home. Home was the reason and the reward. They would have to cross the desert to get there.

Invasion

A full moon glowed in the desert sky the night that the 3rd ID led U.S. and coalition forces into Iraq.

The Iraqi dictator disregarded Bush's ultimatum, and in doing so, he gave the green light to Bush to launch his war. An intelligence tip had suggested that Saddam and his sons were in a bunker at Dora Farms, a compound on the southeastern outskirts of Baghdad, and the Americans took a chance, sending up three dozen Tomahawk cruise missiles from ships in the Persian Gulf and the Red Sea. On March 19, two F-117A stealth bombers dropped four bombs with the hope that at least some of the U.S. warheads would strike the target, decapitating the Iraqi regime by killing Saddam. If the strike was successful, the land war might not be necessary, but defense authorities had prepared a plan to get a force to Baghdad quickly to stabilize the situation if that happened. As fate would have it, the strike failed to take out Hussein. Half a world away, President Bush appeared on television the evening of March 19 to announce that the U.S. was now at war with Iraq.

Bush had asserted that the purpose of the U.S. invasion was to establish a free, democratic, prosperous Iraq that would be an American ally. Removing Saddam Hussein and his Ba'athist regime from power was the first step in writing a new chapter of Iraq's history.[1] The troops of the 3rd ID had their orders. From the berm to Baghdad, the units of the 3rd ID led the Army's drive up through Iraq, with Baghdad, Saddam's seat of power, in the crosshairs. The march up-country was sure to be a long and complicated one, as the spear had to pierce through smaller cities en route to the capital. Iraqi regulars, Saddam's elite forces, and paramilitary units were poised for battle.

Iraqi forces fought back from the start, launching rockets at U.S. positions along the border and igniting oil wells. Setting the oil wells on fire could create an environmental disaster, and CENTCOM's commander, General Tommy Franks, wanted to avoid that. Original war plans had called for two weeks of air operations before launching the land war, similar to the air campaign that had preceded Operation *Desert Storm* in 1991. But concerns about Iraq's oil fields pushed Franks to start with the land invasion instead. The decision did not preclude the "shock and awe" of air strikes; it only postponed them. U.S. airpower demonstrated its capabilities the night after the ground invasion began, raining bombs down on government and military sites in Baghdad, Kirkuk, Mosul, and Tikrit.

Hussein had received a tip that the Americans had information about his regular army, so he secretly had built up his paramilitary Fedayeen. He deployed the fighters to Basra, An Nasiriyah, As Samawah, An Najaf, and Karbala, positioning 3,000 of them in each city. Once in place, the Fedayeen cadres mobilized additional support from local civilians in their areas. Their primary method for convincing civilians to join the militias was to threaten to kill their wives, children, parents, and other family members if they refused. Groups arrived at villages in trucks and buses, militiamen brandishing their weapons. After announcing to bystanders that the Americans had invaded, militia leaders sought out all the local able-bodied men to enlist. When a man refused, a cadre shot his wife point blank as a lesson to other husbands reluctant to join the cause. It was a recruitment tactic that the Fedeyeen used in cities throughout southern Iraq. For the men of those cities and towns, the only motivation to fight was fear. Enlisting with the Fedeyeen was the only way to protect their families from Saddam's henchmen.[2]

The militia leaders handed out AK-47s and rocket-propelled grenade (RPG) launchers to the new "recruits," and they went into battle in their civilian clothes, riding in Toyota pickup trucks, buses, ambulances, and taxi cabs. The Fedayeen had retrofitted some of the Toyotas with a mounted machine gun, recoilless rifle, or air defense weapon.[3] Teams of Fedayeen used backhoes to dig fighting positions along the Euphrates River. Every quarter mile or so heading north, they dug fighting positions and stocked them with weapons. Once the fighting began, Fedayeen fighters could dive into the trenches, pick up the guns, and shoot at U.S. troops. On their side was the element of surprise, as the Americans couldn't predict when a militia would pop up.[4] From what Army commanders and soldiers gathered from their encounters with the Fedayeen, the paramilitaries had received basic weapons handling and fighting instructions but had no tactical leadership or ability to respond to battlefield conditions as they changed. Yet U.S. commanders remained concerned about the Fedayeen because there were so many of them.[5]

On the morning of the invasion, March 19, General Blount boarded a helicopter to observe the 3rd ID's formation from the air. It was the only way he could get a clear view of the massive assembly of military equipment positioned at the border. He wanted to make sure all the parts were in place and note any potential problems before the vehicles rolled. A bird's-eye view was the most efficient way to inspect everything.[6] Once he had gotten a look from all the possible angles and was satisfied, the helicopter delivered him back to the ground, and he returned to his assault command post.

At the initial entry into Iraq, there were no paved roads, so Army engineers used satellite technology to map the area and determine where there were roads and bridges that could accommodate the 3rd ID's heavy equipment. It took several days of work, but the engineers were able to advise the general with confidence about routes that were safe for the tonnage that would pass over them. Before the 3rd ID rolled out, Blount split his division in two. As he envisioned moving some 10,000 Army vehicles from Kuwait to Baghdad along Highway 8, the only major road they had, he foresaw the slow pace it would take to get all of the convoys to Baghdad, especially if vehicles broke down along the way, which was almost sure to happen. Blount consulted with his engineers, and they used their satellite technology again, this time to determine a second route.

It was possible that some of the formations could swing out into the western desert and traverse trails through the sand, but Blount worried about heavy fuel trucks getting bogged down in the sand or while crossing wadis – dry valleys that collected rain during heavy rainfall. If the fuel trucks got stuck, the rest of the vehicles would eventually be stranded once they ran out of fuel. But the quicker the formations could move, he reasoned, the harder it would be for Saddam's forces to launch offenses that could slow the division. Continuous movement as quickly as possible to keep the Iraqis guessing was central to Blount's strategy for the invasion. The satellite imagery and advice from his engineers convinced the general that a segment of the division could make it off-road through the desert. Blount planned that the two segments would eventually link up at As Samawah.

To cross the border into Iraq required crossing a 6-mile barrier made up of tank ditches, barbed wire, electrified fencing, and berms of dirt. Soldiers referred to the whole thing collectively as "the berm." Ironically, the berm's original purpose was to keep Iraqi forces out of Kuwait, yet now it stood in the way of the American advance into Iraq. To prepare for the crossing, the 3rd ID performed an elaborately choreographed production that involved moving 10,000 tanks, Bradleys, Humvees, fuel trucks, and other vehicles from their encampments in the Kuwaiti desert and positioning them on the border with Iraq. The dance, nothing short of an armored ballet, took place under the cover of darkness.

Combat engineers got to work cutting ten passage lanes in the berm. Construction teams also laid down bridges so that the vehicles could pass over the tank ditches. As the engineers worked, the soldiers of the 3rd Squadron, 7th Cavalry Regiment (3-7 Cavalry) stood guard protecting them. Without the Army engineers, bridge layers, and bulldozer drivers, the armored formation would not have been able to cross the border. It wasn't a maniacal rush into Iraq. The work was methodical and required patience and focus. Professional, skilled soldiers figured out how to create safe passage for the thousands of soldiers set to enter Iraq.

Colonel John Peabody's engineers eventually cleared the ten lanes sometime after midnight on March 20, and Blount commanded the vehicles through them with the 3rd ID in the lead for V Corps. Each vehicle carried about three days' worth of water and MREs for those riding in it. The armored formation included 21,000 troops, 250 M1 Abrams tanks, and hundreds of Bradley fighting vehicles, artillery, rocket launchers, and engineering vehicles. Support vehicles for the 82nd Airborne, 101st Airborne, and V Corps including fuel and supply trucks were also part of the convoy. They navigated minefields and barbed wire as they made the crossing. Embedded news crews from CNN, ABC, and Fox filmed the high-tech 21st-century cavalry charge of the 3-7 Cavalry into the vast and empty desert of southern Iraq. As the division began its crossing, an Iraqi missile hit less than a mile away. The 3rd ID needed to hurry and get on the move.[7]

Alexis Perez-Cruz's unit, 2-69 Armor, was the first battalion right behind the division cavalry squadron, 3-7 Cavalry, to cross the berm. Perez-Cruz was both a tank commander and the executive officer for Charlie Company. An international relations junkie, Perez-Cruz had studied up on Hussein, WMDs, and the potential connections between Iraq and terrorist networks like Al-Qaeda. But as his unit crossed the line of departure, the only thing on his mind was preparedness. 2-69 Armor had rehearsed all possible scenarios, in the daytime and at night, in exercises with air support. The soldiers had rehearsed with their hatches closed as though they were in a chemical attack.[8]

When it was "go time," the soldiers packed up and took their positions. Perez-Cruz had managed to buy a radio online and have it shipped to him in Kuwait, and he was able to pick up the BBC's signal. He and his soldiers crowded around the radio and listened as Secretary of State Colin Powell gave a speech and President Bush announced that the U.S. was going to war in Iraq. It was a surreal moment, as though the president was giving orders to the soldiers directly through Perez-Cruz's radio. As the BBC reporter announced that rockets had fired, Perez-Cruz looked behind him and saw the flares of Tomahawk land-attack missiles. As the 3rd ID's vehicles began rumbling across the berm, tank crews played AC/DC's "Hells Bells" and Metallica songs. Although it felt surreal, it was real. The 3rd ID was going to war.[9]

In Charlie Company, 1-64 Armor, commanders gave Staff Sergeant Jabari Williams one of the only two vehicles in the entire company that had a Force Battle Command Brigade and Below system. FBCB2 was a computer-digitized screen with a map and graphics that helped the driver navigate from one point to another. Williams had had an opportunity to train on the system, so his commander gave him a chance to use it at war. The executive officer rode in an M113 personnel carrier with the first sergeant and tracked the company's movement. As the soldiers of C Company sat in their vehicles waiting to go, Williams looked up and saw missiles with "U.S. Army" emblazoned on them. It was his first time going into combat.[10]

Captain Charles O'Brien, commander of Alpha Company, 3-69 Armor, was in a tent with some other commanders discussing Iraq's burning oil fields when he heard cheering outside. The commanders rushed out of the tent and saw soldiers up on the front decks and turrets of their tanks. U.S. rockets were flying through the sky, attacking an Iraqi outpost on the border. It was how O'Brien learned that the war had started. Soon he and his soldiers were moving out.[11]

Blount rode in his command vehicle, the M113 armored personnel carrier nicknamed "Zeus." M113s had been one of the most common armored vehicles the U.S. and South Vietnamese armies used in the Vietnam War. Their lighter weight allowed for increased mobility and made them easier to transport than heavier vehicles, but their lightness meant machine-gun fire could damage them. Blount rode behind the lead battalion. At the top of the M113 was a hatch from which Blount could stand and look out, and he often took that position. It was important to him that his soldiers see him and know that he was up front with them. Brigadier General Lloyd Austin, Blount's assistant division commander, also rode in an M113. Blue Force Trackers allowed Blount and Austin to observe and communicate with division forces about their locations, enemy positions, and battlefield conditions and give orders in response to developments in real time. The awareness that Blue Force Tracker technology gave Blount, as well as his trust in his brigade commanders to respond to what they saw, gave the 3rd ID the flexibility to handle changes on the battlefield that could occur rapidly and unexpectedly. If a vehicle moved out of FM radio range with another vehicle, commanders and crews could e-mail each other via Blue Force Trackers, GPS-enabled technology that gave commanders the ability to watch movement on the battlefield, so they always remained in communication.

When Colonel William Grimsley addressed his 1st Brigade soldiers, he told them to take a deep breath; they knew what to do. He had complete confidence in them and the training they had undergone for this moment.[12] As 1st Brigade passed over the berm, soldiers from the engineering units that had made the crossing possible stood atop the berm and waved American flags. The 3rd ID's tip of the spear had pierced Iraq's border and was on its way north. Army leaders had expected a couple of enemy tanks to be waiting for them as they crossed into Iraq. Intelligence had suggested as much. Intelligence didn't know the half of it. Eleven Iraqi tanks, as well as other vehicles and an infantry unit, met the Americans at the crossing. The enemy soldiers stood their ground and opened fire on the 3rd ID. Yet the Iraqis' element of surprise did little against the thousands of U.S. armored vehicles. Soldiers of the 3rd ID, overwatched by division scouts and attack helicopters, destroyed the Iraqi unit quickly and prepared again to move.[13] Other than that enemy encounter, the vast desert surrounding the column was barren except for the occasional Bedouin encampment. While the vehicles rumbled by, Bedouin adults and children ventured out of their tents to watch in astonishment the advance of American tanks, Bradleys, armored personnel carriers, and other Army vehicles. The Bedouin tribes were the first Iraqis the 3rd ID encountered upon entering Iraq, and the emptiness of the desert belied the urban nature of the war the 3rd ID would eventually fight.[14]

Shortly after the war began, General Tommy Franks, commander of CENTCOM, issued a statement outlining his lofty goals for U.S. intervention in Iraq. Disarming Iraq and removing Saddam's regime would not be the end. Franks declared that U.S. troops would "liberate the Iraqi people" from an oppressive, torturous, and terroristic leader. He also promised that the U.S. would provide humanitarian aid to Iraqis, including food and medical supplies. Ultimately, the U.S. would help the Iraqis start over with a government of their choosing.[15]

Franks offered more than a military victory. He made a long-term commitment to Iraq's political development and to meeting the needs of Iraqis that went beyond fighting a war to take down a dictator. The question was whether the U.S. could deliver on all of it. While America had a proven track record of delivering humanitarian aid to war-torn regions of the globe, it did not have a stellar resume when it came to nation building. The State and Defense departments had not determined who would be in charge of postwar nation building before the 3rd ID led U.S. forces into Iraq, and Franks' commitment to Iraqis after the war foreshadowed a military engagement that would not end when the guns fell silent.

As ground forces pushed further into Iraq, F-117s and B-2 bombers hit targets in Baghdad with no opposition from the Iraqi air force. The air missions were so successful that three days into the fighting, the air campaign shifted focus to targeting the Republican Guard divisions positioned around Baghdad. Most formidable of these forces was the Medina Division. Intelligence reports had indicated that division soldiers had hidden their tanks around Karbala, less than 30 miles southwest of Baghdad. To complement his official military, Saddam distributed ammunition and weapons to villages and towns throughout the country, enabling the development of the Fedayeen. While his air defense systems were not of the most current technology, he had a lot of them, and occasionally they would inflict damage upon U.S. forces.

Guiding U.S. operations in Iraq was a concept known as "effects-based strategy." Instead of fighting a war of attrition, troops would use minimum force to maximum effect by identifying targets that would help achieve the overall political goals of the mission. In the case of Iraq, the political goal was the removal of Saddam Hussein and the Ba'ath Party, which was why U.S. military strategists planned a first strike aimed at Saddam's suspected hiding place. If U.S. forces decapitated the Iraq regime, America could avoid a lengthy war.[16]

Blount's top priority was getting to Baghdad as quickly as possible. A rapid advance and ultimate removal of Hussein would cause the Republican Guard to collapse. The units would not be able to keep up with and continuously prepare for the next encounter with U.S. forces. But he faced a delicate balance between forging ahead to Baghdad and protecting the supply units that were vital to keeping the convoy moving. Without fuel and other supplies, any gains from speed could be lost.

In order to reach Baghdad, the 3rd ID's armored formations had to make their way from objective to objective, mostly along Highway 8 and Highway 1. The objectives were points near cities that the 3rd ID had to pass by and secure on the way to Baghdad. Some harbored hostile forces waiting to attack Americans. Logistics remained a concern throughout the advance to Baghdad, and protecting the lines of communication was of utmost importance to the war effort, especially ensuring safe passage of fuel trucks to the combat units so that they would not get stuck waiting to refuel. Truck convoys bringing supplies to the front of the formation caused traffic jams all the way back to the Kuwaiti border where the reinforcements came in. Crews had to move broken-down vehicles out of formation so that mechanics could repair them. The Americans had established "fuel farms," large bags of JP-8 fuel that were partially buried underground until needed for refueling.

Taking objectives prevented Iraqi forces from moving reinforcements into the vicinity of the cities and also prevented

Iraqis from interdicting operations en route to the cities. Securing the lines of communication, the routes that connect an operating military unit with its supply units, was vital to the 3rd ID's ability to operate effectively. It's why disrupting the lines of communication was an important strategic goal for enemy forces. Before the war, the Iraqi Army had hoarded stockpiles of weapons, and soldiers and militia used them to attack the trail of the armored columns, aiming at supply, maintenance, and communications units to disable them.

Woods' 24th Corps Support Group was spread out and assigned to locations in Iraq and served the refuel needs of the brigades and battalions that passed through. In order to maintain command and control in such a complex environment, Woods placed personnel she trusted in positions to operate independently if needed, and then units reported back to her later. Woods and her deputy commander, Lieutenant Colonel Pat Voller, alternated between two command posts, a main one and a forward CP. She kept one located with the 3rd ID since that was 24th CSG's main customer, and she tried to keep one forward and one to the rear so that she could respond to fuel needs at various points in the troop formations and keep operations moving. Prior to crossing the line of departure, Woods and her deputy had worked out a plan for how each command post would handle fuel supply issues, and she had also established plans with the commanders of subordinate units during training in Kuwait, so by the time they were invading, Woods and the commanders she was working with knew the expectations and unit capabilities. Training and relationship building in Kuwait was crucial to ensuring that the 24th CSG could serve the fuel needs of the 3rd ID over the long distances that developed as a result of some 10,000 Army vehicles moving in formations toward Baghdad.[17]

To establish fueling points for the 3rd ID, soldiers of the 24th CSG built logistics support areas (LSAs) at points along the division's route. The first was forward logistics base Cedar near Tallil Air Base, and the 24th CSG handed it off to another CSG when it was time for Woods' brigade to move on. Next, Woods sent a battalion forward with 2nd Brigade, and those soldiers established

LSA Bushmaster, where they positioned the fuel bags for trucks that needed to draw fuel and take it to the forward vehicles to keep the operation going. Woods ordered a battalion to stay at Bushmaster with the 7th Corps Support Group until all of its elements arrived. The third logistics support area 24th CSB established was LSA Dogwood, which was created in response to Blount's order that support troops not operate east of the Euphrates due to the risks to non-armored vehicles. With the LSAs established, Woods hoped her brigade could meet all the fuel needs of the 3rd ID and other V Corps units her CSG also had to service, but at times, she found herself having to ration the various combat units, something she had not anticipated having to do. If she had two days' worth of rations, should she give both to the 3rd ID, or give one day's worth to another V Corps division such as the 4th ID or the 101st Airborne? To try to meet as many needs as possible, knowing that she wouldn't be able to meet everyone's every time, Woods got creative and split two supply companies, combining the water units and the Class I units and then sending the combined units to where they were needed.[18]

The Iraqi Army had placed six divisions in the Tigris and Euphrates River Valley to defend the region. Farthest south was the 51st Division, while the 6th Armored Division was in position just north of Basra. The 18th Infantry Division had set up in Qurnah, and the 14th Infantry Division and 10th Armored Division were positioned between Qurnah and Amarah. Units of the 11th Infantry Division were around An Nasiriyah. All six divisions were in place on March 19.

By the evening of March 21, the 3rd ID had made it about 100 miles into the Iraqi desert. The next day, soldiers in Colonel Dan Allyn's 3rd Brigade spotted their first target, Tallil Air Base, headquarters of Iraq's 11th Division. It was located next to the ruins of the ancient city of Ur, the birthplace of the prophet Abraham, southwest of An Nasiriyah where Highway 1 turned to cross the Euphrates River, making it a critical point for the Americans. V Corps ordered General Blount's 3rd ID to capture Tallil Air Base and establish a logistics support area to aid the Army's advance north. After completing the mission, 3rd Brigade troops seized the Highway 1 bridge over the Euphrates River northwest of An Nasiriyah. Early in the drive to Baghdad, the methodical nature of the advance and the need for patience was clear. The 3rd ID would have to take each objective one at a time, securing roads and bridges as the units moved forward. Though impressive in size and skill, maneuvering the armored columns required awareness of the geographical surroundings and enemy troop positions in order to avoid delays and unexpected attacks.

Even with flawless preparation, the 3rd ID still confronted surprises. On the advance to Objective Liberty, just south of Tallil Air Base, Lieutenant Colonel John Charlton, commander of Task Force 1-15 Infantry (1st Battalion, 15th Infantry Regiment), sent in a tank team to assess the enemy presence at the location. As Captain Dave Waldron led B Company of Task Force 1-64 Armor toward the objective, he and his tankers were surprised to find an Iraqi armored unit waiting for them. The M1 Abrams thermal detection technology indicated that the enemy tanks' engines were running and thus ready to engage. At once, Captain Waldron radioed Task Force 1-15 Infantry, declaring "Dragon 6, Knight 6. Tanks! Out." Then the fighting began.[19]

The Iraqis' aged T-62 tanks were no match for the M1 Abrams. B Company's main battle tank trained its night vision sight on the enemy tanks, and soon five American tanks fired their 120mm cannons in unison on the Iraqis. In a search and destroy mission that lasted about two minutes, gunners and tank commanders picked off Iraqi tanks and other military vehicles positioned around the perimeter of Objective Liberty. Before dawn on March 22, Task Force 1-30 Infantry (1st Battalion, 30th Infantry Regiment) passed through the southern opening that Task Force 1-15 Infantry had cleared. After a wave of intense artillery and attack aviation strikes, Task Force 1-30 Infantry captured Tallil Air Base. Units cleared the airfield and searched for chemical weapons but found none.[20]

Once Tallil Air Base was secure, units of the 3rd ID continued in the direction of An Nasiriyah, which was about 233 miles southeast of Baghdad. An Nasiriyah, a city of about half a million people, sits at an intersection of roads leading from Kuwait to Baghdad. Its location made it a critical objective for the 3rd ID. It ended up being the scene of some of the fiercest fighting of the war. Blount's strategy for moving his division to Baghdad as quickly as possible centered on avoiding large cities, and the 3rd ID planned to stay west rather than pass through An Nasiriyah. Cities offered hideouts for enemy forces, and urban streets made for challenging paths for the movement of a giant armored column. If supply units got cut off from forward units, parts of the column could find themselves stranded in the desert, slowing down the 3rd ID's drive to Baghdad. The successful movement of the division assumed that its columns would remain intact.

When the 507th Maintenance Company got separated from its marching column on March 23 and made a wrong turn, its members ran into an ambush near An Nasiriyah. The 507th, out of Fort Bliss, Texas, was one of the support units attached to V Corps on the mission to Baghdad. In the darkness of night late on March 23, a segment of the 507th got separated from the rest of the column and could not make radio contact with units ahead. Confusion ensued, and the separated group mistakenly crossed the Euphrates River and headed toward An Nasiriyah. Although the city was still under the control of the Iraqi government, the 507th passed through An Nasiriyah's checkpoints without incident. Yet once through the city, leaders of the company realized they had taken a wrong turn at some point. They decided to retrace their steps and pass back through An Nasiriyah. Vehicles were running low on fuel, so they needed to reconnect with the column quickly. Back they went, rumbling toward An Nasiriyah, hoping to reestablish contact before vehicles ran out of gas.

As the 507th approached An Nasiriyah again, Iraqi irregulars opened fire on the company. Iraqis in civilian clothes carrying concealed AK-47s and rocket-propelled-grenade launchers chased the convoy in pickup trucks. Leaders of the 507th ordered the convoy to speed up, but some vehicles struggled to keep up, causing the convoy to separate. Sensing the Americans' distress, Iraqis continued firing on the company, disabling vehicles and killing one soldier as he tried to rescue fellow soldiers from one of the downed trucks. Amid the chaos, the 507th broke apart even more, but soldiers managed to radio a U.S. Marine Corps unit in the area for help. Task Force Tarawa arrived and rescued some of the 507th soldiers, but Iraqis captured 12, including Private First Class Jessica Lynch. Of the 33 U.S. soldiers involved in the ambush, 11 were killed, nine were wounded, and seven were captured. Taking prisoners from the 507th emboldened the Iraqi forces in An Nasiriyah. Reinforcements poured in, and troops went after U.S. Marines, especially in "Ambush Alley" toward the northern bridge leading out of the city. For the Americans, it was a deadly and discouraging day. It eventually took ten days for the Marines to secure An Nasiriyah.

The drive to Baghdad was one of constant movement. Day and night, the convoys rumbled along in a singular determination to reach the capital city and destroy the Hussein regime. Soldiers took turns trying to sleep in their tanks and personnel carriers, curling into uncomfortable seats with the hope that sleep would take over for a few hours. Keeping thousands of vehicles in formation was a challenging task. Tanks, trucks, and carriers broke down along the way and needed to stop for repairs. Operating vehicles had to stop for fuel, which meant waiting for fuel trucks to make their way up to the position where vehicles nearing empty waited. Stoppages separated units from one another even as drivers tried to maneuver vehicles needing service out of the way. Some units also got bogged down in villages when curious locals swarmed the armored units, hoping for a glimpse of Americans, if not a handout of food or cash. Iraqi boys and young men foraged through trash searching for MREs, while others flashed peace signs and waved to welcome the invading forces. Some even shouted anti-Hussein epithets.[21]

Sleep deprivation took its toll. Drivers nodded off at the wheel, causing their vehicles to swerve out of position before the drivers roused themselves awake again. Other drivers fell asleep during pauses in the movement. Sometimes troops would have to move on foot to approach a vehicle and wake a sleeping driver. Dust and swirling sand made it challenging to see the next vehicle ahead, and some vehicles lacked radios, so drivers had no means of keeping in contact with those in front and behind. Frayed nerves exacerbated by exhaustion caused tempers to flare.[22] The advance to Baghdad was as much a mental game as a physical one.

Artillery booms punctuated the monotonous rumble of tank and carrier motors. Convoys stopped periodically to repair vehicles and assess orders, and soldiers set up makeshift campsites with the hope of taking a break. Yet sandstorms made rest difficult. Soldiers wore goggles to protect their eyes, and they learned to accept the layers of dust that covered every inch of exposed skin. The heaviest sandstorms darkened the sky and obstructed the views of mechanics working to repair tanks and Bradleys. With so many vehicles needing maintenance, some mechanics worked on just a couple of hours of sleep. Mealtimes offered little respite, as grit covered the MREs. Soldiers managed to choke down the sandy food and get on with their tasks, often eating on the go.[23]

Pushing on toward Baghdad, the 3rd ID soon approached the vicinity of As Samawah, about 150 miles south of the capital, on March 22. V Corps planned to use 3-7 Cavalry in a feint through the city and across the Euphrates to trick Iraqis into believing that the entire column was headed the same way. V Corps' Wallace trusted the plan in part because intelligence reports about the majority Shia city indicated that most residents were pro-American. Intelligence suggested that the citizens of As Samawah would greet the Americans as liberators and throw a parade to welcome them. Yet when soldiers of 3-7 Cavalry arrived, the opposite greeted them. Fedayeen units attacked them from the beds of pickup trucks with rocket-propelled grenades and machine guns. Fedayeen cadres had positioned themselves throughout the city and aimed at U.S. supply lines. Disrupting the link between combat units and their support and supply teams was the Iraqi irregulars' best hope for crippling the 3rd ID. About 1,500 Fedayeen guarded a bridge across the Euphrates.[24]

Fedayeen troops positioned in As Samawah held their ground, much to the surprise of the 3rd ID soldiers who encountered them.

A sandstorm reduced visibility, making it difficult for the Americans to find Fedayeen troops under the eerie red sky.[25] A column of tanks and Bradleys on the edge of the city got separated from the larger U.S. formation during the sandstorm, and a group of Fedayeen in a white pickup truck saw an opportunity to attack. As the column made its way to the assembly area, two trucks pulled within about 10 yards of the U.S. vehicles. Once U.S. soldiers realized the Fedayeen were there, a tank round destroyed one of the trucks. But it didn't deter the fighters in the other pickup. They jumped out and began firing back at the Americans. Rocket-propelled grenades and other weapons fire exploded during the middle of the night.

U.S. artillery eventually found and destroyed the Fedayeen compound in As Samawah, but only after friendly fire destroyed two M1A1 Abrams tanks and a Bradley due to the sandstorm's impact on night vision technology and the fog of war.[26] Although not deadly for U.S. troops, the fighting in As Samawah served as a reminder that the Fedayeen fighters were not to be taken lightly. They were not professional soldiers, but they had the desperate will to fight that stemmed from disaffection, isolation, and blind trust in a native leader against a foreign invader. What was supposed to be a welcome parade ended up being a full-scale battle, and on March 23 Blount ordered the 3rd Brigade to As Samawah to try to control the city. 3-7 Cavalry had done hard work, killing more than 500 Iraqi soldiers, destroying 30 antiaircraft systems, and disabling three command and control facilities. As the 3rd Brigade took on the fighting at As Samawah, 3-7 Cavalry began movement north to An Najaf.[27]

The number of Fedayeen the 3rd ID encountered surprised Blount. Prewar planning had focused on the Iraqi regular army and Republican Guard, and commanders had relied on intelligence coming from Jordan and other allied countries in the Middle East. While Blount was in Kuwait training with his division, he got to know CIA agents working with contacts in Jordan and Iraq, and they supplied him with information about the Iraqi military. The information chains were intentionally vague, and details were almost always second- or third-hand. A brother or sister or friend of a division commander passed along a tip that a leader was going to resign or there was an assassination plot afoot. Some of the intelligence made it into the press, and Saddam monitored U.S. media.[28] Hussein also used the Fedayeen to ensure the Iraqi military leadership remained loyal and that villagers would fight the Americans.

Before the invasion began, Colonel Roberta Woods and her brigade were briefed on the Fedayeen and told to look out for Toyota pickup trucks and militias wearing civilian clothes, so the soldiers of 24th Corps Support Group knew to expect the Fedayeen. The biggest threat the Feyadeen posed to the 3rd ID was the possibility that militias could cut the lines of communication, leaving combat units stranded without access to fuel, ammunition, medics, and other supports. For the support brigades such as Woods' 24th CSG, tucking in behind combat units offered protection in times of attack. Woods also made sure her commanders leading convoys knew how to read a map and understood how to stay on the prescribed route. Non-commissioned officers checked in periodically with soldiers to make sure they were alert and not falling victim to fatigue. 24th Corps Support Group did not lose any soldiers during Operation *Iraqi Freedom*.[29]

Fedayeen in plainclothes driving civilian vehicles created challenges for U.S. soldiers and commanders trying to follow the rules of engagement regarding self-defense. According to the Geneva and Hague conventions, a soldier in uniform is a lawful target, but a person wearing civilian clothes is a noncombatant. In dealing with the fedayeen, Cayce advised division commanders to look for hostile intent. Brandishing a weapon was the clearest indication of this. If a weapon wasn't visible, assessing hostile intent was difficult and had to be done in a split second.[30]

One of Colonel Lyle Cayce's legal clerks had to make such a decision. The clerk was at a checkpoint. Earlier that morning, a vehicle had sped toward the checkpoint with no white flag or handkerchief in sight. When the vehicle did not stop, the guards fired a round into the engine block with a .50 caliber weapon, disabling the vehicle. Inside was an armed Iraqi major. Two hours later, Cayce's legal clerk encountered a similar situation with another vehicle speeding toward the checkpoint. The clerk fired a round into the engine block and disabled the car while also hitting the driver's femoral artery. It turned out the driver was an Iraqi civilian who was traveling with his wife to pick up their son, who was trying to desert from the Iraqi army. When they realized that the man was not an enemy combatant, medics fastened a tourniquet around his leg, but it was too late. He died at the checkpoint.[31]

On the night of March 23, V Corps forces came into contact with Iraqi anti-aircraft defenses, which turned out to be coordinated and effective. The 11th Attack Helicopter Regiment of the 101st Airborne was ordered to attack and destroy the armor and artillery of the Republican Guard's Medina Division. Just after one o'clock in the morning, 31 Apaches began taking off from Objective Rams, a position south of An Najaf. As the Apaches flew north, all at once the towns and villages below went black. The power had cut out completely, but only for a couple of seconds. When the lights flashed back on, rifle and machine gun fire pummeled the Apaches. One went down, and both pilots were taken prisoner. Enemy fire was so intense that the remaining Apaches aborted the mission and returned to Objective Rams. The Americans learned later that Iraqi anti-aircraft units had relied on civilian sky watchers on the ground who used cell phones to call in sightings of U.S. aircraft. The quick power outage was the signal to attack. The incident would weigh heavily in decision making regarding the mission into Baghdad.

While Colonel Dan Allyn's 3rd Brigade remained to secure As Samawah, the 3rd ID's 1st and 2nd brigades moved north to establish a forward arming and refueling point southwest of An Najaf. Located on the Euphrates River, An Najaf featured two key bridges across the river. Having encountered the tenacious enemy in As Samawah, Blount devised a plan to encircle and contain An Najaf rather than trying to bypass it in order to protect supply lines and logistics operations at Objective Rams from Fedayeen attacks out of An Najaf. By the time the division had reached the vicinity of An Najaf on March 23, its supply and communication lines stretched 200 miles back to the Kuwaiti border. It wasn't that Iraqi units could destroy U.S. armor, but they could slow the 3rd ID's pace to Baghdad. Long combat operations put a strain on supply lines by bringing more vehicles and weapons into action, causing them to burn ammunition, oil, and fuel more quickly.

Grimsley's 1st Brigade went on to Objective Raiders, a vast desert plain even closer to An Najaf. To reach Raiders, 1st Brigade had to pass over an escarpment nearly 250 feet high running east to west. To cross it, brigade units had to drive on a single-lane road cut between a marsh on one side and a lake on the other. Iraqi troops hoped the terrain would give them an advantage and had dug in artillery and infantry units to attack American vehicles as they attempted the crossing. Grimsley assigned Task Force 3-69 Armor, under the command of Lieutenant Colonel Ernest "Rock" Marcone, to lead the fight up the escarpment. As Grimsley and Marcone expected, the Iraqis shelled the task force and fired artillery rounds as the armored vehicles made the steep climb up the escarpment, but Marcone's soldiers handled the enemy and took the ridge without sustaining any casualties.[32]

From there, Blount ordered 1st Brigade to secure the northern bridge at Al-Kifl, nicknamed Objective Jenkins, while Lieutenant Colonel Terry Ferrell's 3-7 Cavalry took the southern bridge, nicknamed Objective Floyd. Brigadier General Lloyd Austin issued Blount's orders late in the evening on March 24.[33] Meanwhile, 2nd Brigade received orders to go to An Najaf, and Colonel Perkins looked at a map showing a long and circuitous route the brigade was to take. Perkins did the fuel calculation and found that just to get from Kuwait to An Najaf on the proposed route would use up the brigade's entire fuel ration plus about 85 additional tankers borrowed from V Corps. Perkins went to Lieutenant General Scott Wallace, commander of V Corps, and told him how much fuel his brigade would need for the trip. Astonished, Wallace told Perkins there was no way he could give him that much fuel. He had two other brigades, 1st and 3rd, that also would need fuel resupply from V Corps. At that moment, Wallace began to rethink the whole plan, but Perkins also began thinking about a solution.[34]

Perkins called his logisticians together to see if they could come up with a way to get to An Najaf without depleting 2nd Brigade's fuel. Because tank and Bradley fuel consumption was measured by the hour, Perkins reasoned that if the tanks could travel quickly and get to An Najaf in fewer hours, they'd conserve some fuel. The logisticians confirmed that Perkins was right, but they wondered how he planned to move the tanks faster along the winding road. His answer was to not take that road but to send the tanks up a straight shot to An Najaf. Shorter distance, less time on the road, less fuel consumed. Again, the logisticians confirmed that, in theory, a straight shot was more fuel efficient, but that would mean going off-road across terrain for which the logisticians didn't have maps or clear knowledge of what was there. Surely the vehicles would encounter wadis, but they didn't know exactly where, and a unit could run into one while driving at night. The logisticians raised another concern. Tanks and Bradleys could handle a cross-country trek because they were tracked vehicles, but all the support vehicles – artillery, mechanics, medics, logisticians, fuel trucks – were wheeled, so they would not be able to travel as quickly or as easily off road.[35]

Undeterred, Perkins kept thinking. If he split the support units off from the tanks and Bradleys, the heavy armored vehicles could take the direct cross-country route and get to An Najaf quickly, saving fuel, while the wheeled vehicles, which used much less fuel, took the circuitous road to the city. Once at the city limits, the combat vehicles would turn off their lights and wait in the dark for the support teams to arrive. When Perkins took his idea to his logisticians, they responded succinctly: "Sir, that's crazy."[36] Crazy because they didn't have maps of the area. Crazy that the tanks and Bradleys would be sitting out there waiting without artillery, medics, mechanics, or other support nearby. But Perkins sent his brigade to test his idea in the Kuwaiti desert, and the units ran a gallons-per-hour test to determine whether Perkins' plan would work. What the soldiers found was that if the armored vehicles moved at 30 miles per hour, they could make it on the cross-country route without needing any of V Corps' fuel reserves.

It was the job of Lieutenant Colonel Eric Wesley, 2nd Brigade's executive officer, to play the skeptic to Perkins' audacity but also to help execute Perkins' vision. Hearing Wesley vocalize the risks involved in the plan to divide the brigade helped Perkins think of solutions. Wesley and the others were correct to point out that traveling without spare parts or medics was dangerous, and listening to them led Perkins to assign medics to the Bradleys and order units to bring replacement parts for their vehicles. It was all part of managing risk, and that's what commandership was about for Perkins. Eliminating risk wasn't possible, but with proper training and the insights of trusted colleagues, managing risk was.

Perkins briefed Blount and Wallace on his idea, and their response was similar to that of his logisticians. "Separate the brigade? You just don't do that."[37] It was a huge tactical risk in exchange for solving a logistical problem, but Perkins got permission to do it. As the units split up, the tank and Bradley companies nicknamed themselves Task Force Heavy Metal, while the support units called themselves Task Force Rock and Roll. In lieu of maps, 2nd Brigade had satellite photos from the Army Corps of Engineers, and the images showed wadis in the area as Perkins had suspected. The 3rd ID had learned tragic lessons about the danger of wadis during exercises at the National Training Center when vehicles went into wadis and rolled over, killing the soldiers inside.

To avoid similar accidents during combat, Perkins knew his soldiers needed to see where they were going, and thermal sight technology wouldn't help them navigate the wadis. So he made another unconventional decision once it got dark during the journey to An Najaf – he ordered the tank and Bradley drivers to turn their headlights on. In keeping with the previous reactions to Perkins' controversial ideas, his battalion commanders' responses could be paraphrased as "Once again, the Colonel's gone crazy."[38] The ability to see without being seen at night was a major advantage for the 3rd ID, and one of the division's catch phrases was, "We own the night." Now, not only had Perkins separated the combat units from 2nd Brigade's medics, mechanics, and artillery, but he also called for bright white lights to be turned on. From Perkins' perspective, it wasn't a crazy order. He was much more concerned about a driver rolling a tank or Bradley into a wadi than he was about encountering Iraqi troops. His soldiers could handle the enemy; a tank rolling into a wadi was a more dangerous threat.[39] The combat units arrived at An Najaf about a day ahead of the wheeled vehicles and shut the armored vehicles down to conserve fuel. When the HEMTTs caught up, soldiers refueled the tanks and Bradleys, and the brigade prepared to move on.

Though Perkins' ideas were daring, they were not haphazard. Perkins and 2nd Brigade had completed training rotations at Fort Stewart and the National Training Center, and they'd spent months training in the Kuwaiti desert, instilling in Perkins firm confidence in the brigade's ability to learn, innovate, synchronize, and perform complex choreography in battle. In each rotation, the brigade tried a different method of command and control so that brigade personnel had the skills and agility to adjust in response to battle conditions as they played out. Central to Perkins' beliefs about training was getting good at the basics – logistics, command and control, expertise in handling armored vehicles. Once soldiers mastered the basics, they could apply them anywhere.

Task Force 1-64 Armor spearheaded the effort to seize Objective Rams on March 24, with Hilms' Alpha Company in the lead. As lead company, Hilms' soldiers were always the first to make contact with the enemy, and Hilms knew that his battalion commander, Lieutenant Colonel Erik Schwartz, relied on his read of the enemy situation. As night fell, Fedayeen units struck U.S. forces. Soldiers of 1-64 Armor nearly ran into an open field of trench lines filled with Fedayeen and regulars. Hilms mused that it was the first time his company had met the enemy.[40] Alpha Company had only a handful of combat veterans. Of its 100 soldiers, about three or four non-commissioned officers had seen combat back in Operation *Desert Storm*. The rest of Hilms' soldiers were green. One of his gunners identified the Iraqi soldiers who were shooting at them. Hilms was up in the top of his tank commander's hatch, and he dropped down into his commander's station. Peering through his gunner's sight extension, Hilms saw a group of Iraqi soldiers standing up out of a trench line firing at their them. The gunner had the Iraqis in his sights, and Hilms gave him a fire command. The gunner didn't move, so Hilms repeated his order. Still the gunner didn't move, and Hilms realized that the young sergeant was reflecting on the fact that he was about to take another person's life. Hilms put his hand on the gunner's shoulder and calmly told him to fire.[41]

It took the entire night for Alpha Company and other units to clear the trenches. The tanks moved methodically through the area, shooting enemy soldiers as they fired on the armored vehicles. But as Iraqi fighters went down, more popped up and took their places. Hilms suspected that they didn't realize the U.S. tanks and Bradleys were equipped with night vision technology. But the Iraqis, especially the Fedayeen, were persistent fighters, and they might have fought to the death even if they knew what kinds of weapons the Americans had. As the sky brightened the next morning, Hilms and his soldiers observed hundreds of enemy bodies strewn across the desert sand.

In As Samawah and An Najaf, the Iraqis proved to be a different enemy than what U.S. military planners had envisioned in their war games. The Americans had expected to encounter mostly Iraqi regular army forces or Republican Guards, but they had underestimated the tenacity of the Fedayeen fighters. The enemy had no tanks or conventional weapons, but instead fought from trenches and pickup trucks, firing machine guns and rocket-propelled grenades. Later, soldiers discovered weapons caches everywhere – in the desert, in buildings, and on the outskirts of the city. The stockpiles were for Fedayeen reinforcements to pick up and fight the Americans from whatever positions they could find.[42]

While the fighting in An Najaf raged, a massive sandstorm hit on March 25, seriously limiting the division's mobility. General Blount had been in his share of sandstorms. He had trained the Saudi National Guard in desert warfare, and Saudi guardsmen taught Blount how to fight and survive in the desert. He spent many nights in the desert with the Saudis, and he faced sandstorms of various levels of intensity, but nothing was like what the 3rd ID experienced on the road to Baghdad. Before the storm hit, Blount had received a weather report predicting the storm and warning that aircraft would be grounded because of it. The predictions were accurate, and a sandstorm unlike any the general had ever seen hit the Iraq desert.

Soldiers called it "the mother of all sandstorms," as it blinded U.S. surveillance and electronic vision equipment, clogged weapons and air filters, and disabled engines. Sand got into computers, and it caused cameras to malfunction. Dust covered every surface, preventing soldiers from writing on maps or blueprints. Winds reaching 50 miles per hour whipped sand through the air, pelting soldiers as they tried to manage the storm's impact on their vehicles. Sand in the air severely reduced visibility. Blount couldn't see his command post 20 feet from his vehicle. In its fight to secure the bridge at Objective Floyd, 3-7 Cavalry lost its air cavalry support.[43] The storm was so heavy that it seemed as though night had fallen, only it also interfered with night vision technology.[44] From the ground to the sky, a red glow made Iraq look like Mars. For Grimsley, the sandstorm was of Old Testament proportions; all that was missing were frogs and locusts.

Sand covered soldiers, too. It got in their nostrils and ears, clouded their goggles, covered any bit of skin exposed, and even made its way under uniforms. Soldiers wrapped scarves around their faces but the sand was relentless and ubiquitous. Private Lewis Austin, from Jackson, Mississippi, drove an 18-wheel munitions supply truck and marveled at the crippling effect of the sandstorm. If he was needed for a resupply, he didn't know how he would manage to move his truck forward when he couldn't see the road in front of him. Then it started raining, and the rain mixed with the swirling sand to make gobs of mud and transformed the layers of grit on soldiers and equipment into slime. Soldiers took cover inside their vehicles when they weren't outside trying to clear the muck away from engines and moving parts.[45]

The 3rd ID made the best of it, using the operational pause to conduct resupply, repair vehicles, and give soldiers some much-needed rest. Hilms and other commanders spent their days having meetings and discussing tactics going forward. Occasionally a group of Fedayeen fighters converged on the tanks without warning, but their small-arms fire did little damage to the armored vehicles. But the spontaneity of the attacks contributed to the chaotic atmosphere in and around An Najaf during the sandstorm. The Fedayeen kept the U.S. soldiers on edge.[46] The division had been moving nonstop since it crossed the berm five days earlier, and soldiers were exhausted. V Corps' Wallace had already wanted to slow the 3rd ID's movement in order to resupply and prepare before attacking into the Karbala Gap. Stopping due to the sandstorm allowed the logistics units to catch up to the fast-moving forward mechanized units. So, in some ways, the sandstorm was a blessing in disguise.

While division forces conducted their refueling, Colonel Mike Birmingham spoke to reporters about what the troops were doing. Yes, the sandstorm had forced a division that had prioritized speed to slow some of its units down, but some news outlets began turning the story into an indictment of the Pentagon's approach to the war. Rumsfeld was wrong to send a smaller, lighter, force to Iraq, some analysts chided. The 3rd ID would be bogged down until another division, the 1st Armored or 4th Infantry, could arrive to help, others opined on television and in op-eds. It was as though reporters and editors were waiting for the U.S. war effort to fall apart. Editors at *Time* prepared a cover story entitled "Why are We Losing?" *Newsweek* editors planned a cover emblazoned with the headline "Quagmire."[47] Birmingham understood that the coverage reflected the animosity some reporters had toward the Bush administration's decision to go to war, but he also saw that it did not extend to the soldiers.[48] In any case, the division would fight on, and eventually the evidence would disprove the prophecies some of the papers seemed eager to see fulfilled.

Some of the embeds were international, and Woods' 24th Corps Support Group had a Japanese television crew embedded with it. The camerawoman was from the U.S., and she communicated with CGS leadership and soldiers. CSG troops treated the journalists like fellow soldiers, and the news crew rode in the back of a Humvee as the CSG moved. Because the main reporter did his broadcasts in Japanese, Woods never knew exactly what he was saying, so she decided that she would share information with him that she shared with her soldiers, but she did not allow him into meetings with CSG commanders. Woods never did learn what the reporter said about the CSG or the war, but he was a committed journalist. When U.S. forces had their first Scud alert in Kuwait, Woods happened to be in the media tent when the Scud alarms went off. While soldiers rushed to get to their bunkers, the Japanese reporter put on his Kevlar and did a live shot reporting on the Scud attack.[49]

3-7 Cavalry, the division's scouting unit, marched north on Route Appaloosa along the Euphrates heading to the bridge at Objective Floyd. After separating from 2nd Brigade to avoid congestion, 3-7 Cavalry encountered several well-planned ambushes. The first ambush originated at night from a mosque on the west side of the route. First Lieutenant Matt Garrett, Alpha Troop's scout platoon leader, noticed the structure, and he hopped on the radio to note that the mosque reminded him of an Orlando restaurant called Middle Eastern Times. Just after Garrett spoke, Iraqis appeared out of the shadows and fired on the U.S. convoy. For two hours, Alpha Troop fought the Iraqis, who determinedly moved to within 15 meters of U.S. vehicles, eliminating the cavalry's ability to use artillery. Iraqi paramilitary forces fired on U.S. troops from both sides of the road and from on and off ramps. The Iraqis attacked 3-7 Cavalry with small arms, automatic weapons, and rocket-propelled grenades. Enemy fighters also attacked the Americans from vehicles, some of them armed, others ordinary cars and trucks. 3-7 Cavalry battled through the ambushes throughout the night and into the next day.[50] U.S. soldiers nicknamed Route Appaloosa "Ambush Alley" after they'd come out of it. Yet in the end, the armored cavalry emerged from the fighting having suffered no casualties or losses.[51]

On March 26, as the sandstorm continued to pummel An Najaf, Task Force 1-64 Armor attacked through the city and secured a bridge over the Euphrates for 3-7 Cavalry's rearward passage of lines. Hilms received word that 3-7 Cavalry had conducted a feint on the east side of the Euphrates River to distract Iraqi forces. In doing so, the cavalry had lost some equipment and needed 1-64 Armor to cross the river and relieve some of the troops. Team Wild Bunch took the lead as the task force maneuvered toward the bridge. As the vehicles moved down a road just south of An Najaf, Iraqi soldiers ambushed them from both sides. Fedayeen militias fired rifles and rocket-propelled grenades from trenches on either side of the road. The Americans fired on the enemy but continued to move so they could get to the bridge as soon as possible. When the tanks reached a crossroads, Toyota pickup trucks and school buses carrying Fedayeen fighters sped toward the column. As company commander, Hilms was in the fourth or fifth vehicle back in the order of march, and as his lead platoon crossed the junction, Hilms noticed a school bus come screeching out of nowhere. About 20 or 30 Fedayeen were inside, and Hilms thought maybe it was a suicide mission and the bus was loaded with explosives. The bus rammed the Bradley in front of Hilms' vehicle and crumpled upon impact, no match for the fighting vehicle. In response, the Bradley's gunner fired on the bus at close range. The mangled bus began sparking, and then it exploded. Two Fedayeen fighters were thrown from the bus, and one landed on the side of the road next to Hilms' tank. Even in the sandstorm, he could see a white-hot burning ember in the Iraqi. It was a piece of explosive material.[52]

The task force continued to fight through the ambush for several miles, eventually making it to the bridgehead and allowing 3-7 Cavalry to move 400 vehicles across the bridge. The sandstorm had not let up, and Iraqi forces had withdrawn into An Najaf. Hilms did not want to fire into the city because it had a large civilian population. Fedayeen troops tried to coax the Americans into An Najaf by sneaking up to the edge of the city, firing on the task force units, and then running back into the interior. But the task force stayed on the bridge in a blocking position for more than a day, taking mortar and rocket-propelled grenade fire as it came. Troops of the 101st Airborne Division showed up and relieved Task Force

1-64 Armor, which moved out to go further north to Karbala.[53] As the tip of the spear for V Corps, the 3rd ID had to keep moving toward its ultimate mission in Baghdad, and McKiernan wanted to free the battalions of 1st and 2nd brigades from the fighting to secure the lines of communication around An Najaf.[54]

Iraqi reinforcements to An Najaf had been arriving from the north, making it imperative that 1st Brigade secure the Al-Kifl bridge at Objective Jenkins, northeast of An Najaf. The highway through the suburb of Al-Kifl was a key resupply route for Iraqi soldiers in An Najaf. The town and the highway teemed with Iraqi regulars, Fedayeen irregulars, and villagers. Riding in cars, taxi cabs, and pickup trucks, Iraqi soldiers and militia fired on U.S. troops from all directions. Enemy troops had also taken fighting positions along the town's main road, with two stationed atop a schoolhouse. Lieutenant Colonel Will Grimsley, commander of the 1st Brigade, worried that another "Blackhawk Down" situation might occur.

Grimsley and other commanders learned the extent to which the Iraqis had targeted bridges when they received a captured enemy map. All the 70-ton capable bridges, those strong enough for tanks and other armored vehicles to cross, were circled in red. If the Iraqis destroyed any of the large bridges, they could seriously slow the 3rd ID's progress. On March 27, as 1st Brigade units advanced to Objective Jenkins, Iraqi soldiers and armed civilians attempted to destroy the Al-Kifl bridge. There were two battalions of Republican Guards, a brigade commander, and about a thousand infantry troops defending it. They were dug in and fought with small arms, machine guns, and rocket-propelled grenades.[55] As a reconnaissance team and a tank platoon from Task Force 3-69 Armor (3rd Battalion, 69th Armor Regiment) crossed the bridge, two Iraqis under the bridge detonated explosives attached to one of the bridge's piers. The soldiers crossing heard an explosion behind them. The explosion caused the bridge to buckle in sections, temporarily cutting off the platoons that had crossed. When U.S. troops found the Iraqis, they were about to set off another bomb. The Americans killed them, and then they discovered that the entire underside of the bridge was wired with explosives.[56]

Among the technology in the 3rd ID's arsenal was a portable communications system called a TeleEngineering Kit or TEK that allowed combat engineers to communicate with structural engineers at the U.S. Army Engineer Research and Development Center in Vicksburg, Mississippi. At Objective Jenkins, soldiers of the 54th Engineer Battalion, known as "Jungle Cats," used a TEK to assess and repair the Al-Kifl bridge across the Euphrates. The explosion damaged the bridge enough that engineers from the 54th used their TEK to determine whether it was safe for additional U.S. vehicles to cross it. Jungle Cats assessed the damage and sent information with live video footage to the team in Vicksburg. Less than four hours later, the engineers in Mississippi reported back via video conferencing and advised the 54th to add wooden reinforcements to the weakened piers. The 3rd ID's use of TEK was an example of the high-tech nature of Operation *Iraqi Freedom*.[57]

All told, 1st Brigade soldiers in Al-Kifl found themselves engulfed in heavy fighting that lasted 12 hours. When it ended, the bloodied and lifeless bodies of Iraqi soldiers lay in the streets. The Americans had lost no soldiers or equipment. Among the dead, 1st Brigade medics found a wounded Republican Guard soldier, and they treated his gunshot wounds. The man told his captors that he had heard that U.S. forces had already killed thousands of Republican Guard soldiers in northern Iraq.[58] Grimsley had to credit the Iraqis; they had put up a good fight. But 1st Brigade had overwhelming fire power, and the adaptability of his subordinate commanders and soldiers was impressive.[59]

The next stop for 1st Brigade troops was a brick factory just north of Al-Kifl. Acting on intelligence reports indicating that Iraqi forces used the factory as a staging area, B-52s had bombed it, and 1st Brigade soldiers went to handle the aftermath. They found mostly armed civilians in construction trucks, who surrendered themselves to the Americans. Meanwhile, west of An Najaf, soldiers with Task Force 3-7 Cavalry battled with Iraqi troops and ended up taking 50 prisoners of war. They bound the men's wrists with zip ties and sent them off to interrogation.[60] From there, the 3rd ID continued to pierce through the center of Iraq, always aiming for the heart of Baghdad.

After three days of relentless sandstorms, the morning of March 27 brought crisp, clear relief. The 3rd ID's 3rd Battalion, 15th Infantry Regiment (3-15 Infantry) had stopped and set up camp southwest of Baghdad, pausing to bring up supplies and repair vehicles. The desert had been quiet, but soldiers monitoring the perimeter from their M2 Bradley Fighting Vehicles had spotted Iraqis lurking in the distance. Two Soviet-era T-55 tanks and two armored personnel carriers probed the battalion's line, so commanders called in air support. A-10 Thunderbolt II planes did the job of destroying the Iraqi unit.[61] Lieutenant Colonel Stephen Twitty, the battalion commander, ordered his troops to dig defensive positions and remain vigilant. Enemy forces repeatedly engaged the division's combat units, and intelligence indicated that the Iraqis planned to try to retake the bridges over the Euphrates that the Americans had seized. But the Fedayeen militias, the main source of enemy engagement, seemed to have little in the way of a tactical plan other than to rush at American vehicles with the hope of getting close enough to launch rocket-propelled grenades from their pickup trucks. An Abrams tank usually picked them off while they were still far enough away to pose no threat.[62]

As a whole, the 3rd ID's training and equipment gave the division an extraordinary advantage over Iraqi forces. But American soldiers were still vulnerable to deadly attacks like the one that occurred on March 29 at a highway checkpoint north of An Najaf. Sergeant Eugene Williams, Corporal Michael Curtin, Private First Class Michael Creighton-Weldon, and Private First Class Diego Fernando Rincon, all with 1st Brigade's 2nd Battalion, 7th Infantry Regiment (2-7 Infantry), guarded the checkpoint that day. Sergeant Williams hadn't spoken to his pregnant wife, Brandy, since March 15, before the war had started. She was at their home in Hawaii, caring for their first child, three-year-old Mya. He had recently written to his sister in upstate New York, where he was from, saying he couldn't wait to get home and cook for the whole family. Williams shared football in common with Curtin and Creighton-Weldon. All three men had played in high school. Private First Class Rincon had gone the theater route in school, foreshadowing his military career when he earned a role in *A Piece of My Heart*, a play about nurses in the Vietnam War. Rincon was the youngest of the group, a 19-year-old immigrant from Colombia whose family had settled in Conyers, Georgia. Before shipping out to Kuwait, Rincon had spent most of his time restoring an old Ford Mustang. He shared a love of cars with Creighton-Weldon, who enjoyed working on his truck in his spare time back home. Creighton-Weldon lived in Conyers, too. When the 20-year-old joined the Army, he had followed in his mother's footsteps. Sergeant Major Jean Weldon had recently retired from her career in the Army and was living in Palm Bay, Florida.[63] Service in the 3rd ID brought together the four men, whose lives likely would not have intersected otherwise.

That day in An Najaf, the soldiers monitored the checkpoint with the order to detain Iraqi fighters in civilian clothes. At one point in the morning – it was a Saturday – a taxi approached the checkpoint. The taxi driver leaned out of his window and beckoned the soldiers to the vehicle. It seemed as though the man needed help, so the soldiers walked over to him. They did not know that the driver was a suicide bomber. He had a bomb inside the taxi, and he readied himself to detonate it. When the soldiers reached the car, it was time. The driver did his deed, and the bomb exploded, killing him and the four soldiers.

Williams would never meet his unborn child. Jean Weldon lost her oldest son. When Curtin's former Little League coach, Chuck Senna, heard the news, he thought with sadness back to when he had served in the Vietnam War and casualties were reported to their Jersey Shore hometown of Howell. Fernando Rincon's grieving father promised he would finish restoring his son's Mustang for him.[64] The suicide bomber also had a story. His name was Ali Jaafar al-Noamani, and he was a non-commissioned officer in the Iraqi Army. Al-Noamani was also the father of several children. Iraqi state media reported that Saddam awarded the bomber two posthumous medals for his service. In the wake of the murders, Iraqi Vice President Taha Yassin Ramadan declared that it was just the beginning of Iraq's use of suicide bombing as a weapon of war. British and U.S. intelligence agents had reason to believe Ramadan's threat. They had learned of a training camp Saddam Hussein had created for Arab volunteers who were willing to enlist their services to Saddam's cause as suicide bombers.

The suicide bombing in An Najaf foreshadowed the nature of the war to come in Iraq. Danger came out of nowhere. Differentiating between friend and foe was challenging, and being wrong cost lives. The soldiers of the 3rd ID believed they were in Iraq to liberate innocent Iraqis from the clutches of a brutal dictator, but sometimes the people they were trying to save killed them. It was the way of asymmetrical warfare, specific not just to Iraq but common in most of the wars in which the U.S. had fought since World War II. Iraq's Republican Guard, not even the elite Medina Division, could not match the 3rd ID or other U.S. forces in a conventional battle, but a suicide bomber could destroy four lives in an instant.

Grimsley had been at Objective Raiders when it happened. From his brigade command post, Grimsley could look across to the northeast and see the checkpoint in the distance. The possibility of suicide bombing had come up in many conversations among commanders, and they remembered the history of the 1983 Beirut bombing that had killed U.S. Marines and the Khobar Towers bombing in Saudi Arabia. But they understood those things in a macro, dispassionate sense. The incident at An Najaf made it real. When the explosion at the checkpoint happened, Grimsley heard it. He looked out into the distance and saw a plume of smoke, and almost immediately a report came into the command post that a vehicle had exploded, and there were casualties. At the news, Grimsley rushed out of the command post, climbed into his armored vehicle, and headed in the direction of the checkpoint.[65]

When Grimsley arrived on the scene and learned what had happened, he found Captain Rob Smith, commander of Alpha Company, 2-7 Infantry. Smith and his company had already been through a rough fight south of As Samawah, where his company had gotten separated from the rest of the task force and ended up alone for about three days. But Smith had managed to lead his company north, borrowing fuel and other supplies from units his troops passed along the way. He had made it work, and Alpha Company eventually reunited with the rest of 2-7 Infantry. Then the attack on the checkpoint happened. Of a nine-man squad, four were killed and five were injured in the suicide bombing. Grimsley walked up to Smith and saw that he was physically shaken. Grimsley looked him in the eye and asked him, "Are you ok?" Smith replied that he was. Then Grimsley put his arm around Smith's shoulders and told him that he needed him. His company was scheduled to go back into the fight tomorrow, and he had to push through this. "Are you sure you're ok?" "Yes," Smith replied. Grimsley was in awe of the young captain's character and courage.[66]

As the 3rd ID advanced north from objective to objective, Hussein, his son Qusay, and Iraqi military advisors monitored intelligence about the movement of U.S. troops and made several wrong assumptions about U.S. war plans. Hussein and his advisors knew Special Operations forces were in Al Anbar Province, so they assumed that coalition troops would attack from Jordan. Because Marines were maneuvering near Kut, the Iraqis guessed that most U.S. troops operated east of the Euphrates. Hussein was aware of troop movements along the west side of the Euphrates, but he assumed that it was not the primary maneuver. When Republican Guard commanders asked for permission to destroy a main bridge over the Euphrates north of the Karbala Gap, Qusay Hussein, head of the Republican Guard, denied the request, missing a chance to hinder the 3rd ID's movement toward Baghdad.[67]

Karbala was the next stop on the 3rd ID's mission to Baghdad. As Blount pored over a map, he realized that the path through the Karbala Gap would give his division a direct line to Saddam International Airport and an entryway into Baghdad. To traverse the gap would be a risky move. The narrow passage between a lake and the city of Karbala made for easy targeting of U.S. troops with chemical weapons. Yet Blount insisted on the quickest possible approach to Iraq's capital city, and that was through the Karbala Gap. The division prepared to move forward on April 2.

Pushing Through Karbala

General Blount recognized the advantage of going through the Karbala Gap, even with the risks involved. It was the most direct route to Baghdad, and Blount wanted his division to keep moving quickly. Baghdad was so close, and slowing down gave Iraqi forces time to plan and regroup. Blount wanted to keep the enemy on the defensive, always guessing. Going through the Karbala Gap would allow division forces to avoid the cities that lined the Euphrates on the approach to Baghdad. Cities were dangerous, as 3rd ID troops had already discovered in An Najaf and As Samawah. Urban buildings offered hiding places for snipers and bombs. Going through the gap, Razazah Lake would serve as a protective barrier on the left flank, while the Euphrates River sat to the east. Yet passing through the Karbala Gap would not be easy for the 3rd ID. The two narrow roads running through the gap crossed an irrigation canal and agricultural land, two elements that Blount aimed to avoid by not traveling through the Euphrates River Valley. The gap also featured jagged rock quarries, further limiting maneuver space.[1]

Pushing the division through the Karbala Gap also gave the Iraqis their best chance to hit the Americans hard. The space provided useful fields of fire to the enemy and offered limited escape options for the 3rd ID. If the caravan of forces got bogged down in a bottleneck, the Iraqis could unleash chemical weapons or launch artillery and tank fire and wreak havoc on American troops. It almost looked as though the Karbala Gap offered more advantages to the enemy than to the 3rd ID. But Blount focused on what was beyond Karbala and how the division could get there as quickly as possible. If the 3rd ID made it through the gap, division forces would be on Baghdad's doorstep. Given the speed with which the 3rd ID had advanced toward the capital city since departing Kuwait less than two weeks earlier, Blount did not want his division to lose any momentum.

Blount expected that his troops would face Saddam's own armor, the Medina Division, at Karbala. If the general was correct, it would be the first major armor-on-armor fight of the war. U.S. air attacks, including strikes by V Corps attack helicopters, had weakened the Medina troops, but they remained a threat to the division.[2] Blount was right to suspect the enemy would be present. Iraqi military leaders understood that the Karbala Gap was a main entryway to the Baghdad area, and they positioned the elite Medina and Nebuchadnezzar divisions of the Republican Guard to defend the gap against U.S. forces. Blount refused to underestimate the Iraqis, and in planning for Karbala, he assumed that the 3rd ID would need to be prepared for dangerous fighting.

In the context of V Corps' overall strategy for the final drive into Baghdad, attacking into the Karbala Gap was part of a cluster of five operations on March 31 involving the 3rd ID, 101st Airborne, and 82nd Airborne to secure more tightly the 3rd ID's lines of communication to its supply units to the south and to deceive Iraqis into believing that the 3rd ID was going to cross the Euphrates south of Karbala, not through the Karbala Gap. The 101st Airborne's 2nd Brigade made a feint to Al Hillah, while 3rd ID's 2nd Brigade sent two mechanized task forces, 1-15 Infantry and 3-15 Infantry, to Al-Hindiyah. The task forces arrived at the Al-Hindiyah bridge crossing the Euphrates and found it wired for explosives. As the task forces moved into blocking positions near the city and bridge, Iraqi intelligence mistook the Americans' positioning as evidence that the U.S. was planning to fight there. The feint worked by holding the Iraqis' focus on Al-Hindiyah and the bridge so that they didn't notice the 3rd ID moving on the Karbala Gap.[3] Back in An Najaf and As Samawah, troops of the 101st and 82nd continued their efforts to secure the cities and prevent Iraqi forces from disrupting the 3rd ID's supply lines.

The 3rd ID also wanted to locate and destroy the Medina Division's artillery before moving into the gap. Colonel Tom Torrance had the division's artillery radars in position to quickly acquire the Iraqi artillery as they engaged 2nd Brigade forces in Al-Hindiyah. With modern technology, they were able to rapidly destroy the Iraqi guns, preventing the enemy from impeding the 3rd ID's movement through the Karbala Gap, the fifth in the cluster of attacks. If fuel trucks and other supply units could travel north uninterrupted, and if Iraqi forces fell for the feints, then the 3rd ID would have a clear path through Karbala on which to launch its final assault into Baghdad. Blount and Lieutenant General Wallace of V Corps also knew that the Karbala Gap was in what was known as the "red zone." This was the area where Saddam had authorized chemical weapons attacks to counter a U.S. advance. American and British forces had received intelligence from members of the Iraqi National Coalition in late 2002 and early 2003 that Hussein planned to use chemical weapons against Western forces. The information was of no surprise, considering that Hussein's use of chemical weapons had killed 100,000 Iranian troops during the Iran–Iraq War, and he had used chemical warfare against Iraqi Kurds in the late 1980s, killing 5,000 civilians. Mustard, sarin, and VX gases were in Hussein's arsenal. UN weapons inspectors had reported that the Iraqis also possessed biological weapons, including anthrax, botulinum toxin, and aflatoxin.[4] Armed with this knowledge, U.S. forces arrived in Iraq prepared for the worst.

Equipment and clothing provided barriers to nerve agents and other poisonous substances. M1A1 Abrams tanks and Bradley fighting vehicles were pressurized to prevent chemical and biological weapons from seeping inside. Troop units were equipped with protective suits that included special helmets, boots, and gloves. The equipment was called MOPP – mission-oriented protective posture – and it was designed to protect against contact with skin and lungs.[5] MOPP gear was cumbersome and uncomfortable.

The mask was difficult to wear, but a mechanism using activated charcoal had the capability to break down and absorb the types of chemicals Hussein could unleash. In addition to the clothing, footwear, and masks, troops were also equipped with several different kinds of autoinjectors that were antidotes to nerve gases. Prior to deployment, troops received smallpox and anthrax vaccines to protect against biological weapons, and they carried an antitoxin to counteract botulinum toxin.[6] Air strikes would attempt to eliminate as much of the enemy as possible in the area, but chemical warfare remained a concern. Wallace asked Blount what he planned to do in the event of a chemical weapons attack. Blount replied that the division was trained to operate in a chemical environment and had established several decontamination sites already, but the 3rd ID would not immediately halt the mission. Units would continue on with the fight and then decontaminate at the first chance.[7]

On an open battlefield, chemical weapons were less effective because they would disperse into the air, and units could move out of the area or upwind to escape their strength. But if elements of the 3rd ID were crowded into the Karbala Gap as vehicles snaked through the area, chemical weapons would be more potent. Prior to the 3rd Brigade's assault, the division had unleashed massive amounts of artillery fire on the area, eliminating much of the Iraqi forces positioned in the area around the gap. The attack destroyed enemy artillery units as well as those potentially tasked with unleashing chemical weapons. At midnight on April 1, the 3rd Brigade, commanded by Colonel Dan Allyn, led the 3rd ID's offensive by attacking the city of Karbala.

The next day was a Friday, the Muslim day of worship, and Perez-Cruz marveled at the throngs of people walking to the local Shia mosque to pray. It was a war zone, yet the faithful still pressed on and went to services. It was another surreal moment which made Perez-Cruz stop and look around at where he was and what he was doing. He'd been in Kuwait, but Kuwait was all skyscrapers and glistening modernity. This was the Middle East of Perez-Cruz's imagination. As the worshipers walked by, some of them stopped to thank the soldiers, and Perez-Cruz thought about how long they had been oppressed by Hussein's regime and how they just wanted to go to their mosques and pray.[8]

While Blount prepared the 3rd ID to attack into the Karbala Gap, Wallace at V Corps received reports about the locations of Iraqi troops. Reports indicated that armored vehicles and artillery were moving out of their hiding positions and moving into defensive positions along Highway 8. UAVs also identified Iraqi formations. Intelligence regarding the Karbala Gap indicated that there was no substantial enemy presence in the area. Wallace was surprised that the Iraqis didn't even seem to be trying to defend the Karbala Gap.[9]

As the elements of 3rd Brigade approached Karbala, troops captured Iraqi soldiers who claimed to be from the Nebuchadnezzar Division of the Republican Guard, one of the main divisions from this unit. The Americans hadn't expected to see them, believing the Nebuchadnezzar elements were fighting in the north. Based on how they looked, 3rd Brigade soldiers thought they were deserters. The Iraqis wore civilian clothes and traveled in trucks instead of tanks. American interrogators learned that the Iraqis had been ordered to go south to defend Baghdad, leading V Corps to believe that Saddam had enforced the Baghdad area with Republican Guard troops. The dictator had saved his best soldiers to make a final stand at Baghdad. Even if the Americans captured everything else, the dictator held on in desperation to keep control of the capital city.[10]

While 3rd Brigade isolated the city, elements of the 69th Armor Battalion led 1st Brigade into the gap. At about 2am, troops advanced on the west side of Karbala toward a dam the Americans named Objective Muscogee. They encountered Iraqi infantry troops, most of whom fought on foot. Planning to push through the Karbala Gap at night, the 1st Brigade's fighting units fell into place. The 3rd Forward Support Battalion moved up to the front, carrying fuel, ammunition, medics, a chemical decontamination unit, and a chaplain. Commanders worried that any or all of these support services might be needed depending on how the battle went. The units waited in pitch-black night. Fighting at night made sense, and night vision goggles made it possible, but the problem was sleep. The air war began first, and the sounds of exploding rockets and artillery made it difficult for soldiers to catch some sleep before their units rolled. Added to the noise was anxiety about the upcoming battle, especially the possibility of chemical weapons. Sleep was a prized commodity that was out of the reach of many of the soldiers waiting to head into battle that night.[11]

For two hours, the trail convoy stood still in the pitch-black desert night. Some soldiers noticed the scent of onions. It was pungent, but they couldn't identify the source in the dark. Then the horizon began to glow red, announcing the sunrise, and as the sky brightened, the troops discovered the source of the odor. The lead elements of the convoy had stopped near an onion patch. Dogs ambled around the yard of a small, quiet farm house. The convoy got moving again after sunrise. U.S. tanks and Bradleys rolled past a factory and an abandoned military post. The convoy made it across a dam and a bridge through the Karbala Gap with minimal fighting and no chemical weapons attacks. By dawn, the 3rd Brigade had seized Objective Muscogee and the Highway 28 bridge. On the east side of the city, Colonel David Perkins and his 2nd Brigade had advanced through the wetlands toward Highway 9. Air Force and Navy aircraft supported the 3rd ID with strikes that destroyed an Iraqi armored column that had approached the dam at Objective Muscogee.

Lieutenant General Ra'ad al-Hamdani commanded the II Republican Guard Corps, covering the area south of Baghdad to An Najaf. Despite the beliefs of the Iraqi high command that America's main assault on Baghdad would come from Jordan to the west and also from the north, al-Hamdani knew they were wrong. As the 3rd ID led the V Corps' move on Karbala, al-Hamdani tried to convince his superiors that the main U.S. threat was south of the capital. On April 2, al-Hamdani traveled to Baghdad and met with senior military leaders including Qusay Hussein. Al-Hamdani told them what was happening in Karbala, but his superiors insisted it was a feint. The defense minister and other leaders refused to budge from their position that the main U.S. attack would come from the north and the west, and the defense minister ordered al-Hamdani to begin moving his forces north of Baghdad starting at five o'clock the next morning.[12]

Al-Hamdani asked for permission to address the group, and then he led them to a large map. He pointed to the Karbala Gap and described the 3rd ID's push through it, insisting that the Americans' next stop was Baghdad. Their first stop would be the airport, he told Iraq's military leaders, and then they'd descend on the presidential palaces. If the Americans crossed the al-Kaed bridge, there would be no stopping them. Qusay Hussein asked al-Hamdani if it was really true, and al-Hamdani said yes. Qusay turned to the other military leaders. Could al-Hamdani be right?[13]

But the rest of the group refused to believe it. The Republican Guard chief of staff demanded they follow the plans emanating from high command and shift troops to the north of Baghdad as quickly as possible. Al-Hamdani's heart sank. The decision sealed Baghdad's fate. He asked Qusay if he could take his leave. His men were fighting on both the Tigris and the Euphrates, and he needed to be out there. On his way out, Al-Hamdani stopped Qusay one more time and told him that if the Iraqis did not send more troops to Karbala immediately, the Americans would be in Baghdad within 48 hours. As the lieutenant general walked out onto the street, he knew the end was near.[14]

It was mid-afternoon as al-Hamdani made his way to his headquarters in Yusufiya, a town on the outskirts of southwestern Baghdad. He couldn't get out of his head the way Qusay had looked at him when he described the situation in Karbala. Qusay had believed him, but the pull of high command's orders was too great. When Qusay told al-Hamdani to move his troops north, he acted as a mouthpiece of high command, not on his own understanding of where the American threat was. When al-Hamdani arrived at headquarters, he briefed his commanders on the orders from high command. Then he told them that Baghdad would fall in two days. Prepare for the worst, he said.[15]

Then al-Hamdani got to work. He sat down with his commanders and assessed what they could do with the forces they had left. Al-Hamdani ordered special forces units to positions along the Tigris, and he sent other units to Karbala, in defiance of high command's orders to withdraw from the city. He placed the troops in Musaib, outside of Karbala, to give the illusion of withdrawal. That night, al-Hamdani heard that U.S. troops had crossed the Euphrates over the al-Kaed bridge and were nearing Baghdad. Another of his warnings had gone unheeded. Some ten days earlier, al-Hamdani had requested that the bridge be demolished so that the Americans couldn't cross. He had ordered his commander of sabotage force, Major Rawkan Al-Ajeeley, to wire the bridge with explosives. When Al-Ajeeley's men were finished with it, they had applied enough explosives to render the bridge unpassable if detonated. But as al-Hamdani waited for approval from high command to destroy the bridge, the Americans drove their armored vehicles across it and trained their weapons on Baghdad.

In response to the Americans crossing the Euphrates, the Iraqi Republican Guard chief of staff ordered al-Hamdani to launch an offensive near the bridge on April 3. The lieutenant general had one brigade, but he called in elements of the 10th Armored Brigade and special forces of the Medina Division, as well as the 22nd Armored Brigade of the Nebuchadnezzar Division. He also deployed available artillery units. The troops seemed to be in good spirits and willing to fight. Al-Hamdani rode into battle with the commander of the Medina Division. Everything seemed to happen so quickly. Al-Hamdani watched an Iraqi commander fighting with a machine gun. The soldiers and officers who remained while others fled seemed to have a personal reason for fighting beyond any government directive. The lieutenant general couldn't help but feel proud despite the chaos and destruction swirling around him.

With the communication lines down, al-Hamdani's cell phone wasn't working, so he wanted to return to his headquarters in Yusufiya. He asked a Medina Division security officer to bring him a vehicle, and soon a major drove up to meet him. As they drove toward the town, they found themselves following the same route as an American convoy. U.S. fire hit the car, blowing out all four tires so that the car drove on metal wheels. Al-Hamdani made it to his headquarters just before U.S. troops arrived. As 3rd ID tanks bore down on the headquarters, al-Hamdani ordered his commanders and soldiers to save themselves. As for the lieutenant general, he considered himself the captain of a sinking ship and remained at headquarters. He managed to evade capture and eventually snuck away to see if anything was left of the Medina Division. All he found were burned-out tanks and the remnants of army vehicles. America's destruction of the division was utterly complete. From there al-Hamdani went into hiding at a relative's house and waited for the end.

Blount's second in command, Brigadier General Lloyd Austin, hoped to capitalize on the 3rd ID's momentum going through the Karbala Gap. He wanted the division to get across the Euphrates, and that meant securing the al-Kaed bridge, nicknamed Objective Peach. Surrounded by palm trees, rice paddies, and canals, the al-Kaed Bridge was a key entry point to the greater Baghdad vicinity. The successful taking of Objective Peach would put the 3rd ID within 25 miles of Baghdad. Lieutenant Colonel Rock Marcone, commander of 3-69 Armor of 1st Brigade, thought it looked like Vietnam, a jarring contrast to the desert conditions the 3rd ID had trained for and battled through up to that point.[16] It was a reminder of why ancient Mesopotamia was nicknamed the fertile crescent despite the expanse of desert in southern and western Iraq.

While 3rd Brigade finished the job in Karbala, 1st Brigade moved on to Objective Peach on April 2 with the mission to secure it so that 2nd Brigade, and eventually 3rd, could pass through and head on to Baghdad. The capital city was so close, yet dangers lurked from hiding places such as under the bridges. Iraqis had rigged explosives up under the concrete structures in hopes of turning them into giant concrete bombs. Part of the Al-Kaed bridge was already blown up, which tipped Blount and his commanders off to what the enemy had done. The section still standing was passable, but it would become a literal ticking time bomb once 3rd ID tanks and Bradleys started making their way across. If Iraqis detonated the explosives mid-crossing, the carnage and destruction would constitute a major setback for U.S. forces. If the Iraqis blew up the bridge before the 3rd ID began to cross it, the division would lose its passage to the vicinity of Baghdad.

Marcone's 3-69 Armor was tasked with the job of leading 1st Brigade in taking the bridge. Securing Objective Peach involved a two-phase operation that drew on what 1st Brigade had learned in the fight at Al-Kifl. First, 3-69 Armor would seize the ground on the near side of the Euphrates and generate smoke to obscure the crossing site from enemy eyes. After that, Marcone's forces would cross the bridge and expand the bridgehead. He sent scouts to assess the area, and they fought an Iraqi infantry battalion and elements of a reconnaissance battalion near the western approach to the bridge. To combat the enemy units, Marcone relied on artillery support and a company of Apache helicopters to attack as his troops advanced toward the bridge.[17] In just over 30 minutes, 3-69 Armor had reached the bridge and encountered Fedayeen troops. Marcone called in fire missions to clear the area of Fedayeen as well as those enemy units positioned to demolish the bridge. By mid-afternoon on April 2, the soldiers of 3-69 Armor had secured the west shore of the bridge. Air support then worked to clear the far side of the bridge. Engineers began checking for explosives.[18]

Marcone expected the bridge to be mined, and he had experienced an engagement with an explosive bridge back at Objective Jenkins, which crossed the Euphrates at Al-Kifl, just north of An Najaf. He ordered engineers into RB-15 inflatable boats and sent them out to the bridge columns to disarm the explosives so that 1st Brigade could take the bridge intact for follow-on use by the rest of the division. Just after four o'clock in the afternoon, the Iraqis detonated charges intended to destroy the bridge. The explosion damaged the northern span, but three lanes of the southern span remained passable. Engineers climbed out of the RB-15 boats and into the waist-deep waters of the Euphrates. They waded through the river toward the bridge columns where wires connected dynamite to the concrete structures.[19]

For Captain Charles O'Brien, Alpha Company commander, the fight to secure Objective Peach encapsulated all the training and learning his company had done up to that point. The soldiers of Alpha Company fought through Iraqi forces and artillery for about 6 miles as the enemy tried to slow the movement of 3-69th Armor toward the bridge. At one point, O'Brien saw Iraqi civilians come of out their houses and wave their arms. A second later, field artillery rained down on Alpha Company. O'Brien would never know if the civilians were signaling Iraqi artillery units to fire or warning Alpha Company to take cover. What he did know was that his and every other commander's blanket order was to avoid shooting civilian targets. During the fight for Objective Peach, Alpha Company destroyed a couple of vehicles that could have been civilian or military, but it was the nature of a war in which the Fedayeen used civilian vehicles to attack U.S. troops. There was a cemetery on the far side of the Euphrates River, and Alpha Company soldiers did not fire into it even though they received enemy fire from it.[20]

Using aerial photographs of the bridge and surrounding buildings, Marcone and his troops made a plan to neutralize the exploding mechanisms that were wired to the bridge. Close air support and artillery prevented enemy troops from advancing as the soldiers of 3-69 Armor disabled some of the mines. One fearless engineer hung upside down, suspended under the bridge, in order to reach wires that he needed to disable. The work was dangerous but vital. It required a steady hand and a calm disposition under the most intense pressure. Marcone ordered some of his infantry across the bridge to secure the other side, and then he sent three companies after them.[21] 3-69 Armor held the bridge through the night until the rest of the 3rd ID crossed it.[22]

While the soldiers of 3-69 Armor worked to take the al-Kaed bridge, 2nd Brigade units passed through the Karbala Gap after 3rd Brigade had seized the city of Karbala. As the tanks and Bradleys emerged from the gap and moved north away from the city, they ran into Iraqi regulars manning Russian infantry fighting vehicles. Iraqi soldiers fired on 2nd Brigade units as they advanced. Soldiers of 2nd Brigade dispatched the enemy and kept moving, and the units pushed on as quickly as they could toward Baghdad. The soldiers of 2nd Brigade had orders to cross the al-Kaed bridge and move toward the southern approach to the city.[23]

It was a long night getting there. At one point during the trek, an HEMTT broke down, blocking the road. Colonel Eric Schwartz, commander of 1-64 Armor, told Hilms to have his soldiers move the truck to the side of the road and destroy it. A crew did so and threw a grenade in the cab, which exploded as the soldiers left the scene. That way the Iraqis wouldn't be able to use the truck.[24]

Irrigation canals lined the terrain south of Baghdad, and some were too narrow to support a tank or Bradley. As 2nd Brigade trekked toward Baghdad, drivers sometimes reached points where they realized they couldn't safely drive their vehicles forward anymore. They radioed the vehicles behind them and told them to back up, pushing the column back so that they could try an alternative route. 2nd Brigade soldiers arrived at the intersection of Highway 1 and Highway 8 south of Baghdad on the afternoon of April 3. An order came down the next day that there were Republican Guard units further south away from Baghdad, and the soldiers of Task Force 1-64 went out on an attack back the way they had come to destroy them.[25]

Alpha Company and others traveled about 15 to 20 miles south and discovered what looked to be Medina Division units. Upon inspection, the soldiers found that it was mostly the division's abandoned vehicles. Hilms speculated that some of the Medina troops had decided that it wasn't worth it to continue fighting. As the Americans moved south along the highway, they found entire battalion formations of T-72s and Russian infantry fighting vehicles, air defense weapons systems, and other military equipment, along the edge of the road. The Medina troops had covered some of it, using palm tree leaves as camouflage. Hilms ordered his soldiers to fire on the equipment in order to destroy it.[26]

After making it to the destination point, the Wild Bunch turned around to meet back up with the 2nd Brigade at the junction of Highway 1 and Highway 8. As the soldiers headed north again, they had to pass the Medina equipment they had shot up. The vehicles and artillery were exploding at that point, ignited by 1-64 Armor's firing. Medina troops had loaded all of the equipment with ammunition and explosives. On both sides of the highway, 1-64 soldiers dodged shrapnel and flying debris as they went by.[27]

By that point, Hilms' soldiers had been in combat of some kind every day since the second day of the invasion. As a commander, Hilms averaged about two to three hours of sleep each day, mostly in the forms of a cat nap here and there, rarely several hours in one stretch. He and his soldiers got by on adrenaline and the quick realization that complete situational awareness was life-saving. Most of Alpha Company had never been in combat, but the soldiers learned quickly that they had to stay ahead of the enemy in order to survive. No amount of training enforced that fact like combat action did. Anything could be a threat, and so Hilms and his troops operated in a constant state of hypervigilance. It took a toll on their bodies, with most of them losing 20 to 30 pounds during the drive to Baghdad. They had MREs, but the stress and lack of sleep drained their bodies.[28]

Well into the evening on April 2, as 3-69 Armor received artillery and mortar fire, Marcone got word that 2nd Brigade had run into trouble and would not make it to the bridge until morning. It would be up to 3-69 Armor to defend the bridge all night with the disconcerting intelligence that an Iraqi commander brigade was coming from the airport to retake the bridge. Soon assistance arrived from 37th Infantry of 1st Brigade, and that battalion took the southern part of the bridgehead so that Marcone's forces could concentrate on the north and east sides, the direct lines of attack. In the middle of the night, Marcone began receiving reports of Iraqi tank sightings. The battle began around 3am and continued until around 6am on April 3. Charlie Company, commanded by Captain Gerald Robbins, handled the bulk of the fighting, and it turned out that one tank company had actually fought two brigades – the 10th Medina Brigade as well as the commander brigade. The Iraqis had tried to launch a coordinated armor attack with tanks and armored personnel carriers reinforced with artillery mortars, but Charlie 3-69 Armor's long-range-vision technology allowed the tank company to fire on the Iraqis effectively.[29] When the fighting ended at daybreak, the U.S. companies had destroyed Medina's 10th Brigade.[30]

Robbins' Charlie Company consisted of ten tanks and four Bradleys. In the light of day after the battle, Marcone walked out onto the road to assess the damage. As far as he could see, body parts and burning Iraqi tanks and personnel carriers littered the road. It had been a major tank battle, but in the darkness of night and early morning, it had been hard to tell what they were fighting, even with long-range-sight technology. Charlie Company had done its job on the enemy brigade.[31]

With Objective Peach secured, 3rd ID forces closed in on Baghdad. Around nine o'clock in the morning on April 3, Perkins' 2nd Brigade began crossing the al-Kaed Bridge en route to Objective Saints, the intersection of Highway 1 and Highway 8. Control of Saints would cut off Iraqi forces in Baghdad from reinforcements coming from the south and would also prevent troops in the capital from reinforcing units positioned south of the city. There 2nd Brigade met remaining elements of the Nebuchadnezzar and Medina divisions, as well as Fedayeen troops at about one o'clock in the afternoon. For 12 hours, 2nd Brigade fought through enemy forces to push on toward the city. In the middle of the night on April 4, 2nd Brigade secured Objective Saints on the south side of Baghdad, putting V Corps into the position of controlling the southern approach to Baghdad.

While 2nd Brigade fought for control of the key intersection of Highways 1 and 8, 1st Brigade advanced on Saddam International Airport – Objective Lions. Blount planned to use the airport as a base of operations for continued attacks into Baghdad. The 3rd ID had moved through the Iraqi desert so much more quickly than V Corps, CFLCC, and the Pentagon had expected, and Blount reflected on his division's accomplishments and recognized the momentum it had. In about a day, the 3rd ID had pushed through the Karbala Gap, seized the al-Kaed bridge, and secured a major highway intersection just outside Baghdad. There was no reason to stop now. Blount decided to capitalize on his division's forward progress and attack the airport on April 4.

Closer to Baghdad, Iraqi forces were positioned east of the Euphrates River. Units included the 2nd Medina Armored Division, brigades from the 1st Hammurabi Armored Division, and the 6th Nebuchadnezzar Mechanized Division. 1st Hammurabi was mostly located west of the city, while the 6th Nebuchadnezzar operated south of the city along with elements of the Medina Division and held Objective Saints. War planners had expected

Republican Guard units to defend the airport and the city. They also estimated that the 17th Brigade of the Hammurabi Division would move to defend the roads leading into Baghdad. As many as 15,000 irregulars might also defend the city.

V Corps originally had the 101st and 82nd Airborne divisions taking the airport, but Blount knew the 3rd ID was better suited for the job. Iraqi antiaircraft units had executed successful attacks against American aircraft, making an air assault a risky choice. An example was the Iraqis' successful assault on the 11th Helicopter Regiment. On March 24, V Corps ordered the unit of AH-64 Apaches to attack the Medina Division near Karbala to eliminate Iraqi forces positioned there before the 3rd ID began its trek through the Karbala Gap. What the Army didn't know was that Iraqi spies had been watching the helicopter preparations for the battle. An Iraqi general in An Najaf called antiaircraft unit commanders and told them of the Americans' planned air assault. Based on this intelligence, Iraqi anti-aircraft units attacked the U.S. helicopters.[32]

V Corps commanders had worried that Baghdad's dense urban setting would prove too difficult for the 3rd ID's armor to maneuver through. Blount had no such worries, and he made that clear. He radioed Wallace from the tactical command post and asked for permission to advance to Baghdad. "Sir," the general said to the Corps commander. "We trained for this. We prepared for this. We're ready for this. We need to go now."[33] Silence fell on the command post as Blount and his commanders waited to for Wallace's reply. Then Wallace's voice came through the radio as he offered his blessing: "Have a good fight. Victory 6, out."[34] The 3rd ID would take the airport, the west side of the city, and the city center, while the Marines would come in and handle the east side.

Blount expected Baghdad to be heavily defended, with brigades from the Hammurabi and Adnan divisions positioned to fight along the northern and western approaches to the city around the airport. He also figured that Special Republican Guard and Fedayeen troops would fight within the city. In order to advance more 3rd ID elements toward the city, Blount ordered the 54th Engineer Battalion to erect a ribbon bridge across the river to offer another means of crossing since Iraqis had disabled a segment of the al-Kaed bridge at Objective Peach. 3-69 Armor was set to lead 1st Brigade's advance to Saddam International Airport. Soldiers called their battalion "the tip of the tip of the spear" as they drove toward the capital city.

As the 3rd ID made its approach, the view from Baghdad was one of dread. Thick clouds of black smoke hung over the city, emanating from oil trenches Saddam's forces had set on fire. The hope was that doing so would prevent U.S. missile guidance systems from locating bomb targets. Then a sandstorm hit the city. Winds were so strong that they bent the palm trees along the Tigris River nearly flat, and the storm clouded the already polluted skies with yellowish-brown sand. Saddam's propaganda machine worked hard to deny the presence of U.S. troops in Iraq, but shortwave radio transmissions and the rumor mill conveyed the truth to the citizenry. The Americans were almost at the city gates.[35]

Tanks rolled toward the capital city, and curious residents from a town just outside Baghdad lined the streets and cheered as the armored formation passed by. To the citizens, the hulking tanks and Bradleys likely formed an awesome sight. Some surely understood that the appearance of the U.S. military signaled the imminent downfall of Saddam Hussein, while others may have looked on in fear or interest. Yet even as Iraqi citizens watched U.S. military equipment rumble by, Iraq's minister of information, Muhammed Saeed Al-Sahhaf, held a press conference and told a different story. "Baghdad Bob," as Americans had nicknamed him, declared that Republican Guard troops had expelled U.S. forces and controlled the Baghdad airport. It was an act of desperation on the part of a regime under siege, one that had no chance in the face of the U.S. military. But the act made sense. Iraqi citizens were accustomed to receiving only one perspective on their country's state of affairs emanating from Saddam's authority. Baghdad Bob had reason to expect that some citizens who had not seen the Americans with their own eyes might believe him. But soon the 3rd ID's tanks would descend on the city, and no amount of state-controlled media lies could silence their roar.

The General's Gamble: Seizing Baghdad

General Blount had convinced his V Corps superiors that the 3rd ID was the division best suited to seize Saddam International Airport. Iraqi antiaircraft units had proven their ability to disrupt U.S. air attacks, rendering too risky an airborne operation on Objective Lions, the airport's nickname. Grimsley's 1st Brigade troops had just come from the intense fighting at Objective Peach where they had crushed the Iraqi counterattack. Units of 2-7 Infantry were still making their way to link back up with the rest of the brigade as they navigated irrigation canals that broke up the terrain. It was strange to go from brown desert to the lush green foliage along the Euphrates. It reminded Grimsley of Florida or coastal South Carolina. To an older generation of soldiers, it might have looked like Vietnam.[1]

Blount called Grimsley on the morning of April 3 and asked him when his soldiers could be ready to move on to the airport. Grimsley replied that they could be ready that day, which was what Blount had hoped to hear. "I want you on the road by four o'clock," Blount told Grimsley, and with that, 1st Brigade had its next mission.[2] Following his conversation with Blount, Grimsley gathered his subordinate commanders near a house on the banks of the Euphrates River, and they sketched out their plan of attack. Task Force 3-69 would get to the wall surrounding the airport and find the southwest gate to enter the airport grounds. Other brigade units would get into position, overwhelm the Iraqis with firepower, and secure the near side of the airport. 3-7 CAV would set a screen on 1st Brigade's left flank from the west and north along the highway to Jordan and the roads to Fallujah and Ramadi. Meanwhile, Task Force 2-7 would take the east side of the airport and block the main entry to the airport from downtown Baghdad. Grimsley expected that if the Iraqis were going to launch a counterattack, it was going to come from downtown. Once on the airport grounds, company teams would each take one of the four runways, while others would set up positions near storage facilities and other buildings. The goal was to have all units in position before daylight.[3]

By four o'clock on April 3, 1st Brigade was ready to move out as ordered. Lieutenant Colonel Rock Marcone's 3-69 Armor led the convoy. Traveling mostly on paved two-lane roads, elements of the brigade passed through small towns and across narrow bridges that left the formation vulnerable to ambush. Grimsley noticed groups of young Iraqi men in civilian clothes glaring at the Americans angrily. The road to the airport wasn't straight – it meandered – and 3-69 began taking enemy fire almost as soon as they began to move.[4] Gunfights continued all the way to the airport. While trying to avoid an ambush, one of the vehicles fell into a canal, resulting in the deaths of Staff Sergeant Wilbert Davis and *Atlantic* reporter Michael Kelly, who had been embedded with the 3rd ID.[5]

When 3-69 arrived at the concrete wall surrounding the airport, the troops couldn't find the entry gate, so Marcone ordered a tank to knock the wall down. It was eerily dark and quiet. There was no natural light because it was a new moon, and there was no light coming from Baghdad because all the electricity was shut off. The only light came from wreckage burning on the runways, the result of close air support from the Navy via the USS *Theodore Roosevelt*. There were no Republican Guards that Grimsley could see on the grounds. The quiet was unexpected and unnerving. It appeared that the Iraqis had given up on the airport, and Grimsley called Austin and told him that Objective Lions was secure.[6]

At dawn on April 4, Marcone, who had been asleep on his tank, awoke to the thudding sound of a 25mm firing. In a moment of mutual surprise, the Americans and the Iraqis had discovered each other, but not where either side had expected the enemy to be.

Special Republican Guard brigades had each taken a runway, and guardsmen had dug trenches in the marsh between the access road and the runways. It was there, concealed by the tall marsh grass, that they had established their headquarters, laid communications wire, and stored mortars. They had expected the Americans to launch an airborne attack on the airport, and from the trenches, Iraqi soldiers were positioned to launch a counterassault against U.S. attack helicopters and troops falling from the sky. The Iraqis had not planned for an armored task force to come rolling onto the airport grounds. As the sun came up on April 4, Republican Guard soldiers awakened and climbed out of their trenches only to come face to face with American tanks.[7]

Because Task Force 3-69 Armor had not expected the Republican Guards to have dug trenches at the airport, tank commanders were surprised to look down and see Iraqi soldiers coming up out of the marsh and appearing right below their tanks. Once they realized what was going on, the tank commanders worked quickly and started from their tank hatches, firing pistols and throwing grenades into the trenches. There wasn't time to start their tanks and get them moving into fighting positions. For about 90 minutes, the two sides engaged in fierce fighting. U.S. tanks took RPG fire, and grenades exploded all around. Task Force 3-69 Armor eventually managed to destroy both of the Republican Guard command posts, killing the commanders inside. Once the Iraqi soldiers knew their commanders were dead, they began surrendering.[8]

Throughout the morning, 1st Brigade troops continued to arrive at the airport. Task Force 2-7 Infantry established blocking positions at an area called "four corners," the main entrance on the east side of the airport. As soldiers set up the blocking position, they took small-arms fire from all directions. While some Iraqis surrendered, others remained in position and fought. Exhausted U.S. soldiers who had been traveling all night to get to the airport continued to battle their way to one of their most crucial objectives.

Iraqi Special Republican Guard tanks lay in wait as 1st Brigade elements combed the grounds. Late morning on April 4, a Fox chemical reconnaissance vehicle from 2-7 Infantry traveled on an overpass near the four corners and just missed being hit by a tank main gun round. It was a reminder that the enemy remained staked out at the airport. First Lieutenant Paul Milosovich sent a Bradley onto the overpass to look for Iraqi tanks, and just as he reached the top of the bridge a main round from a T-72 hit his vehicle with an impact so forceful that the rucksacks strapped to the outside of the Bradley exploded. Burning boots, shirts, and equipment flew into the air, and the commander of the Bradley was thrown out of the turret.

The crew managed to back the Bradley down off the overpass, preventing it from being hit again and saving the lives of those inside. An infantry squad equipped with Javelin antitank weapons arrived on the overpass and located three Iraqi T-72s on a road inside the airport compound. The antitank team fired a Javelin, hitting one of the tanks and causing it to explode in a massive fireball as its turret flew into the air. When the tank's ammunition storage compartment caught fire, secondary explosions engulfed the tank next to it in fire. A second Javelin hit the tank, ensuring its destruction. It was the first enemy kill by a Javelin missile, one of the Army's newest weapons. The driver of the third Iraqi tank began to move his vehicle in a desperate search for an escape route. Private First Class Jefferson Jimenez of the antitank unit fired a third Javelin, missing a killing hit but damaging the tank anyway.[9]

It took two more days of fighting to fully secure the entire airport property and adjacent palaces. Soldiers of 3-69 Armor searched for bunkers and fighting positions and captured any Iraqi troops they encountered. Military buildings and concourses serving commercial flights had provided cover for Iraqi forces, and U.S. soldiers swept through those areas before declaring the airport secured. Soldiers found Iraqi troops hiding throughout the airport grounds. Sergeant First Class Richard Fonder and Specialist Joseph Ramsel of Alpha Company, 3-69 Armor drove their vehicle near a bunker and tossed a grenade in to clear it out. Twenty Iraqi soldiers emerged from the bunker to surrender, and while Fonder and Ramsel processed the prisoners, they discovered another area where enemy troops were in position and ready to fight. After a brief battle between Americans and Iraqis, about ten additional Iraqi soldiers surrendered.[10]

Bravo Company of the 11th Engineer Battalion set out to build an enclosure to keep prisoners for processing. Sergeant First Class Paul Smith led the team of soldiers building the enclosure in a former Iraqi military compound at the airport. An armored combat earthmover smashed a hole in the concrete wall surrounding the compound, and engineers entered the area and began clearing away debris. As they moved through the compound, the engineers spotted about ten Republican Guard soldiers with small arms, rocket-propelled grenades, and mortars. Smith moved quickly, calling in a Bradley for support and ordering his soldiers to move into fighting positions. As Bravo Company prepared to fight, Smith realized that there were nearly 100 Republican Guard troops, a company-sized unit, in the compound. The Iraqis regained control of the compound's two watchtowers and began firing on the Americans. Bravo Company soldiers scattered to avoid the rocket-propelled grenades and small-arms fire that rained down on them.

In the chaos, Smith threw a grenade over the wall near the gate, driving back the Iraqis. He ordered his fire team to engage the enemy. The Bradley had arrived and fired on enemy positions, and Smith also called in an armored personnel carrier for additional fire support. When it arrived, it took a direct hit from a mortar round, which wounded the three soldiers inside. Smith dragged the wounded soldiers to a safe position, and they were evacuated. Then Smith ran to the armored personnel carrier, climbed in, and drove it, under heavy fire, to the center of the compound. He manned the vehicle's .50-caliber machine gun and fired on Republican Guard soldiers in the watchtower as well as those rushing the gate. Meanwhile, Bravo Company's first sergeant planned a counterattack that eventually drove the Iraqi unit out. Had the Republican Guard troops succeeded in their mission, they might have attacked the 2-7 Infantry's tactical operations center.[11]

But the cost was Sergeant Smith's life. During the fighting, Iraqi fire mortally wounded Smith. He had stood his ground as he took fire from automatic weapons, not retreating even when rounds shattered the ceramic breastplate in his flak jacket. A shot to the head killed him. It hadn't been Smith's first time in Iraq. He was a veteran of Operation *Desert Storm*. He was also a 33-year-old father of two. His death left his wife, Birgit, a widow. Smith's decision to man the armored personnel carrier's machine gun from an open position saved the lives of about 100 U.S. soldiers and ensured that he was the only American to die in the battle.[12] When Colonel Lyle Cayce got to Baghdad International Airport around 2pm on April 4, the temperature was about 115 degrees. The tanks were still smoking from the battle. Soldiers had attached their duffel bags of clothes to the sides of the tank, and Cayce saw the smoldering remains of the duffel bags on the tanks. The soldiers looked ashen. They had wiped the enemy out.[13]

As the 3rd ID closed in on the capital, the strength of enemy forces within the city was unclear. Based on the number of abandoned vehicles on the roads leading to Baghdad, intelligence analysts estimated that anywhere from nine to 12 Republican Guard units had left their positions outside the city and moved inward to defend the capital, especially Saddam's palaces and government buildings. Analysts also warned that the Fedayeen would not surrender easily. They concluded that the Iraqis would take full advantage of what urban warfare had to offer them and establish fighting positions on the top floors of buildings, inside schoolyards, near mosques, and dug in along major highways. The Iraqis had knowledge of the city that the Americans did not, and their willingness to fight from civilian sites clashed with Americans' reticence to fire on such structures. Some U.S. analysts worried that the fighting in Baghdad could mimic the First Battle of Grozny, where Chechen irregulars battled Russian armor units for more than a month before the Russians occupied the city during the First Chechen War of the mid-1990s. The fighting in Grozny resulted in thousands of military and civilian casualties. Grozny, along with Somalia, made some commanders reticent to engage in urban warfare.

Differences among the U.S. service branches regarding the rules of engagement made it difficult for the Americans to identify legitimate military targets. The Army accepted radar intercept as a positive identification, but the Air Force required eyes on a target or confirmation from a ground unit it was a legal target. Because of that difference, if an Army unit was fired on and only had radar confirmation of the source of fire, the unit would have to rely on Army equipment to take out the target. If Army artillery didn't have the range needed to attack the target, the Army unit would have to use the multiple launch rocket system (MLRS). Each one of the rockets in the MLRS contained about 640 bomblets the size of a tennis ball. MLRS was effective, but with a blast radius of about 250 yards, it didn't allow for pinpointing a precision target. There was a great potential for collateral damage. Hussein knew this, and he put his artillery next to mosques and schools because he knew the Americans would be reluctant to fire on those types of targets. He used international laws of war against the U.S. and to his advantage.[14]

The relative speed with which the 3rd ID took the airport, which CENTCOM called "a gateway to the future of Iraq," convinced Blount that the 3rd ID could make an armor thrust into the heart of the city. A "thunder run" was a reconnaissance raid aimed to take Baghdad's pulse and determine how Iraqi forces would respond to the arrival of U.S. troops. If 3rd ID soldiers could fight their way in and stay, and move freely in downtown Baghdad, it would prove to Iraqis and the international media that the U.S. was in control of the capital city. The name "thunder run" came from the Vietnam War, a reference to combat missions to secure supply routes.[15] In Operation *Iraqi Freedom*, thunder runs were designed to give Blount and his commanders knowledge about how Iraqis planned to defend Baghdad so that the 3rd ID could successfully overcome enemy defenses. Since intelligence reports about the fortification could only tell Blount and V Corps leaders so much, thunder runs would give them a direct look at the interior of the city to see how willing and able Iraqi forces were to fight the Americans.

Since March 20, the U.S. had bombarded the city with hundreds of "smart" bombs. The weapons contained global positioning systems that could guide them to within 40 feet of a pre-programmed target. Yet the precision of the bombs was irrelevant when Hussein turned schools, hospitals, and mosques into military sites while civilians remained on the grounds or nearby. Buildings, parking structures, and private homes served as hideouts and fighting positions that left Americans vulnerable to attack as their hulking armored vehicles negotiated city streets.

V Corps commander Lieutenant General William Scott Wallace hadn't expected the division to attack into the heart of the city so quickly. He wanted to take things slowly in order to get a feel for the condition Iraqi troops were in and what they were capable of. One of the things that worried Wallace was that he didn't know how many Fedayeen or Republican Guard troops were in Baghdad. But Blount convinced him that they should go in and find out. Blount pushed for a quick drive into the city in part because he was tired of hearing Iraq's minister of information publicly insist that U.S. troops had not taken the airport. Once again, Baghdad Bob appeared on television insisting that American forces weren't in the city, hadn't taken the airport, and other falsehoods. Blount wanted to prove that Baghdad Bob was wrong. His soldiers had done a masterful job from the moment the division had crossed the line of departure from Kuwait into Iraq and had pushed through enemy fire, crippling sandstorms, and intense fatigue. The formation of 10,000 tanks, Humvees, Bradleys, and armored personnel carriers never lost pace despite slows and stops. Blount, as well as V Corps' Wallace, wanted Iraqis to know once and for all that their media lied to them. The 3rd ID was going to attack into the heart of the city.

Although the conditions that led to the thunder runs developed in the moment, the decisions made by 3rd ID leadership were grounded in more than a year of training at Fort Stewart and NTC and in Kuwait. Instead of focusing on one way to conduct desert and urban warfare, the brigades had tried different tactics and maneuvers and learned from each exercise. One had Perkins running 2nd Brigade's command and control from a helicopter, with the idea being that he could see everything from above and that omnipotence would be an advantage. But they learned that it actually wasn't.[16] The risk of enemy antiaircraft fire shooting down an American helicopter outweighed the advantage of omnipotence. Understanding the pros and cons of various tactics and learning to adapt through long periods of training had made Blount, Perkins, and other leaders within the 3rd ID confident in the division's ability to handle a mission into the city.

Blount chose 2nd Brigade, under Perkins' command, to conduct what was to be the first thunder run on April 5 by sending a battalion of M1A1 Abrams tanks and Bradley fighting vehicles up Highway 8 from the brigade's headquarters at Objective Saints. Perkins had decided to lead with a tank battalion because he knew the vehicles could sustain big hits, they moved fast, and they had major firepower. It required sacrificing standoff capability; the tanks were incapable of raising their guns high enough to shoot into tall buildings which the enemy would undoubtedly use as fighting positions. Speed was the key, then, as it had been on the drive to Baghdad. Commanders set the pace at about 15 miles per hour – a good speed that allowed gunners to shoot steadily as the tanks were moving. What they didn't want to do was stop, because then the Iraqis could close in, and if they did, it would be very difficult for the Americans to get out.[17] The battalion would enter southwest Baghdad and then turn and head west to link up with Colonel William Grimsley's 1st Brigade at Saddam International Airport.

Perkins selected Lieutenant Colonel Eric Schwartz's Task Force 1-64 Armor to attempt the thunder run. Schwartz had desert experience, having commanded a company in 1-64 Armor during Operation *Desert Storm*. On April 5, Schwartz led more than 700 soldiers and officers and 30 tanks, 14 Bradleys, and 14 engineer vehicles from Objective Saints and traveled north to Baghdad. The journey from Objective Saints into central Baghdad was about 10 miles, and Schwartz's vision for the attack was concise. He told his chief planners, "Let's look at the start point and the end point. We have one road to travel and let's just look at all the bad things that could happen on the way."[18] Schwartz knew that his battalion would not stay in Baghdad. The purpose of the April 5 operation was a combination of reconnaissance and a display of the U.S. military presence in the city. Schwartz hoped to report back with a sense of what urban warfare in Baghdad would be like.[19] He and his planners knew to expect Fedayeen, and they knew the irregulars would fight from civilian vehicles and shoot at U.S. soldiers from hospitals, schools, and mosques. Fedayeen troops also held up women and children as human shields in battle. Mid-afternoon on April 4, Schwartz called together his company commanders and specialty platoon leaders and put together some quick plans to rehearse for the operation. They needed to finish rehearsing before sunset.[20]

As dawn broke on April 5, the vehicles rolled, and the thunder run began. Perkins went into battle with his soldiers, riding in his M113 armored personnel carrier. Soon after the mission began, Task Force 1-64 Armor encountered disorganized resistance from Republican Guard soldiers in uniform, and plain-clothes Fedayeen troops attacked American forces with rocket-propelled grenades and small-arms fire. Although the preferred formation for an armored brigade was a wedge so as to achieve 360-degree coverage of the battlefield, entering a city on a road required 2nd Brigade to move in a line, what Perkins called "ducks in a row."[21] Among the problems with the formation was the potential for a tank to hit the tank in front of it when firing. But taking a highway was the only way for the brigade to get into Baghdad.

Overpasses were especially dangerous to the task force, as the infrastructure provided cover for Iraqi fighters, and they had taken the on and off ramps as fighting positions. The ramps gave the enemy a means of cutting off the lines of communication from the forward fighting units, which was what had happened in Mogadishu. Iraqi troops had stored weapons caches in ditches and dug fighting positions along the roads into the city. Republican Guards had also positioned tanks and Soviet infantry fighting vehicles in alleyways so that as the U.S. column moved up the highway, Iraqi vehicles could come out of an alleyway and shoot at the American flank. Instead of using air defense weapons to shoot down U.S. aircraft, the Iraqis had placed them on the side

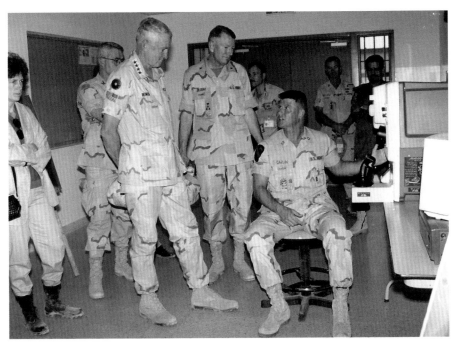

General Dennis Reimer, U.S. Army chief of staff, visiting OPM-SANG in Saudi Arabia in May 1999 during General Buford Blount's second appointment. (General Blount's personal archive)

Saudi Arabia's Crown Prince Abdullah, along with Anita Blount, pinning on General Blount's 2nd Star in Jeddah. Blount's time as the program manager for the Saudi Arabian National Guard modernization program instilled in him a deep interest in and respect for the Arab world. (General Blount's personal archive)

Crown Prince Abdullah presenting Blount with the King Abdul Aziz Medal. Blount's vision for an armored invasion of Iraq crystalized during his service in Saudi Arabia. (General Blount's personal archive)

General Blount with President George W. Bush at Fort Stewart, the 3rd ID's home base. (General Blount's personal archive)

General Blount attending the Thanksgiving dinner at Fort Stewart in 2001. Blount made it a point to interact with 3rd ID soldiers as much as possible and often ate in the dining hall with them. (General Blount's personal archive)

An Apache Longbow returning from a combat mission. An Iraqi attack on Apaches in March 2003 was one of the events that convinced Blount that a ground attack into Baghdad would be more effective than an air assault. (General Blount's personal archive)

General Blount briefing the final attack plan for Baghdad. The original invasion plans did not have the 3rd ID going into the city, but Blount convinced his superiors at V Corps that his division was the one for the job. (General Blount's personal archive)

ABC news anchor Diane Sawyer talking with General Blount while on assignment in Kuwait. The Army's embedded media program gave journalists close access to the war. (General Blount's personal archive)

3rd ID Bradley fighting vehicles from 3-7 Infantry take a brief stop during their move deeper into Iraq, March 21, 2003. (Photo by Scott Nelson/Getty Images)

A 3rd ID M1/A1 Abrams tank rolls deeper into Iraqi territory on March 23, 2003, south of the city of An Najaf. (Photo by Scott Nelson/Getty Images)

3rd ID vehicles navigate their way through "the mother of all sandstorms." The sandstorm temporarily slowed the division's progress but also created time for tank crews to conduct maintenance on their vehicles. (General Blount's personal archive)

A U.S. soldier practices drinking water from a canteen while wearing a chemical suit. 3rd ID personnel wore chemical suits during the entirety of the invasion due to concerns about Saddam Hussein having chemical weapons.
(General Blount's personal archive)

The 3rd ID's armored column approaching Baghdad. The division made history when it arrived in Baghdad only three weeks after it invaded Iraq.
(General Blount's personal archive)

Division Operations Officer Peter Bayer, General Blount, and Major Erik Berdy, Blount's aide-de-camp, in front of Blount's M113, which he nicknamed "Zeus." (General Blount's personal archive)

Iraqi people welcoming American soldiers on the outskirts of Baghdad. From Blount's perspective, locals viewed U.S. troops as liberators when they arrived. (General Blount's personal archive)

Soldiers of the 1st Brigade Combat Team (BCT), under the command of Colonel William Grimsley, wait for 2nd BCT troops at the end of the first thunder run at Saddam International Airport. (General Blount's personal archive)

2nd BCT tactical operations center at Objective Saints after an Iraqi missile attack. The attack occurred as Colonel David Perkins was leading 2nd BCT troops into the heart of Baghdad on the second thunder run. (General Blount's personal archive)

An Iraqi orphan tries to sell a pack of cigarettes. U.S. soldiers were told to avoid buying items from locals they encountered during Operation *Iraqi Freedom.*
(General Blount's personal archive)

U.S. soldiers at Saddam Hussein's VIP Parade Field in central Baghdad after the second thunder run, which solidified the 3rd ID's control of Iraq's capital city.
(General Blount's personal archive)

3-7 Infantry soldiers use a Bradley fighting vehicle for cover as they conduct a neighborhood patrol on the outside perimeter of Baghdad International Airport, April 8, 2003. (Photo by Scott Nelson/Getty Images)

Brigadier General Lloyd Austin, General Buford Blount, and Colonel Jack Sterling on Easter Sunday 2003 in Baghdad. (General Blount's personal archive)

On Firdos Square in central Baghdad, in front of the Shahid mosque, a U.S. Marines
tank helps the population to take down a statue of Saddam Hussein.
(Photo by Patrick ROBERT/Corbis via Getty Images)

Private First Class William Mersereau of
the HHC 2-69 AR Scout Platoon, 3rd
ID, helps an Iraqi woman as troops assist
in the distribution of household gas
canisters in Baghdad, May 25, 2003.
(Photo by PATRICK BAZ/AFP
via Getty Images)

A soldier reads a letter included in a
long-awaited care package from home.
Delivery of mail to U.S. troops was a
logistical challenge but also an important
morale booster.
(General Blount's personal archive)

Republic Bridge over the Tigris River after the thunder runs. Highways in and out of
Baghdad served as transportation conduits even as troops fought on them.
(General Blount's personal archive)

A memorial to Private Gregory Huxley, who was killed when a rocket-propelled grenade penetrated the M113 personnel carrier in which he was riding. (General Blount's personal archive)

Memorial service in Baghdad for fallen 3rd ID soldiers. The division lost 44 soldiers, with more than 300 wounded. (General Blount's personal archive)

Infantry soldiers shifting from desert warfare to clearing a jungle-like area along the Tigris River. The palm trees and lush greenery were a jarring contrast to the brown dry desert conditions U.S. soldiers experienced during the attack into Baghdad. (General Blount's personal archive)

Iraqis look on as U.S. Army soldiers keep watch after an attack killed one U.S. soldier and wounded five others on June 5, 2003 in Fallujah. The 3rd ID moved into the town in an effort to quell anti-American attacks in the area. (Photo by Mario Tama/Getty Images)

General Blount leads a group of soldiers back from Iraq on August 22, 2003, at Fort Stewart in Hinesville, Georgia. Blount returned with the division's colors, signaling the return of most of the unit based at Fort Stewart. (Photo by Erik S. Lesser/Getty Images)

General Blount (left) and Lieutenant General David Mc Kiernan, commander of all coalition ground forces in Iraq, walk in front of Iraq's Hands of Victory monument as they tour territory captured by the Army during the U.S.-led war against Iraq.
(Photo by Rick Loomis/Los Angeles Times via Getty Images)

General Blount gives up command of the 3rd ID in 2003. The change of command ceremony was held at Fort Stewart, the division's home in Georgia.
(General Blount's personal archive)

of the highway. Enemy air defense cannons now shot at Task Force 1-64 Armor vehicles in direct fire mode. Hilms had his headset on to monitor the conversations across the task force net, but that meant he couldn't hear what was going on around him, including bullets whizzing over his head as he stood up in his turret. He soon realized it was why his loader kept trying to shove him down into the hatch.[22]

In the midst of the barrage of fire, Hilms realized that Alpha Company, Task Force 1-64 Armor's lead company, would run out of ammunition if his soldiers fired at everything pointed at the column. To conserve ammunition, Hilms ordered his soldiers to only engage and shoot at an enemy or weapon that was capable of hurting the tanks, rather than waste bullets on an Iraqi soldier firing an AK-47. On the other hand, a rocket-propelled grenade could damage a tank's engine, so it was worth neutralizing. Hilms communicated with the commanders behind him and described what he saw to the battalion commander to explain the orders he had given Alpha Company.[23]

The endpoint of the April 5 thunder run was Baghdad International Airport, and some of the Alpha Company tankers realized that trying to get there was like trying to get to an airport in any big city. They reached a "spaghetti junction" – Sergeant First Class Ronald Gaines, 1st Platoon's platoon sergeant thought it looked like interchange to get to the Louisville airport; it reminded Captain Ryan Kuo of Chicago. It was hard to tell which part of the ramp to take. There were signs, but smoke from all the gunfire obscured some of them. One of the tanks got separated from the platoon and had to make a U-turn in order to rejoin the others. As tankers, they hadn't expected to go into a city, let alone Baghdad, but they adapted to their environment and kept moving.[24]

As the battle raged, civilians drove their private cars and trucks on the same highways where U.S. and Iraqi forces fought each other. State-controlled media had kept the public from knowing how quickly American troops had arrived at the gates of Baghdad. Baghdad Bob had used his television appearances to convince Baghdad citizens that the Iraqi Army had fought off the American advance, and so they had gone about their business on the morning of April 5 as though it were a normal day. The presence of both civilians and plain-clothes irregulars made it difficult for U.S. soldiers to differentiate between hostile forces and noncombatants. When an Iraqi vehicle crashed into a Bradley that was blocking a ramp, the car behind it stopped, and U.S. soldiers discovered an Iraqi general who was the Baghdad logistics chief inside. They captured the general and took him along on the rest of the thunder run.[25] He kept insisting that the Americans were not supposed to be there. Out of respect for a fellow general, Blount let the Iraqi use his satellite phone to call his wife and tell her he wouldn't be home that evening.

U.S. tanks and Bradleys rolling into Baghdad drew curious residents out onto the streets. In some areas, residents cheered the arrival of the Americans. Others waved white flags. But as the task force moved along Highway 8, Iraqi regulars and Fedayeen fired on the column from all directions. About 20 minutes into the run, a shot from a recoilless rifle hit an external generator on a tank in the rear, causing burning fuel to start a fire in the engine compartment. Schwartz made the decision to stop the advance and give the crew a chance to try to put the fire out. An abandoned American tank was fodder for Baghdad Bob's propaganda machine that continued to churn out stories of Iraqi victory over U.S. forces despite the presence of American armor in the capital city. But the hit occurred near a major overpass, and stopping there gave Iraqi soldiers a prime target on the U.S. column.

They tried, in any case. While the task force was stopped, Iraqi regulars and paramilitary troops descended on the column in pickup trucks and buses, but seemingly without leadership or order. For 20 minutes, the tank crew worked to put out the fire while also shooting back at the Iraqi attackers, numbering more than 200 by that point. But fuel kept leaking onto the engine, causing the fire to flare up again. A frustrated Perkins ordered the crew to abandon the tank, and crew members scrambled to retrieve maps, electronics, and other sensitive materials from the tank before evacuating. Then they rushed through enemy fire to get to an M113 for transport. As the soldiers boarded the vehicle, one member of the tank crew got shot in the eye, another in the shoulder.[26] Once the crew had left the disabled tank, Iraqis climbed upon it, smiling and waving as they stood on it.

Task Force 1-64 Armor pressed on, receiving persistent enemy fire as the tanks, Bradleys, and armored personnel carriers moved through the city. About an hour into the trek, Alpha Company rode into intense small-arms and rocket-propelled grenade fire. As Alpha Company fought through enemy fire, Hilms and the other tank commanders leaned out of the hatches of their tanks and fired their M4 rifles on the opposite side of where their gunners were firing. That was what Staff Sergeant Stevon Booker was doing when he got hit.

Sergeant Booker ordered his platoon to return fire, and he fired his tank's mounted machine gun. As the fighting raged, Booker's machine gun malfunctioned, but it did not stop the tank commander from doing all he could to repel the enemy. Booker grabbed his M4 carbine, climbed onto his tank's turret, and shot unprotected at Iraqi soldiers. If Booker was scared, he didn't let his crew members see it. He shouted orders encouraging them to keep fighting, always leading and modeling leadership for the soldiers under his command even during the most harrowing moments. Booker's decision to risk leaving the relative safety of his tank and engage Iraqi soldiers protected his platoon's flank and pushed back what would have been another wave of enemy troops before it could crash down on the American convoy. From his position on the turret, Booker spotted an Iraqi personnel carrier. His accurate aim and fire destroyed the vehicle before enemy troops could dismount.[27] It took an Iraqi bullet to stop Booker from fighting, and only because the hit was a deadly one. In Hilms' estimation, Booker was the best staff sergeant tank commander in Alpha Company.

Booker was 34 years old and from a town outside of Pittsburgh. He had joined the Army after high school. He cared mostly about being a good soldier, but in his spare time, he liked to play basketball, throw darts, and play video games. In letters home, he'd asked his family to send turkey jerky and cupcakes, touches of home that might have seemed incongruous in a desert war zone but were deeply comforting to Booker and his comrades who shared in the contents of the care packages. He typed his last e-mail to his aunt Linda Hargraves about a month before the 3rd ID crossed the border from Kuwait into Iraq, describing the "miles and miles of sand" that surrounded him and telling her that he was ready to get the job done so he could come home.[28] Booker's sheer bravery and commitment to his platoon left his family waiting for a homecoming that would never arrive.

When they learned Booker was down, commanders stopped the column while Booker's crew tried to save his life. Task Force 1-64 eventually subdued the enemy forces and moved on. Iraqi troops made one last effort to get in the task force's way, creating a barrier of 3-foot-high concrete slabs across the highway. But an M1 Abrams tank rammed into it and crushed the barricade enough for the rest of the task force to push through it. The next stop was Saddam International Airport. The soldiers of Task Force 1-64 had completed their mission.

There was little jubilation as the tanks and armored vehicles entered the airport grounds. The exhausted soldiers evacuated their wounded and dead. Some broke down in tears, while others stood in shock as they surveyed their battered vehicles. Tanks were littered with hundreds of brass cartridges. A Bradley and a tank were still on fire. Medics evacuated Booker and put him on a flight, but he had already died. Several other wounded soldiers were evacuated. Crews took about four hours to rest and repair their equipment, and then it was back to work. Schwartz looked on at his soldiers and marveled at their ability to survive as their vehicles took multiple rocket-propelled grenade hits and bullets rained down on them. The lieutenant colonel had lost a tank commander and a tank, and five wounded soldiers fought for their lives.[29] The 3rd ID had managed to keep its casualty rates low, but each individual death was a cruel blow and a reminder that even with the strongest equipment and most advanced technology, soldiers still died in battle, and survivors pressed on with the sadness and guilt that came with losing comrades. The next day, April 6, Task Force 1-64 held a memorial for Booker, and shortly after his comrades had paid their respects, they learned that they would be going back into central Baghdad.[30]

Typical to the character of the 3rd ID, Blount, Perkins, and other leaders used the April 5 mission to learn about the battlefield and the enemy. The highway overpasses were critical points where Iraqi troops could shoot down on the American column. Especially vulnerable were the M113 vehicles like the one Perkins had ridden in during the initial thunder run because of the vehicle's open hatch. An Iraqi soldier could lob a grenade into it from an overpass and cause catastrophic damage. Maintaining speed of movement was key. If units stopped, that allowed the enemy to swarm like ants on stationary U.S. vehicles. Perkins and his soldiers also learned that every vehicle would likely get hit. Traveling in a line along a major highway allowed the Iraqis to concentrate their firepower on one avenue of approach. But 2nd Brigade also learned that a successful armored thrust into Baghdad was possible.[31]

Despite the casualties, Blount was satisfied with the thunder run. Blount and his commanders learned that Iraqi forces had not given up and continued to defend the city, but Iraqi defenses were haphazard and desperate. The enemy also seemed to have been taken off-guard by the thunder run. Baghdad Bob had not given up, though. He made his usual television appearance and insisted that Iraqi troops had defeated the Americans and pushed back the invasion. Blount was tired of Baghdad Bob's antics. One more thunder run would prove beyond a shadow of a doubt that not only were the Americans in Baghdad to stay, but they were able to move freely throughout the capital city.

Blount proposed his plan to Wallace. The V Corps commander wasn't worried about whether Blount's troops could make it to downtown Baghdad – he knew they could. Wallace's major concern was the safety of the lines of communication. 2nd Brigade support troops would have to get ammunition and fuel to the combat units downtown, and they would have to have a route for evacuating casualties via armored vehicle. Air evacuations would not be possible in Baghdad's urban environment. Wallace suggested that 2nd Brigade go back in, but only as far as the second intersection and then turn left and head to the airport like in the first thunder run.[32] Yet Blount and Perkins had formulated a plan to use 3-15 Infantry to secure three major intersections on 2nd Brigade's route to downtown Baghdad. Someone in the planning conversation nicknamed the intersections objectives Moe, Larry, and Curly. If the soldiers of 3-15 Infantry secured the intersections, the lines of communication and supply would remain open.

Blount gave the order for the second thunder run to roll on April 7. This time, all of Task Force Heavy Metal, the brigade's combat units, would go, while the wheeled vehicle support teams, Task Force Rock and Roll, stayed back at 2nd Brigade's headquarters at Objective Saints, ready to be called forward as needed. Brigade leaders had learned from the first thunder run that the units needed to move quickly while fighting to control Moe, Larry, and Curly on the way to central Baghdad. Division leaders identified the regime district near Hussein's palaces and parade grounds as the specific location within downtown Baghdad that 2nd Brigade needed to get to. If a vehicle broke down or was otherwise immobilized, Perkins ordered his soldiers and commanders to leave it immediately and move on. The worst that could happen was that images of it made it into Iraqi propaganda, but Perkins reasoned that if his troops couldn't use it, the enemy couldn't either, so leaving it posed a much smaller threat than wasting time trying to repair it.[33]

Another issue was fuel, as it had been for the entire division since commanders had planning conversations in Kuwait. Perkins knew that a tank burned 57 gallons of fuel an hour and held 550 gallons, so he calculated that the combat battalions had about eight to ten hours of burn time before their tanks were empty. If the battalions got stranded in Baghdad, Command Sergeant Major Robert Gallagher would never let Perkins forget that he'd created another Mogadishu, and Perkins had that in mind when he conceptualized his plan for going downtown. With approximately eight hours of fuel, Perkins would have to decide around hour four whether the brigade was going to make it or needed to turn around and go back to Objective Saints. If the brigade pushed beyond four hours and then realized it couldn't keep going, it wouldn't have enough fuel to make it back to headquarters, and that's when Baghdad could become another Mogadishu. It was another example of how logistics drove the tactical decision-making process.[34]

Crews spent April 6 working on their vehicles, making repairs and ensuring that everything was ready to operate at full capacity. While soldiers got their equipment in order, Blount and Perkins mapped out their plans for the second thunder run. Both men understood that the success of the first thunder run depended on flexible decision-making by the commander on the ground. Blount and Perkins established objectives in open areas within the city, wide boulevards and parks where Iraqi troops had fewer places to hide. There was a psychological angle to the plan. By exploiting the open areas of the city, the Americans would prove that Hussein could not successfully defend Baghdad despite what the national news media reported.[35]

Numbers-wise, the population of Baghdad dwarfed 2nd Brigade. It was a city of more than six million people, and Army estimates indicated that as many as 50,000 Republican Guards would defend the city, while at most the brigade was bringing 1,000 troops. Perkins' military education had taught him that defenders already had three-to-one odds from owning and knowing the terrain and being already stationary there. To neutralize the advantage, typical strategy called for the attacking side to establish six-to-one odds by bringing six times the expected number of attackers. Yet 2nd Brigade was going to attack with a miniscule fraction of the potential defending population. Even if a quarter or less of the city's residents took up arms against the Americans, by the typical rules, the Iraqis would still have the advantage.

Since the plan was to attack all the way into downtown, Perkins wanted his brigade to stay overnight downtown if conditions were right. Blount agreed with Perkins but knew it would be a hard sell at V Corps. A 3rd ID unit in Baghdad overnight would signal decisively to Hussein and his lackeys that their time was up; the U.S. Army was there to stay. If 2nd Brigade made it downtown, seized symbolic sites, and could secure an open resupply line, Perkins would keep his soldiers in the heart of the city rather than going to the airport or trying to turn around and go back to Objective Saints where the brigade began its attack. Once the combat battalions were established in the regime district and an open road for transporting ammunition, medics, fuel, and other supplies was secured, then the brigade could fight to expand its perimeter farther and farther out.[36]

Along the road to Baghdad, 3rd ID forces had learned that the conventional Iraqi Army and Republican Guards were well trained in conventional warfighting tactics and fairly well armed with Russian T-72 tanks and BMD fighting vehicles. During one battle on the way, 2nd Brigade had captured an Iraqi company commander and confiscated his battle plans. Perkins found them to be solid, complex tactical plans, not just a call for irregulars running around with AK-47s. But the captive company commander had no idea what the other company commanders were doing because Hussein discouraged crosstalk among military commanders, fearing it would foment a coup. It was then that Perkins realized that the Iraqis' Achilles' heel was lack of communication. Individual commanders may have had good defense plans, but they had no contact or situational awareness of any other commander. They could execute the plan they had, but because they didn't know what the other commanders had planned or experienced, they didn't have the ability to learn or innovate. Armed with this knowledge, Perkins realized that while he couldn't outnumber the Iraqis or know more than they did about Baghdad, he could out-innovate them.[37]

To do so, Perkins had to come up with a fight the Iraqis hadn't planned for. They didn't expect the Americans to enter the city and engage in urban warfare, so the Iraqis set up concentric rings of air defense on the tops of buildings facing out of the city. But if the U.S. troops fought into the city, the outward-facing air defenses would be useless. If 2nd Brigade attacked like a needle piercing a membrane and drove straight into the regime district in the city center, the Iraqis would have to rethink their battle plans, which would be challenging if not unfeasible given the lack of communication among Iraqi commanders. Once in, Perkins' brigade would secure the major traffic circles to prevent Iraqi troops from piling on the Americans, and they would secure three key bridges to keep Republican Guards out. Although decisions were made within 24 hours about the second thunder run, they were grounded in learning, planning, and training that had occurred over many months. The thunder runs were not spontaneous.[38]

A major debate in planning the second thunder run was over whether infantry or tanks should go first. Those who favored leading with infantry argued that securing the overpasses and ramps was critical for the successful passage of the rest of the brigade. To control the terrain, the Americans needed to have infantry troops on the ground. Perkins vetoed that plan. All the training his brigade had conducted from the National Training Center to Fort Stewart to Kuwait pointed to speed as a major factor in a successful invasion. The brigade had to maintain speed. If infantry troops went first and got bogged down fighting in foxholes, 2nd Brigade would lose its momentum, giving the enemy time to bring in reinforcements. Perkins wanted his tanks to blast through Highway 8, dealing with the fire from overpasses and ramps as it came. The tanks and Bradleys were heavily armored and could handle it. What he really needed the infantry to do was secure the overpasses and ramps for the support units traveling behind the armored forces. Getting the tanks into downtown Baghdad as quickly as possible would provide a shock effect and allow the brigade to lock down the traffic circles so that Iraqi troops couldn't swarm the Americans in the regime district. Leading with tanks and sending infantry last would also minimize incidents of fratricide, Perkins reasoned to his incredulous commanders when he explained that he wanted armor to go first. If infantry troops took the overpasses first, and then the tanks went through, the chaos that ensued when forces converged could result in Americans accidentally shooting Americans.[39]

Given the lethal accuracy of U.S. weapons systems, if an American soldier fired a tank gun, it was likely to hit its target. In a situation where U.S. forces converged, Perkins told his soldiers to not fire the first shot so as to avoid a friendly fire incident. It was counterintuitive to how soldiers had trained, and he faced resistance when he gave that kind of order. But he knew the Iraqis' Russian equipment wasn't nearly as precise, and fratricide was a more dangerous threat when forces converged. The Iraqis were less likely to deliver a lethal hit. All of this justified Perkins' decision to send the infantry in last.[40]

On the night of April 6, as 2nd Brigade prepared for a second thunder run, Perkins had told Wesley that there were two things required for the brigade to make it to the regime district and stay there overnight. The first was command and control. A brigade of 5,000 soldiers was planning to take on a city of six million people, and all of the brigade's weapons systems had to be choreographed correctly in order to succeed. The second requirement was that Perkins needed to be able to call in the resupply packages when fuel and ammunition got low. Both of those requirements relied on coordination via the TOC, and Perkins was determined. When Wesley told him that reconnaissance from an unmanned aerial vehicle had shown that Iraqis were placing obstacles along the highway to block 2nd Brigade's passage, Perkins replied that there would be no change in his plans. The brigade would move forward. Understood, Wesley said, but was there any condition that would cause Perkins to change course and come back? Perkins pointed at Wesley and declared, "We're going to Baghdad tomorrow, no matter what."[41]

Task Force 1-64 and Task Force 4-64 Armor led 2nd Brigade with the mission to secure Objective Diane, the regime district of downtown Baghdad that included Hussein's parade grounds, palaces, and historical sites. As part of the mission, Perkins ordered 1-64 Armor to seize the Tomb of the Unknowns, while 4-64 Armor would capture two of Hussein's palaces on the Tigris River. Brigade elements started at Objective Saints and advanced toward downtown Baghdad and objectives Moe, Larry, and Curly, the three main interchanges on Highway 8. Perkins assigned Task Force 3-15 Infantry to secure the interchanges in order to ensure that Iraqi troops would not be able to disrupt the supply lines to the units in the city center. The column order would have 1-64 Armor and 4-64 Armor taking the lead and 3-15 Infantry taking the trail.

To prepare for the second thunder run, Lieutenant Colonel Stephen Twitty, commander of 3-15 Infantry, created three company teams, nicknamed Team Gator, Team Rage, and Team Zan, out of portions of his battalion to attack at the objectives and secure the interchanges. Zan was named for Captain Harry "Zan" Hornbuckle, the team's commander. Hornbuckle was a graduate of the Infantry School's Captains' Career Course and an instructor in the Ranger Training Brigade, and Twitty trusted him completely.[42] On the night of April 6, Twitty had called his commanders into a bombed-out building to discuss the battle plan. Soldiers pulled a tarp over the top of the walls to create a makeshift roof and hung ponchos over the broken windows to conceal the meeting from enemy sight. The teams would attack at six o'clock in the morning, Twitty ordered, as he used yellow post-it notes to create a visual image of the plan for maneuver. Moving south to north, the teams would attack Curly first, then Larry, and then Moe near downtown Baghdad. Twitty could tell that his commanders were nervous. They all knew how intense the fighting had been during the first thunder run.[43] But securing the three objectives was crucial for keeping a supply route open for the brigade units attacking into the heart of Baghdad.

Perkins ordered Task Force 1-64 and 4-64 Armor to go speeding into downtown Baghdad. If they took fire from overpasses or other positions, they were to push through and keep going. If a tank became disabled, Perkins instructed crews to abandon it. Artillery support conducted preparatory fire on each objective to eliminate resistance before the task forces arrived.[44] But as Blount and Perkins had predicted, the Iraqis were still defending the capital city.

As 1-64 Armor was preparing for the second thunder run, an infantry team discovered a minefield on the attack route. Upon closer inspection, they found that the minefield contained 440 antitank mines spanning a section of the road. Schwartz discussed options for clearing the minefield with Captain David Hibner, commander of Alpha Company, 11th Engineer Battalion, and Hibner suggested that his company manually remove the mines from the road. They had six hours to clear the road before the task force would go, and Schwartz wanted assurance that Hibner could get it done and, more importantly, get it done safely. Hibner said his company would get it done, and by 5:15 on the morning of April 7, the road was clear. The soldiers had worked through the night, lassoing the first few mines and then later removing them by hand, picking them up one by one and moving them to the side of the road. The mines all had an anti-handling device on them, but the Iraqis had not engaged the device, so the engineers could pick them up without setting them off. It was a risky, dangerous, and intense mission, but Hibner's engineers pulled it off. Had their mission failed, the second thunder run would have been halted indefinitely.[45]

At about 5:30am on April 7, the 2nd Brigade advanced along the cleared highway and headed to downtown Baghdad.[46] Almost immediately, Iraqis began firing on the task forces. Two rocket-propelled grenades hit a tank, temporarily disabling it. The drive north on Highway 8 was a firefight involving tank and Bradley crews engaging with Iraqi military vehicles while enemy troops on foot approached the convoy and fired at it. Iraqi troops attacked the brigade's supply convoy and descended on the Americans from all sides, using highway overpasses, civilian houses, schools, mosques, and offices as bases and fighting positions. Iraqis fired on and hit U.S. ammunition trucks while other units tried to block supply lines, cutting them off from forward units. Iraqis fought from ditches just a few feet from U.S. tanks. Enemy fighters lay on the ground as if dead, only to leap up holding live grenades when U.S. soldiers approached. There was the memory of Mogadishu again – Americans caught in urban conflict where militias isolated U.S. units on city streets, attacked from behind, and brought in waves of reinforcements to counter the American operations.[47] Schwartz called the urban battle "a head-on-a-swivel fight" because soldiers needed to have 360-degree awareness at all times. It seemed that a more frantic nationalism motivated the soldiers and Fedayeen defending Baghdad than Schwartz and his soldiers had witnessed at An Najaf and Karbala.[48]

Task Force 1-64 Armor got pummeled as it advanced. Each one of its vehicles was hit with direct fire during the fight for Baghdad, and one of the Bradleys took five RPG hits during the first thunder run. The gas-guzzling M1 Abrams tank had a menacing appearance, but it also had some limitations. They could only elevate their guns 20 degrees, which gave them aim about three stories up a building. Enemy troops who were smart positioned themselves much higher in buildings to avoid tank fire. It was why the integration of combat power between tanks, Bradleys, and engineers in urban warfare was so important to Schwartz. Despite is limitations, an M1 Abrams tank projected a clear and compelling image of U.S. power. Schwartz reflected on this, concluding, "When you take an M1 into an urban area, you are showing that you care to send the very best."[49]

Alpha Company was the lead company again, and Hilms saw the Iraqis fighting just as they had the previous two days. But because of what Task Force 1-64 Armor had learned in the first thunder run, the highway overpasses that the Iraqis had used to their advantage were now planned targets for 2nd Brigade's field artillery battalion. Knowing that the Iraqis had used the overpasses as fighting positions allowed U.S. commanders to order their artillery to attack the positions before the ground forces passed them. As Alpha Company led 2nd Brigade into the heart of Baghdad where Hussein's presidential palace was, enemy resistance was lighter than Hilms had expected. Iraqi soldiers hadn't expected the Americans to make it that far into the city.[50]

Iraqi troops had placed overturned 18-wheelers on the highway as makeshift barriers, leaving U.S. commanders surprised that the Iraqis had not taken the time to set up better defenses. Perhaps Hussein's propaganda asserting that the U.S. Army was nowhere near Baghdad had left Iraqi forces lazy. Or perhaps Iraqi war planners had given up on conventional warfare and shifted entirely to unconventional urban fighting. As the lead elements of the 2nd Brigade battled into the city, the reason mattered little to the soldiers facing intense enemy fire. Iraqi troops attacked the American tanks and Bradleys from buildings, alleys, and bunkers they had built along the road. At one point, soldiers recognized a tank as the disabled Abrams that their comrades had abandoned during the first thunder run. They saw some Iraqis trying to recover the tank, and Task Force 1-64 Armor troops picked the Iraqis off as the American column rumbled by.[51] Perkins radioed Brigadier General Lloyd Austin and told him he believed his soldiers could make it into the city center, and Austin relayed the message to Blount.

Despite enemy efforts to resist the advance of the task forces, 1-64 Armor and 4-64 Armor made it to Objective Diane within about two hours from their 6am departure on April 7. Soon those at the front of Task Force 1-64 Armor could see the Swords of Qadisiyyah, an archway made of concrete, steel, and bronze marking the entrance into Baghdad's city center. The structure was opened in 1989 to commemorate the Iran–Iraq War and slain Iraqi soldiers. The name Qadisiyyah refers to an older history. In the 7th-century battle of Qadisiyyah, Arab soldiers drove the Persian Sassanid army out of Mesopotamia in what might accurately be called the first Iran–Iraq war. Passing under the Swords of Qadisiyyah was a triumphant moment for Task Force 1-64 Armor and the rest of the 2nd Brigade. U.S. troops and tanks had claimed the ground on which some of the most powerful symbols of Hussein-era Iraqi nationalism stood, and no amount of small-arms fire or militia attacks had halted the advance of the 2nd Brigade. The journey into the heart of Baghdad had not been easy, and the soldiers knew that their lives were on the line the entire way. They had lost some of their own, and several others lay wounded in hospitals. But the soldiers set up blocking positions at the site where Hussein had once looked on military parades in his menacing glory, vindicating the mission that had begun weeks ago.

Wallace had been watching the thunder run on his Blue Force Tracker. When Perkins' vehicle got to the intersection leading into the city, instead of turning left to head to the airport, he turned right towards downtown Baghdad and the regime district. Though it might have appeared that Perkins was disobeying orders, Wallace didn't see it that way. He saw a young leader taking advantage of the situation presented to him on the battlefield. It was an example of the trust and autonomy that leaders from the corps level on down had cultivated in the training leading up to the invasion. Wallace called Blount, and Blount expressed his confidence in Perkins to make the right call based on the conditions surrounding him. They agreed to let Perkins go on. Not long after his conversation with Blount, Wallace glanced up at a television monitor and saw CNN broadcasting live footage of Perkins walking around the presidential palace. He heard conversation on the radio between Perkins and Blount: Perkins was asking what kind of calling card his soldiers should leave for Hussein.[52]

When Schwartz's soldiers made it to Hussein's viewing booth on the parade grounds around ten o'clock in the morning, Perkins ordered them to shoot the statue of Hussein on a horse in front of the viewing booth. Fox News reporter Greg Kelly went live with the shot. Kelly's monitor showed a side-by-side of the Fox broadcast and Baghdad Bob's broadcast on Iraqi television. Baghdad Bob was in the middle of a press conference where he insisted that U.S. forces were not in the city when a Charlie Company tank shot the statue. Baghdad Bob's newscast disappeared from the screen, and he did not appear on Iraqi television again. Shooting the statue achieved Blount and other commanders' goal of silencing the Iraqi minister of information.[53]

After seizing Objective Diane, Perkins communicated to Blount that he wanted to stay downtown and hoped to get V Corps' approval to do so. Perkins was with the two tank battalions that had made it to the regime district, and he needed to know how the fighting at the interchanges Moe, Larry, and Curly was going. Only if U.S. troops secured all three would the supply units be able to reunite with the tank battalions. Failure to secure them could result in a Mogadishu-type situation where U.S. tanks were stranded in a city center without fuel or ammunition. He reached Twitty, commander of 3-15 Infantry, and Twitty told him he needed time and reinforcements. The fighting at Moe, Larry, and Curly was some of the most intense of the war and also some of the most crucial. Without a secure supply line to move fuel, ammunition, food, and other supplies to the forward units, Task Force 1-64 and Task Force 4-64 Armor would not be able to stay in downtown Baghdad. Soldiers would have to turn around and return to Saints, go west to the airport, or, worse, get caught stranded in the city center without supply units. As elements of 3-15 Infantry traveled north on Highway 8, Iraqi forces fought as expected from ramps, overpasses, and fighting positions dug in along the road. Task force engineers driving armored combat earthmovers knocked lamp posts down and pushed piles of rubble onto the ramps and roads leading to the objectives to block enemy forces.

The soldiers of 3-15 Infantry weren't just fighting Iraqis. At Objective Curly, an infantry platoon and a mortar platoon encountered enemy fighters who were mainly jihadists from Syria. The foreign troops were disorganized, but they came at the task force in large numbers with a determination to fight to the death. The Syrians and Fedayeen kept coming, seeming to either not know or not care that they were charging to their deaths. Bullets rained down from the rifles of Iraqi regulars positioned in buildings around the interchange, and Iraqi soldiers hurled grenades out from trenches and from behind cement pillars. Explosions set off chain reactions as fires sparked ammo and fuel tanks. The soldiers of Team Zan, the unit Twitty had sent to Curly, found themselves under fire from all directions. It seemed as though an inferno had engulfed the entire interchange, and black smoke rose up in thick, suffocating clouds.[54]

Captain Josh Wright, commander of Alpha Company at Moe, was dangerously low on ammunition, and the battle was still raging. Perkins decided to send two reserve Bradley platoons along with the refuel and rearm package to reinforce Moe. Refuel and rearm consisted of aluminum HEMTTs, the fuelers carrying 2,500 gallons of JP-8 fuel, and the munitions trucks hauling 8 tons of ammunition. In both cases, the drivers of the HEMTTs were basically driving tons of explosives into the eye of the storm.[55] Most of the HEMTTs never made it to Moe. Iraqis ambushed them at Curly, killing a platoon sergeant and resulting in other U.S. casualties. Rounds cooked off and missiles fired from the ammunition trucks, and a concrete bridge burned after one of the fuelers exploded.

Around the same time, Perkins got a call on his satellite phone from Colonel Eric Wesley, brigade executive officer, who was at the brigade's tactical operations center (TOC). The call was brief, and Wesley was matter-of-fact. "Sir, we had an incident at the TOC," he told Perkins over the phone. "I'm going to be off the net for a while. You're going to have to take the fight. You're going to have to do all the logistics, all the close-air support, all the utility. You've got to do it all from there, from your vehicle, and I'll let you know when we come back up." That was it. It wouldn't be until much later that Perkins found out what had happened at the TOC.[56]

After sending the reserves to Moe, Perkins did the tanks' fuel calculations in his head. They had made it to Baghdad, but they wouldn't be able to refuel until the infantry units had secured the interchanges so the resupply could enter Baghdad. He called the tank battalion commanders, Colonel Eric Schwartz and Lieutenant Colonel Philip DeCamp, and they met in front of DeCamp's tank to discuss options. Never afraid to buck convention, Perkins suggested that the tanks shut their engines off. Since the tanks burned fuel by time, not miles, every hour they weren't running was an extra hour that the battalions could stay downtown.

It came as no surprise to Perkins when Schwartz and DeCamp responded with disbelief. Shutting off the engines meant losing thermal sights and other defenses. But there was still a lot of daylight left, Perkins replied, and in any case, shutting off the engines was the best option for conserving fuel while waiting for the infantry troops to secure the interchanges. Perkins knew his plan to shut off the tanks in the middle of a city of six million people would likely not get a passing grade at the Command and General Staff College, but it wasn't the first time he had taken a tactical risk in hopes of a logistical success. The battalion commanders ordered their tanks to shut down, and then all they could do was wait, hoping that the infantry soldiers would secure the lines of communication before nightfall.[57] In some ways, the 3rd ID had made the fight to Baghdad look easy. But as Perkins sat with his tank shut off in the middle of Baghdad knowing that the resupply package he had sent to the beleaguered troops at Objective Moe was destroyed and something disturbing had occurred at the TOC, the battle for Baghdad felt anything but easy. It seemed eerily like Mogadishu times ten.

What Perkins didn't know was that the decisions of individual soldiers in the moment salvaged enough of the resupply package at Curly so that the surviving HEMTTs could continue on to Moe. Soldiers darted around burning trucks, jumped into ones that weren't on fire, and drove them away from the inferno. The soldiers saved enough HEMTTs to supply Alpha Company at Moe through the night and to eventually deliver fuel to the tanks in downtown Baghdad. When Perkins saw one of the ammunition trucks that made it downtown, he was astonished to see its front window completely shot out. He asked the driver how he had managed to get the truck through the fighting at Moe, Larry, and Curly without a front windshield, and the soldier replied that he knew the ammunition needed to get to Baghdad, so anytime the enemy shot at him, he ducked below the dashboard while pointing his M16 out the open windshield and firing back. Whatever it took to complete the mission. Luckily the road was fairly straight. As Perkins mused on the bravery of that soldier and others like him, he realized that what had happened in that moment reflected the months of training that included placing trust in commanders and soldiers to do their jobs even when the job wasn't clearly delineated.[58]

Trust also extended up through the levels of command. Blount and Wallace let Perkins take risks because they knew he had thought through the pros and cons. They knew this in part because they could hear him. When Perkins called Brigadier General Lloyd Austin, assistant commander of the division, to discuss his plan for staying in downtown Baghdad, he used V Corps' tactical satellite communications. There was one channel for the entire corps, so all corps leaders, including Blount and Wallace, could hear conversations broadcast over it. They heard Austin ask all the necessary questions: "Do you have a plan for fuel? Do you have a plan for casualties? Do you have a plan for ammunition?" Wallace heard those conversations, which confirmed that Austin and Perkins were addressing the same issues he would have. It gave Wallace the confidence to trust the commander on the ground, and he did.[59]

Communication among the levels of command also helped V Corps know how to help the units that were fighting. When combat intensified at Objective Curly, V Corps sent one of 1st Brigade's infantry battalions to reinforce the battalions already there. V Corps used its single Predator unmanned aerial vehicle, or drone, new technology at the time, to send situational information to Perkins and other 3rd ID commanders. Trust and communication up and down the chain of command were as critical to the mission as the ability to operate weapons. Perkins trusted his battalion commanders and did not second guess them, and Blount and Wallace placed the same kind of trust in him.[60]

Wallace had not been fully in on the plan for the second thunder run. He had believed that 2nd Brigade intended to advance as far north as Objective Moe and then turn around and go back to Saints, and it wasn't until he watched the brigade's progress on his Blue Force Tracker System that Wallace realized the soldiers were going into the city. Astonished, the Corps commander called Blount for an explanation, and Blount asked Wallace for his trust. Perkins and his soldiers had made it into Baghdad quickly and handled the enemy resistance they faced. Blount described Perkins' plan to spend the night in central Baghdad and park an Abrams tank in front of Hussein's palaces as an extraordinary symbol of the regime's collapse. Wallace considered what Blount had told him, and then he granted 2nd Brigade his blessing. Blount's gamble had resulted in initial success, and Wallace trusted Blount and Perkins in their knowledge of conditions on the ground and what 2nd Brigade could handle.

On arrival at Objective Diane, the soldiers of Task Force 1-64 Armor set up blocking positions around government buildings while fighting Iraqi regulars and Fedayeen militiamen. The

2nd Brigade's task forces now controlled key intersections and roads near the Al Rasheed Hotel, Tomb of the Unknowns, and the city's parade zone and VIP stand. Hussein no longer had a place up there to review his soldiers passing in parade. Iraqis continued their attacks, uncoordinated as they were, and remained persistent in the face of U.S. armor. Yet the Iraqis could not stop units of Task Force 4-64 Armor from reaching Hussein's palace on the Tigris and clearing it before eight o'clock in the morning, just two hours after the second thunder run began. Another company seized ground at the intersection near the July 14th Monument and bridge across the Tigris. The monument paid tribute to the revolution that occurred on July 14, 1958, against King Faisal II's monarchy. Military leaders of the bloody coup ordered the executions of Iraqi royals and proclaimed the founding of the Republic of Iraq. Now, nearly 45 years later, 3rd ID forces held the monument as part of a larger mission to depose a dictator and return Iraq to republican government. Jabari Williams looked at his fellow soldiers of Charlie Company to his right and to his left and realized that the real shock and awe was what an armor company could do in combat.[61]

As Task Force 1-64 Armor and Task Force 4-64 Armor set up positions in the regime district, the fighting at Moe, Larry, and Curly continued. Until U.S. troops secured the three objectives, the Iraqis still could disrupt the communication and supply lines to 2nd Brigade's combat units downtown. Were it not for U.S. armor, the fighting at Objective Curly might have seemed disturbingly similar to what had occurred in Mogadishu in 1993. It was a resemblance that would not have been lost on Command Sergeant Major Robert Gallagher, who was with Team Zan at Objective Curly. Gallagher's nickname was "Blackhawk Bob," earned as a tribute to his intense fighting in Mogadishu in 1993. Perkins had hired him when 2nd Brigade was still at Fort Stewart. Gallagher was a Ranger by training, and Perkins knew the good-natured rivalry between mechanized units and special ops soldiers, who were known to tease their mechanized brethren for having it easy riding around in armored vehicles while Rangers jumped out of airplanes.[62] Perkins liked Gallagher immediately and appreciated his tell-it-like-it-is attitude when he interviewed Gallagher for the job. The problem was that Gallagher had all of zero experience with mechanized infantry. In keeping with his no-nonsense attitude, he was upfront with Perkins about that. When Perkins asked Gallagher if he had ever worked with tanks or Bradleys, Gallagher told him the truth: No. But he also told Perkins that if he got the job, he'd make himself an expert in armor, and Gallagher was true to his word. Perkins hired him, and Gallagher set up camp in the motor pool, learning everything he could from the master gunners and other soldiers. After a couple of months, Perkins was confident that Gallagher knew more about a Bradley than most of the others in the battalion.[63]

When Gallagher was in Mogadishu, he was a staff sergeant in the quick reaction force that went to rescue the Rangers in one of the helicopters that was shot down. Gallagher's experiences in Mogadishu made him acutely concerned about U.S. soldiers getting stuck in urban warfare in Baghdad. During training in Kuwait, Gallagher went to Perkins' tent every day, sometimes at sunrise, to enforce his concerns. "Make sure it does not turn into a Mogadishu," Gallagher repeated to Perkins like a mantra.[64] What he meant was, don't let the brigade's lines of communication get cut. Ensure a solid connection to ammunition and fuel supply units. Retain the ability to extract casualties. Don't get stranded in the middle of the city. Perkins likened a tank running out of fuel in an urban battle to a helicopter crash. It was just a tank on the ground that could do nothing. Getting cut off from the supply lines was the worst fear of a commander in an urban environment. All of this informed the strategy that drove the plan for the invasion of Baghdad. Perkins saw it almost as an "anti-Mogadishu plan."[65] Perkins wasn't worried about tank-on-tank fighting with the Iraqis. He knew that if U.S. forces had the freedom to move within Baghdad with lines of communication intact, they were unstoppable. But in the nightmare version, the enemy cuts off American combat forces from their supply units and isolates them, and that's when the kidnappings and casualties occur. If it happened in Baghdad, it wouldn't involve a few helicopters like in Mogadishu; it would affect about a thousand vehicles.[66]

As Team Zan of 3-15 Infantry fought at Curly, Gallagher was wounded again, but he continued fighting Iraqis and Syrians, firing his M4 carbine as a medic bandaged his hurt leg. When Twitty radioed the team to check in, Gallagher called for help. Weighing their options, Twitty and Perkins agreed to send Bravo Company of Task Force 3-15 Infantry, which was still in a blocking position just north of Objective Saints, to aid Team Zan. Blount ordered 3-7 Cavalry into position at Saints where Bravo Company had been.

Bravo Company made it from Saints to Curly in about 15 minutes and found Team Zan desperately holding on in the fight. Medics had taken up arms to defend their patients, while some wounded soldiers continued fighting. The soldiers of Bravo Company jumped into battle without hesitation, and soon the forces began running low on supplies. Twitty ordered the supply convoy forward, but enemy troops ambushed it. Two soldiers, Staff Sergeant Robert A. Stever, 36, from Pendleton, Oregon, and Sergeant First Class John W. Marshall, 50, from Los Angeles, were killed while fighting from their turrets near Objective Curly.[67] When the convoy finally arrived at Curly, Captain Aaron Polsgrove circled the supply trucks like a wagon train to protect soldiers as they ran back and forth with ammunition. But the vehicles' close proximity to each other also proved dangerous. An enemy rocket-propelled grenade hit an ammunition truck, and the explosion caught four more trucks on fire. Iraqi and Syrian forces kept on relentlessly as Team Zan scrambled to keep up. To help the struggling unit, Blount sent Task Force 2-7 Infantry from the 1st Brigade to Objective Curly. The reinforcements turned the tide in favor of the Americans and ensured that the resupply route remained open and secure. In the aftermath of the battle, a soldier passing by Curly marveled at how the brass casings covering the ground made the highway look like it was paved with gold.[68]

Meanwhile, north of Curly at Objective Larry, Twitty was positioned with the soldiers of Team Rage. While Iraqi infantry regulars fought at Larry, the major threat Team Rage faced was from irregulars and suicide bombers. Waves of fighters in pickup trucks, city buses, and taxis approached American positions from the south. Some of the enemy vehicles were filled with explosives, like the car that came speeding at an intersection with Highway 8. The driver seemed singularly focused on ramming his vehicle into a tank or Bradley. But then the driver swerved the car onto a ramp and barreled towards Task Force 3-15 Infantry's tactical operations center. It was too late for the driver when he realized that combat engineers had built a berm near the command post. The car struck the berm at such a high speed that the driver flew through the windshield, and his body landed by the post. A Bradley fired on the crashed car, and the explosion was so great that it shook the armored vehicles on a nearby overpass. The soldier who had operated the armored combat earthmover that built the berm likely saved the lives of Twitty and his crew.[69]

Objective Moe, the intersection of Highway 8 and the Qadisiyah Highway, was the closest interchange to downtown Baghdad, and it was there that U.S. forces met primarily with Iraqi regulars and Republican Guard troops. The Iraqis had armor, including T-72 tanks and BMP-1 armored personnel carriers, as well as antiaircraft weapons. Iraqi troops had taken positions in buildings near the highway interchange at Moe and had built a bunker concealed by palm trees. Others had dug a trench along the road. Yet even with regulars in position to fight, irregulars still swarmed the area in pickup trucks carrying explosives. As was the case at Curly and Larry, the troops of Task Force 3-15 Infantry at Objective Moe found themselves fighting a 360-degree battle with Iraqi troops all around and outnumbering them. Every vehicle took at least one RPG hit.[70]

Engineers and sappers of Task Force 3-15 Infantry's Team Gator took to the task of creating obstacles to keep Iraqi troops away from the supply line while also keeping Highway 8 open. Soldiers in armored combat earthmovers dug ditches and mowed down palm trees to create barriers. They pushed destroyed vehicles and dirt into piles to make berms. Sappers connected explosive charges to lamp posts and large signs, set them, and then rushed to take cover behind personnel carriers to await the blasts. Meanwhile, gunners inside Bradleys and tanks fired on enemy troops that tried to approach while the sappers and engineers worked. At one point, a bus loaded with explosives sped toward Objective Moe, but the obstacles slowed it down enough to give the Americans time to fire at and destroy it. It took nearly 18 hours of fighting and 11 wounded U.S. soldiers, but Team Gator finally secured Objective Moe on April 7. When the battle was over, Sergeant Jason Millett drove his earthmover to the fields near the interchange where the bodies of dead Iraqi soldiers lay scattered. He used his vehicle to dig trenches and bury the enemy dead.[71]

While the teams of Task Force 3-15 Infantry battled through objectives Moe, Larry, and Curly, the Iraqis set their sights on 2nd Brigade's tactical operations center at Objective Saints. Brigade personnel had set up the TOC in an abandoned Iraqi military compound encircled by 10-foot-high walls. The TOC was a mobile headquarters housed inside tents extending from M577 armored carriers to create a workspace equipped with computers and high-tech communications systems. Lieutenant Colonel Eric Wesley, 2nd Brigade's executive officer, considered the tactical operations center as the place where brigade staff choreographed the symphony of all the capabilities of a brigade and integrated the capabilities in such a way that the total was greater than the sum of the parts. He liked the symphony analogy because when the notes are right and the musicians are in rhythm, it creates an amazing effect, and the same was true of combat. The TOC synchronized the weapons systems, the electronic warfare, the direct fire and indirect fire, the air assault – everything else that was part of a combat maneuver.

The TOC was the conductor of 2nd Brigade's combat symphony, and on the morning of April 7, Wesley and his staff were wired with anticipation as the brigade began its trek. Things were going as planned, and the battalions that went downtown were set. Task Force 3-15 Infantry was fighting, but the soldiers were doing what they needed to do. Sometime between 9:30 and ten o'clock, Wesley decided he wanted to check in with Perkins and have a one-on-one conversation, so he left the TOC and went to his Humvee, which was parked in a cantonment area outside the command post. He had a satellite phone in the Humvee, and it would allow him to talk privately with Perkins rather than broadcast a conversation on the radio. It wasn't that Wesley needed to say anything confidential, but he wanted to congratulate Perkins, just the two of them. He took off his helmet and placed it on the hood of his Humvee, then he picked up the satellite phone and placed the call. "Sir, congratulations," Wesley said when he got Perkins on the phone. "Everything is going as we expected. It's everything that we dreamed of." Perkins' tank was on the steps of one of Hussein's palaces. It was a moment the two men had discussed over meals and imagined for months while in Kuwait, and they had achieved it.[72]

Just as Wesley said that, he heard what sounded like a low-flying jet screaming overhead. Wesley assumed it was an American aircraft. Then, in a split second, the TOC exploded with an energy so intense that it shocked him to his bones and knocked him to the ground. When he got his bearings, he realized that the call hadn't dropped, so he quickly told Perkins, "Hey, Sir, we just got hit. I've got to call you back." Wesley got to his feet and surveyed the area. Of the 35 vehicles parked near the TOC, more than half were destroyed. Fires were burning all around him. Soldiers inside the tents were thrown from their feet and plunged into darkness when the power snapped off. Explosions continued outside as vehicles caught fire from the blast.[73] He knew there were wounded soldiers, and probably some dead, and he needed to get people away from the fires. Wesley took a deep breath. He knew he had to take control of the situation, and he had learned that composure was more effective than urgency in times of stress. He would have to convey orders clearly to the soldiers, and those who were able would need to get the TOC running again because the brigade's combat units in downtown Baghdad needed the command post's support.[74]

As surviving soldiers regained some sense of their surroundings and staggered to their feet, they began to take in what had happened. When Captain William Glaser, the brigade's headquarters and headquarters company commander, crawled out from under a collapsed tent, he saw that his soldiers who hadn't sustained serious injuries were slowly kicking into crisis mode and surveying the damage to determine a plan of action. The top priority were the casualties, and soldiers went about looking for friends and checking on the wounded. For First Sergeant Roderic Dalton, the 2nd Brigade's Headquarters and Headquarters Company first sergeant, everything seemed to move in slow motion at first. Sergeant First Class Stanley Griffin, who had been knocked to the ground by the blast, wandered through the wreckage of the operations center looking for a friend. The heat of the burning fires mixed with the desert temperature to create stiflingly hot air that wrapped around Griffin as he walked the perimeter looking for his fellow soldier. The periodic explosions of burning vehicles punctured the air. Griffin ventured closer to the vehicles and found his friend's remains on the front seat of his truck. He had been in it when the rocket hit.[75]

Wesley had no Kevlar, he couldn't find his helmet, and he had no radio, but he started walking around, and to any leader he found, he repeated three orders: They needed to evacuate wounded, reestablish security, and rebuild the TOC. He kept it simple and repeated the orders over and over. The sergeants and lieutenants were as stunned as he was, and Wesley knew directness and clarity were critical for getting people moving. Headquarters commander Glaser found a Humvee that was still intact and drove around the compound with Wesley so that Wesley had access to a radio. Wesley soon found that enough of his communications personnel were okay and were able to establish FM and satellite communications fairly quickly. Many of the communications vehicles, though, had been engulfed in the inferno that raged in the parking lot.[76]

As catastrophic as the attack on the TOC was, staff personnel had it back up and running about an hour after the missile had hit. Wesley knew it was because Perkins had established an environment of empowerment and trust in 2nd Brigade, just as Blount had at the division level and Wallace had at the corps level. Wesley trusted that the brigade's soldiers and commanders knew their skills and how to apply them to the situation at hand. Soldiers searched the wreckage for computers and other electronics that seemed to still work and brought them to Wesley, who had selected a spot to erect a new tactical operations center. Communications personnel knew how to reconnect the wires and get the TOC back online. First sergeants had the training to identify which of their soldiers should take security duty. That allowed Wesley to give broad guidance and not micromanage the people he was leading.

When all were accounted for, Wesley learned that 23 soldiers were wounded and five killed. The five who died had perished instantly in the blast. Wesley learned how close he had been to death. A missile had slammed into his Humvee right where he had set his helmet on the hood. Someone who had been about 10 feet away from him had been killed instantly. If Wesley hadn't wandered away while talking on the satellite phone to Perkins, the missile would have killed him, too. As he stood looking at the crater, 10 feet deep and 20 feet in diameter where the TOC once stood, Wesley felt a profound sense of the randomness of combat. The hood on which he had set his helmet only minutes before the attack was obliterated. Yet somehow Wesley had been spared.[77]

The fires in the compound burned for hours after the attack. Later that evening, Wesley and his driver surveyed the blackened and burned wreckage. As they walked around, they found an engine block that had flown about 30 feet. Connected to the engine block was a portion of the bumper that said "headquarters five." Wesley knew immediately that was his Humvee's bumper. It was all that was left of the vehicle he had been near to when the missile hit. Then Wesley's driver knelt down and pulled something out from underneath the engine. "Sir, what's this?" the driver asked. Wesley was astonished to see that what his driver had pulled out of the rubble was a small pocket Bible that his father-in-law had given him. Wesley had put the Bible in a Tupperware container that he then placed inside a wooden box in his Humvee. It was the only belonging of his in the Humvee that survived the attack. Every page still existed. Some were frayed, and a piece of shrapnel had pierced through the first part of the book, but not a word was missing. For a long time after that day, Wesley often pondered the chance nature of life and death.[78]

As a result of the attack on the TOC, 2nd Brigade ramped up security around the compound. Wesley finally reached Perkins in the afternoon, several hours after the attack, and explained what had happened. Loss of command and control had been one of the criteria that would have caused Perkins to consider turning around and pulling out of Baghdad, but the TOC staff had managed to rebuild and reconnect so quickly that the attack did not result in a loss of command and control long enough to affect the thunder run. But the other factor that Perkins had considered vital for staying downtown was resupply, and just as soldiers were piecing the TOC back together, Wesley got word that Iraqi troops at Objective Curly had ambushed and destroyed the resupply package that had been traveling north to meet the combat units in Baghdad. As that information came in, Wesley heard over the radio Perkins telling Blount that he felt safe staying in the regime district. "Sir, I think we can stay here," Wesley heard Perkins say. "I think we can hold downtown Baghdad and stay the night." In that moment, Wesley made a quick decision. He and Perkins had worked together for two years and knew each other well, and Wesley understood the colonel's vision and intent for the thunder run. Therefore, he chose to not mention what he had learned about the ambushed resupply package and figure out an alternate way to get supplies to downtown Baghdad.[79]

Even though everyone at the TOC was still on edge from the attack and worried about security, Wesley decided to send the company that had been reinforcing security at the TOC to secure instead the area where the enemy had ambushed the resupply package. Without a safe line of passage for fuel and ammunition to get to Perkins and the combat units, the mission would fail. So Wesley called the company commander, Captain Ronny Johnson, and told him to move out to Objective Curly. As Wesley watched Johnson's Bradleys drive away, he wrestled mentally with the anxious knowledge that the TOC was on its own. He had just sent his primary security element to Objective Curly. But he had little time to dwell on the unknowns. He needed to find another resupply package to send to Baghdad, and so he called Brigadier General Austin, and Austin found a package and also sent a security company from a battalion in another brigade to reinforce the TOC. Captain Ronny Johnson's company, which Wesley had dispatched to Curly, would escort the resupply package to Baghdad.[80]

The fighting was so intense at Objective Moe that Captain Josh Wright had called and said that he was running out of ammo. Wesley radioed Johnson and told him to stop with the resupply package at Moe before continuing on to Baghdad. But Johnson somehow missed the stop and drove right past Moe. Wright watched him go and then called him, knowing he had missed the stop. Wesley was aware of the mishap, but instead of getting involved to try to straighten things out, he held back and allowed Wright and Johnson to do so. Wright knew Johnson's position, so he told Johnson to stay there, and he sent a few units over to get fuel and ammunition. The culture of trust that Perkins had created in 2nd Brigade had empowered junior officers to make decisions based on their understanding of conditions on the ground. It was that same culture that compelled a non-commissioned officer who was in the vicinity of the resupply package that had gotten ambushed to rush to a 2,500-gallon fuel tanker and drive it away from the vehicles burning near it so that it didn't explode. No one had instructed the NCO to do that. He saw a problem, and he fixed it, knowing that his superiors would support his decision-making in the moment.[81]

Back in the city, Perkins awaited the arrival of supply units, hoping they would show up soon so that he could confirm that the brigade would stay downtown. The tanks were beginning to run low on fuel, but the soldiers of Task Force 3-15 Infantry were still fighting at Moe, Larry, and Curly to secure the supply route. About an hour more of burning fuel without resupply and Perkins would be faced with having to turn the tanks around and send them back to Objective Saints lest they run out of fuel and wind up stranded in central Baghdad. Perkins ordered the task forces to shut their tank engines off and only turn them on periodically to charge the batteries. Even then, fuel levels were getting dangerously low.

Around dusk on April 7, supply vehicles finally began entering Baghdad. Fighting in the city had continued throughout the day as soldiers of 1-64 and 4-64 Armor had worked to secure the downtown area. Alpha Company made it to its objective, a traffic circle next to the Al Rasheed Hotel in the Baghdad Convention Center. Hilms' soldiers secured the objective, and Hilms ordered his soldiers to shut off half of the company's vehicles in order to conserve fuel. Perkins had warned his commanders to monitor fuel consumption in case they needed to move their units back out of the city. Iraqis opened fire on Alpha Company as soon as the soldiers reached Diane, but Hilms stuck to his plan to rotate engines on and off to save gas. On the night of April 7, Hilms got word that 2nd Brigade was staying downtown. Under the cover of darkness, fuel resupply convoys began running up Highway 8 and through objectives Moe, Larry, and Curly, which Task Force 3-15 Infantry had secured. When fuel arrived, Hilms knew that the fighting was about to end.[82]

Hilms reflected on the past two days, and he found himself marveling at the courage of his soldiers. They were 18, 19 years old, a year out of high school, not old enough to buy a beer back home. He knew the "chicken vests" that passed for body armor couldn't stop a bullet, but that didn't stop his soldiers from giving their all to the fight. To Hilms, the young soldiers were fearless, leaning out of tank turrets, firing at the enemy. They had to have been terrified at times, but they never showed it. "Why are these soldiers so brave?" he wondered, awestruck. They volunteered, they signed up, they weren't forced into the Army by the draft. They all had their reasons why, but they chose the Army. Then Hilms thought about leadership. He had learned throughout his career that if soldiers believed that their leaders had their best interests in mind, the soldiers would not let their leaders down. Hilms hoped he had been that kind of leader for the soldiers of Alpha Company.[83]

As the sky grew dark with night, the tank battalions reunited with their ammunition and fuel trucks. Perkins knew his brigade had enough fuel and ammo to spend the night in the city center.[84] Blount called Wallace and once again said that he trusted Perkins' assessment of the situation, and if Perkins was confident that the brigade could safely stay downtown, then Blount believed it and wanted to approve him to stay. In turn, Wallace trusted Blount's decision.[85] The presence of 2nd Brigade would shut down Baghdad Bob's propaganda machine and signal the end of the Hussein and Ba'ath regime. There would be no more denying the 3rd ID's destruction of Iraqi forces. Iraqi citizens would see for themselves U.S. soldiers and military vehicles moving freely throughout the capital city. Blount and V Corps commanders hoped Iraqis would welcome the 3rd ID as liberators for defeating their nation's oppressive and murderous leader.

Blount wanted to see what Perkins and 2nd Brigade had accomplished, so he, his G-3 Lieutenant Colonel Pete Bayer, and his aide-de-camp Berdy drove the thunder run's route into downtown Baghdad. It was moving to see American soldiers on the parade grounds where Iraqi troops had once marched. Blount passed under the Swords of Qadisiyyah, and it was then that he realized the 3rd ID had done it. He went up into Hussein's box overlooking the parade grounds and looked out onto the grounds, feeling a great sense of accomplishment and pride in his soldiers, who had made it to Baghdad from Kuwait in 21 days, much more quickly and with far fewer casualties than the war planners had predicted.

While the 3rd ID took control of Baghdad from the west, the Marines handled the eastern approach to Baghdad along the Tigris River. On April 8, the Marines finally cut off the access roads in the northeast. The 3rd ID was fanned out through the western half of the city. Intense fighting continued as the Americans pushed through the city. Mid-morning on April 8, Iraqi resistance was so severe that U.S. military officials called in air strikes. Around the same time, two M1A1 Abrams tanks from Alpha Company, 4-64 Armor, approached the Al-Jumhuriya bridge spanning the Tigris River and, believing he was under attack, one of the tankers fired a round on the Palestine Hotel, home base for many of the international journalists who had come to Baghdad to cover the war. RPG, sniper, and mortar fire had pummeled the tanks all morning, and attacks were coming from the east side of the Tigris where the Palestine Hotel was located, but it was the wrong target, and the round killed two journalists – Reuters cameraman Taras Protsyuk, a Ukrainian based in Poland, and Jose Couso, a cameraman for the Spanish television network Telecinco – and wounded three others. Blount and CENTCOM authorities told reporters that the tanks had received RPG and small-arms fire from the hotel, but the incident raised concerns throughout the media about the safety of journalists in Baghdad. In terms of the broader character of the war, the event showed the danger of urban warfare, where civilian buildings doubled as fighting positions.

The next day, April 9, the Marines entered Baghdad from the east and linked up with the 2nd Brigade downtown. Meanwhile, Hussein, Baghdad Bob, and other Ba'ath Party leaders had vanished. The Americans had isolated Baghdad, and members of the Ba'athist regime and its associates fled the city. Soldiers from elite Republican Guard to Fedayeen irregulars shed their uniforms, abandoned their weapons, and slipped away into the crowds of civilians who came out onto the streets to see the Americans. Others quietly made their way back to their homes. Yet the war was not over for the 3rd ID. The division's new mission was to stabilize the capital city.

Now What?

On April 9, 2003, jubilant Iraqi citizens pulled down the statue of Saddam Hussein that had lorded over central Baghdad's Firdos Square. The event signaled not just an end to Hussein's rule but the beginning of a U.S. military mission aimed at improving the lives of Baghdad citizens and restoring civil society after more than two decades of dictatorship. Commanders and soldiers of the 3rd Infantry Division had decisively taken Baghdad, a task for which the armor division was well trained. On May 1, 2003, President Bush declared "mission accomplished." That's what 3rd ID soldiers had thought, too, on April 9. They had decisively achieved their mission to seize Baghdad from Saddam Hussein. Yet the 3rd ID's job still was not done even when Bush made his declaration. After the fall of Hussein, U.S. troops embarked on a more challenging and less clear mission. They had to determine citizens' needs, identify existing security threats, and figure out how they could win Iraqi hearts and minds while remaining vigilant to danger. Lieutenant Colonel Jeff Ingram of 2nd Battalion, 70th Armor Regiment, succinctly noted the difference between the two missions when he declared that peace was "much harder than combat."[1]

The 3rd ID was fully prepared for the mission to seize Baghdad, and it showed in the swiftness and relative ease of the operation. But the division had not prepared for a humanitarian mission, yet the soldiers of the 3rd ID played the roles of humanitarian aid workers for months after they had completed their original mission. It was as though with the flip of a switch, U.S. policymakers expected soldiers to shift from being battle-ready to running civic action projects. They were now expected to help the people they had been trained to kill. Soldiers were combat engineers one day, civil engineers the next, without any training on how to switch roles. With no local police in place because of Hussein's directive to not report to work, Blount sent his soldiers out on neighborhood patrols. Tanks were unwieldy in those situations, so he brought in Humvees and sent soldiers out on foot. From the time they crossed the berm until they captured Baghdad, 3rd ID soldiers wore their chemical suits 24/7 in case Hussein really did have WMDs and used them on Americans. Once in the city, division commanders believed WMDs to be less of a threat, and soldiers could remove that layer of protection.

Operation *Iraqi Freedom* was launched on March 20, 2003, with two objectives. The immediate mission was to topple the Hussein regime and destroy its ability to use weapons of mass destruction or give them to terrorists. A longer-term objective was to help build "a new Iraq that is prosperous and free." The objective of major combat operations was clear. What to do next was the question that Bush administration officials had not answered definitively before U.S. forces crossed into Iraq. An obvious answer still had not emerged after the 3rd ID had captured the capital. State Department and Pentagon officials in Washington wanted the military to handle the initial phase of nation building after achieving its combat objectives because they worried about security. The question of whether nation building was the job of the military would not be answered in Iraq.

Prewar planning had determined that America's postwar mission in Iraq would include military and civilian elements, each of which would have particular responsibilities. CFLCC set up its headquarters in Baghdad at Camp Victory, which U.S. forces had established at Hussein's Al Faw Palace. To manage humanitarian efforts, the Defense Department created the Office of Reconstruction and Humanitarian Assistance (ORHA) and appointed retired Lieutenant General Jay Garner to run it. Garner was respected in policy circles for his experience working with Iraqi Kurds after Operation *Desert Storm*, but the task before him when he took the helm at ORHA was daunting. Garner had to build ORHA from the ground up and coordinate with CENTCOM, CFLCC, other agencies, and the yet-to-be-determined military unit that would lead the postwar operations in Baghdad.[2]

Soldiers of the 3rd Infantry Division and other units who had trained for conventional combat later found themselves working as humanitarians. They were the face of U.S. intervention and had close contact with Iraqis. Soldiers talked with community leaders, responded to requests for municipal service support, repaired and rebuilt infrastructure, and worked to convince skeptical Iraqis that they were there to help. Having the additional mission of aiding postwar recovery kept the 3rd ID in Iraq longer than the soldiers and their families had expected.

Even though the 3rd ID had not trained for postwar stability and humanitarian operations, some of the division's NCOs and officers had served in Bosnia and Kosovo, and so they had experience in post-combat missions. They understood how peacekeeping missions worked, which allowed Blount to assign units to jobs with confidence that the jobs would get done. Observing soldiers in the transition from war to peacekeeping, Major Darryl Rupp, an intelligence officer with the 3rd ID's Division Artillery, was impressed but not surprised at the ease with which the division's soldiers handled a meeting with a local leader and interacted with citizens they met while out on patrol. Their immediate supervisors had conveyed to them how to act in those situations, based on their experiences in the Balkans, and the soldiers did it. Yet because there was no streamlined process for sharing wisdom across units, there was no guarantee that all soldiers were trained for postwar missions.[3]

Known by the acronym MOOTW, "military operations other than war" had been part of U.S. interventions abroad since the 19th century. Counterinsurgency was central to America's Vietnam

War strategy, and while some troops fought, others built schools and administered vaccines to civilians in hopes of winning the hearts and minds of the Vietnamese. At the same time, the U.S. Embassy and USAID tried to identify political leaders, implement agricultural development programs, and thwart Viet Cong infiltration into student groups. When U.S. troops withdrew from Vietnam, the Saigon government collapsed under the weight of North Vietnam's military advance and both rural and urban communist insurgencies. South Vietnam wasn't stable when the U.S. military left, but Americans had lost the political will to keep fighting a war that no longer seemed to have anything to do with U.S. interests.

The late 20th and early 21st centuries saw conflicts that foreshadowed the difficulties the U.S. would face in Iraq. An effort that began as a humanitarian one in Somalia morphed into a skirmish that resulted in American casualties. In 1992, the Army's 10th Mountain Division deployed to the Horn of Africa to provide security for UN organizations distributing food. By 1993, U.S. Army units were still in Somalia, now training police, resettling refugees, and working to develop political institutions. Somali militias threatened the Army's efforts, and later that year, the U.S. suffered casualties in an operation to capture militia leader Mohammed Farah Aideed.[4]

In 1994, U.S. troops including Marines, Army Special Forces, and the 10th Mountain Division deployed to Haiti and spent 18 months conducting stability operations including security patrols, democratic political development, infrastructure repair, and healthcare assistance. The UN took control of the operations in 1995, and U.S. forces withdrew having fulfilled the mission as they understood it. Not long after American troops left Haiti, other U.S. forces deployed to Bosnia under the auspices of NATO to conduct peacekeeping missions between Serbians and Muslims. Stability operations included improving the infrastructure at a local market where both adversaries conducted business and assisting in the 1996 national elections process. As one U.S. Army report on Bosnia noted, "American soldiers were involved in hundreds of projects that relied far more on negotiating abilities and coordinating nongovernment organizations (NGOs) than on combat skills."[5]

The end of the 20th century saw U.S. forces again deployed under the flag of NATO, this time to Kosovo. Serbia's president, Slobodan Milosevic, had called for the expulsion of ethnic Albanian Kosovars from the province. After an initial mission of providing security, U.S. troops shifted their focus to new objectives, including providing logistical support for local elections, training a new police force, and repairing infrastructure.[6] A factor that united U.S. operations in Haiti, Bosnia, and Kosovo was the lack of local resistance to U.S. efforts. Insurgents did not rise up and challenge the U.S. Army's presence, so counterinsurgency and counterterrorism did not factor into the Army's analysis of those engagements.[7]

The first Gulf War had shown that U.S. forces could execute a mission quickly, with few U.S. casualties, and get out. In November 2001, Donald Rumsfeld authorized CENTCOM commander General Tommy Franks to develop a plan for removing Saddam Hussein from power. Later, in January 2003, President Bush made the Defense Department responsible for operations after U.S. forces seized Baghdad. Nation building was not at the forefront of postwar planning, reflecting Bush's dislike of lengthy military occupations and Rumsfeld's desire to deploy a smaller, lighter, more agile force to conflict zones. General Eric Shinseki's interest in Blount's successful use of light armor in Saudi Arabian National Guard training was part of a broader mindset shift in the Army in favor of less cumbersome deployments.[8]

What Blount observed in the days after U.S. forces toppled the Hussein regime was that most Iraqis treated the Americans as liberators. Saddam Hussein had many of his citizens living in misery, if not fear, and having him gone gave Iraqis the courage to imagine a future where they had control over their neighborhoods, towns, cities, and lives. If the U.S. handed control to Iraqi leaders soon, the Americans could leave as liberators. The problem was that U.S. advisors had not identified a George Washington or

Abraham Lincoln type to inspire Iraqi citizens to follow him or her into a politically stable future. There was Chalabi and the INC, but they were exiles. They didn't have on-the-ground experience to know the mindset of Iraq's populace. Hussein had murdered the oppositionists who had stayed.

Ever since Edward Lansdale had groomed Ramon Magsaysay for the Philippine presidency in 1954, U.S. policymakers had believed they could identify "their man" in whatever country they hoped to nation build. Lansdale found Magsaysay because he had spent years in the Philippines after World War II getting to know the people and learning about the culture. It was what Blount had done in Saudi Arabia, but while Shinseki had been impressed by what Blount had accomplished training the Saudi National Guard, Army authorities missed an opportunity to use Blount as a diplomat. He had earned the trust of Abdullah; why not an Iraqi leader? Maybe there was someone who had stayed and managed to avoid Hussein's purges. The only way to know was to put an American on the ground who had the confidence and the curiosity to gain entry into local circles. Blount had shown off his diplomatic skills well in Saudi Arabia.

But a 3rd ID-led occupation had not been part of the war planning. Part of the problem was that strategists had expected it to take three to six months for the Army and Marine Corps to reach Baghdad and then another three months to take the city. Therefore, war planners had not established a clear blueprint or goals for "Phase IV," the postwar effort, by the time the 3rd ID arrived in Baghdad just three weeks after crossing the Kuwaiti border into Iraq. They expected to have more time and were caught off-guard by the 3rd ID's swift charge through southern Iraq to the capital city. For the soldiers, "We're here. Now what?" was a mantra that foreshadowed the disconnect between the Army's near flawless combat operations and the disorder that ensued after the fall of Hussein.[9]

While the policymakers argued over what to do next, Blount set out to get Baghdad up and running again, with functional utilities and civil services to meet residents' ordinary needs. He established his headquarters and division command center at Baghdad International Airport. Soldiers set up cots in a former VIP terminal, and Blount created an office there. He parked his vehicle in a hangar and sometimes slept there, too. The airport provided a sense of security, especially in the first week of the division's arrival, when the fighting in the city remained heavy. Convincing occupied locals that the foreign troops in-country were there to help, not hurt, was a difficult task. To earn the trust of Baghdad citizens, U.S. troops spent time getting to know community leaders to ascertain local needs. Security was the 3rd ID's main responsibility in Baghdad, but Blount believed someone also had to make sure citizens' basic needs, such as access to electricity and water, were met. Ignoring those needs would defeat the security efforts by breeding resentment against U.S. forces that could develop into an insurgency. If citizens didn't have to wonder whether the lights would come on or the cooking stove would work, they might be less likely to risk the upheaval of insurgency. From there, they would be more likely to support rational political institutions instead of insurgencies.[10]

One of the first things Blount did in the city was turn the power back on. The Army had issued clear orders not to bomb power plants or sewer and water infrastructure so that Baghdad could operate normally after Hussein was gone. Hussein had wanted the opposite, hoping that if the Americans arrived to a city in shambles, their postwar occupation would be all the more difficult. If the war destroyed any infrastructure, Hussein could blame U.S. aggression. Power grids in every neighborhood were down, and in order to start them back up, teams of 3rd ID soldiers needed to find the person with the keys to get in. Without a name or any other way of identifying that person, division personnel began going door-to-door in the neighborhood surrounding the power plant, asking if any residents worked there. About five houses in, they got a name. Then they got an address. The man's name was Mohammed, and he had the keys to the power plant, but he was afraid to defy Hussein's directive. The soldiers convinced him that they would keep him safe, and Mohammed took them at their word. He unlocked the plant, and 3rd ID engineers restored power to the neighborhood. Then they repeated the same effort until the entire city regained power. To measure progress, Blount went up in a helicopter every other night to see how many lights were on. It was a long, slow process.

When Blount woke up each morning, he went out and looked to see if the smokestacks at the power plants were operating. If they were, it meant the stations were generating power. Then he traveled throughout Baghdad, checking in on brigade and battalion headquarters. Downtown, near the palace grounds, was the green zone, the area that served as the seat of the provisional government the Americans established after taking Baghdad. Blount assigned units to various sections of Baghdad and put soldiers to work restoring electricity and power, reopening banks and gas stations, and providing neighborhood security. Engineering and construction units went to work repairing buildings and infrastructure, some of which had been damaged in battle, while others suffered from neglect. Colonel John Peabody, the division's engineer, also took a helicopter up over Baghdad some nights to see where the lights were on and what areas of the city were still dark.[11] Maintaining the goodwill of Iraqis who were glad to see Hussein gone and who viewed the Americans as liberators was what Blount hoped would be the 3rd ID's final act before the division returned home.

Iraqis came to the brigade and division headquarters offering to share information and sometimes brought food as well. Talking over meals built mutual trust between the Americans and Baghdad citizens, which sometimes led to the sharing of surprising intelligence. An Iraqi man who had gotten to know Wesley and other 2nd Brigade personnel brought his brother to brigade headquarters one day and stated that the brother had some information he wanted to share. Wesley took the brother aside and could tell he was nervous, sweating and clutching his worry beads. On April 6, the day before 2nd Brigade attacked into Baghdad, representatives from the Russian Embassy had come to Iraqi Army headquarters and shared satellite photos of where the main U.S. command posts were. Wesley couldn't believe what he was hearing. He had been there, 10 feet away from death, and the Iraqi was telling him that the Russians had given the enemy the locations of American command posts. He couldn't confirm that the Iraqis had identified 2nd Brigade's TOC from the images, but it seemed to be more than a coincidence that the Russians brought satellite photos to the chief of the Iraqi Army, and then the TOC was hit the very next day. A CIA agent was present during Wesley's conversation with the Iraqi man, and the agent promised that the information would make its way through the proper investigative channels, but Wesley wondered if anything would really be done with it.[12]

Soldiers of Grimsley's 1st Brigade went out from the airport into adjacent neighborhoods and established patrols block by block. The areas near the airport were wealthier and heavily Sunni. Small gunfights still erupted on the streets, and U.S. soldiers found pockets of resistance. As Grimsley explored Baghdad, he found it to be a beautiful city that reminded him of Paris with its broad boulevards and squares. He learned that Baghdad was once a place of poets and artists and cafes, of learning and culture. It was a diverse city that boasted a populace comprised of multiple ethnicities and faiths. Yet, in Grimsley's mind, Saddam Hussein and his Ba'ath Party cronies had destroyed Baghdad's culture and bastardized religion according to Hussein's whims. It was as though Hussein saw himself as King Nebuchadnezzar III.[13]

At the company level, Captain Charles O'Brien, commander of Alpha Company, 3-69 Armor, 1st Brigade, understood that his soldiers were to restore basic municipal functions and develop Iraqi confidence in the Americans as being there to help transfer authority over to a new and democratic government. Companies were assigned to zones within Baghdad and focused their operations in their zone. O'Brien had served in Haiti and Kosovo, and he shared wisdom from those deployments with his young platoon leaders. They had trained for combat but not for stability and support operations. O'Brien gave the platoon leaders some tasks that they could do on repeat as a way to develop understanding of the issues at hand and skills in addressing them. The platoons needed to ensure that routes into their zone remained open and violence did not erupt. While some soldiers established security, others went with O'Brien to contact local political and religious leaders and school and hospital officials. O'Brien's zone was modern and somewhat wealthy, home to doctors and business owners. The neighborhood included about seven houses of worship, and the religious affiliations of the citizens were fairly evenly split between Sunni and Shia, with some Christians mixed in. A group of retired Iraqi military officers had set up a neighborhood watch program, and the officers met with O'Brien and agreed to work with his soldiers on security patrols. O'Brien recognized that from an Iraqi citizen's perspective, the outlook was, "How do I put my life back together?" Building trust and relationships with locals was a vital component of stability and security operations.[14]

There was an uneasy feeling that settled over O'Brien's company in the early days following the 3rd ID's entry into Baghdad. O'Brien thought about Mogadishu and even the Soviet Army in Afghanistan, both examples of wars in which soldiers weren't sure if they were occupiers or liberators. Some Iraqis liked the American soldiers, but others surely hated them. All expected something from them. O'Brien felt vulnerable in the city. The tanks were shut off to conserve fuel, and in any case, the urban environment wasn't ideal terrain for tanks should large-scale hostilities break out again. Soldiers who were used to being inside their tanks now found themselves on foot or riding in soft top Humvees. The feeling of being exposed took some getting used to.[15]

The Bush administration's insistence that the U.S. was a liberator, not an occupier, frustrated SJA Lyle Cayce. "Liberator" and "occupier" were terms loaded with cultural connotations, but from a practical standpoint, international law granted certain powers and authority to an occupier. If an invader could prove that it had sufficient resources to control and protect the local population, the invading nation could proceed to establish stability and control to avoid a power vacuum according to international law. Cayce argued that the U.S. was an occupying power of parts of Iraq and thus could legally exercise the occupying power authority. As an occupier, the U.S. had the legal power to order citizens back to work, impose curfews, and control the government and population. Efforts by an occupier to bring stability could prevent looting, murder, and other problems that occur in a power vacuum.[16]

As the division's public affairs officer, Colonel Mike Birmingham's days in Baghdad followed the 24-hour news cycle. He'd get up at 4 or 5am and be up until midnight or 1am the next day, usually going to bed with *BBC World* on to catch the early morning coverage out of London. Birmingham tried to stay engaged with the reporters on the ground and keep up with what they were covering. He had become close with Major Erik Berdy, Blount's aide-de-camp, and Berdy made sure Birmingham knew when Blount was going out into the city to observe division units or meet with local leaders so that Birmingham could arrange interviews. Blount was willing to engage with the media and accepted on-camera interviews whenever possible. The Army wanted to convey that its mission had been to liberate Iraq, not occupy it, and the 3rd ID's work in Baghdad was aimed at turning control over to Iraqis as soon as troops stabilized the capital.[17]

After 3rd ID units had taken Baghdad, 1-64 Armor had set up camp in one of the Ba'ath Party headquarters. The soldiers didn't have much other than what was on their vehicles. Soon some residents approached the troops and offered to cook for them. It took locals a while to engage the Americans, and usually children broke the ice. Then people began venturing over to the compound with fresh baked bread or a plate of food. Charlie Company Staff Sergeant Jabari Williams enjoyed interacting with Baghdad citizens because it made him feel like he had done something good. The people seemed happy to be rid of Hussein, to have their country and their culture back.[18]

When major combat operations ended, support units such as 24th Corps Support Group shifted their mission away from combat support. Woods no longer had to focus on fuel resupply because fuel needs dropped once tanks and Bradleys were not continuously moving. Since the 3rd ID had established a headquarters at Baghdad International Airport, Woods sent a forward logistics unit to set up a base there. Units other than those of the 3rd ID were also positioned at the airport, and Woods' brigade supported them as well. Water replaced fuel as the primary need, not just for drinking but for shower and laundry facilities now that U.S. forces were settling into Baghdad. Woods assigned units to purify water out of palace lakes and the Euphrates River.[19]

Jabari Williams hadn't expected Baghdad to be such a modern city. He was a country boy from Charleston, South Carolina, and as Charlie Company rolled down a wide thoroughfare into the capital, he was in awe of the skyscrapers and giant statues. Despite the bullet holes and the war debris, Baghdad was vibrant, and Williams saw that parts of it, at least, were prosperous. Gazing at the city's lush parks and shiny glass buildings, Williams imagined the potential of Baghdad and its residents to prosper. Hussein's picture was everywhere, painted on billboards and buildings; photographs of the dictator hung inside offices and storefronts. It wasn't because the people loved him, but because they feared him.[20]

When Blount first arrived in Baghdad, he went to check out Hussein's downtown palace. It was clear that Hussein and his family had rushed to go into hiding. Dogs were chained up outside lying next to empty food and water bowls. Parrots and other exotic pets wandered the grounds. The drawers of file cabinets hung open, their contents gone. Gas masks lay on the beds in all of the bedrooms in case of a chemical attack. Six empty Rolex boxes were strewn on the floor of a bedroom. On one of the beds was an empty aluminum box that Blount later would learn had held millions of dollars. Hussein's fedora sat on a bedside table.

In the days following the U.S. capture of Baghdad, Blount and his team settled into the city only to discover empty government offices in Baghdad City Hall and no city officials or civil service employees anywhere. Hussein had ordered all civil employees to stay home so that no one would be there to collaborate with the Americans when they arrived. More than five million people lived in the city, but the only city office still functioning was the oil ministry. This upended the unfinished Phase IV planning, which had assumed that most police officers, firefighters, and other civil servants would have remained at their jobs through the fight for Baghdad. When it turned out that the city's municipal sector was a ghost town, Blount had to improvise. Without a figurehead in place to oversee the city's transition from war to peace, Blount became the mayor of Baghdad. Every operation that City Hall handled now fell under Blount's control. He had to manage public services, employee payroll, and city security, and there were other issues that he discovered as he assumed his latest leadership role.

As soon as the fight for Baghdad ended, the looting began. Thieves stole money, medical supplies, pharmaceuticals, computers and other electronic equipment, and expensive items from the homes of wealth Ba'ath Party officials who had fled. Looters set fire to government buildings and industrial warehouses, frenzied acts of destruction. Blount assigned security units to banks, gas stations, and hospitals throughout the city. Gunfights sometimes broke out in the midst of the looting, but U.S. troops in Baghdad had orders to hold back in response. Blount's soldiers were not to intervene, and certainly not to shoot, unless the looters were stealing weapons, which were still stockpiled throughout the city. Sporadic violence against U.S. military patrols still occurred in Baghdad, and armed offensives to stop looting would only increase the violence. This meant that some Baghdad citizens who were not participating in the plunder became frustrated at what seemed to them to be a lack of action by the U.S. Army.[21]

Looting was a chronic problem in the postwar city, and nearly any item was fair game. Determined looters absconded from commercial buildings, government offices, and private homes with electrical wiring, appliances, toilet bowls, and whatever else they could get their hands on. Any abandoned building was fair game. To a certain degree, U.S. soldiers understood why the looting occurred. As Private First Class Michael Ruzbarsky, tank driver with A Company, 4-64 Armor, put it, "Everybody's poor."[22] Iraq's economy was in shambles, and many Baghdad citizens had not received a paycheck since the war began. For some, there was nowhere to go to work and no one to issue checks. Some of the looters carried AK-47s, so stopping them required caution. Usually, they gave up their goods and weapons to the arresting soldiers. There was not much else they could do. Soldiers parked their tanks and other armored vehicles in front of banks, schools, government buildings, and hospitals, all of which were on the 3rd Infantry Division's priority list for protection. In some abandoned buildings they found families squatting, having lost their homes due to the war. When U.S. troops on patrol found them, the squatters often asked for permission to stay. They had nowhere else to go.[23]

There were two main schools of thought regarding looting. One was that U.S. troops should come down hard and suppress it immediately. The other one saw looting as a natural correction by citizens who had been oppressed by a dictatorial government. Blount instructed 3rd ID commanders to adhere to the latter way of thinking. The division was not there to crush minor criminal behavior.[24] Looters descended on Hussein's Sajide Palace, removing elaborate furniture, artwork, rugs, and gaudy fixtures that had adorned the palace's rooms. Mobs crowded Baghdad's streets as looters pulled trucks up to department stores and dragged merchandise into their truck beds. Others emptied the Rashid Hotel of its beds and stole the hotel's refrigerator and some tennis racquets as well. Propane tanks were especially in demand, as there was a shortage in the city, and most people relied on propane for cooking in their homes. Children helped their parents carry whatever they could out of stores. Looters reflected a cross-section of Baghdad's population and included those of the professional class as well as poor residents. One pharmacist, who, along with her obstetrician husband and two children, carried furniture out of Sajide Palace, told a nearby reporter, "I paid for these a thousand times."[25]

Soldiers of 1st Brigade patrolled Baghdad neighborhoods to curb lawlessness in the absence of an official city police force. They mostly stopped curfew violators, but the soldiers sometimes had to deal with looting and other kinds of theft, unauthorized weapons possession, and violence against troops. When 1st Brigade troops encountered someone violating curfew, they detained the person, confiscated any weapons, and held the violator until dawn. AK-47s and 9mm pistols were the most common weapons the soldiers found on detainees. Sometimes they confiscated large sums of money, like the 1.8 million dinar, approximately $240,000, members of Task Force 3-69 Armor took from detainees about a month after combat had ended. Suspected criminals fought back at times. When Task Force 2-7 Infantry raided a car shop rumored to be hiding stolen vehicles, two soldiers and an accompanying reporter were injured in fighting that broke out during the raid. In another incident, members of Task Force 1-41 Artillery responded to a tip that a group of private residences housed Saddam Fedayeen militants. Soldiers searched the houses and arrested eight men. They also confiscated guns, ammunition, explosives, and cash.[26]

In addition to confiscating weapons from looters and squatters, 3rd ID units also worked to clear weapons and munitions caches from various hiding places throughout Baghdad. Weapons searches became part of the 3rd ID's daily patrols through Baghdad's neighborhoods. Soldiers stopped to talk with locals they encountered, and in the course of some conversations, citizens led them to weapons stockpiles in hospitals, schools, and homes. Residential neighborhoods were powder kegs, and if someone wanted to make a statement against the actions of the U.S. in Iraq, all it would have taken was a spark to ignite a pile of explosives tucked into a building that ordinary civilians used every day. A blast in a school while children sat at their desks, or an explosion in a hospital ward where sick and injured patients lay in beds, would have called into question the idea that Iraqis were better off under U.S. occupation than they were under the Hussein regime. Clearing the weapons caches was one of the most important tasks the 3rd ID faced in the immediate postwar days and weeks.[27]

Explosive ordnance disposal experts did the most dangerous work in the removal process. They were already on the scene, clearing unexploded ordnance from Baghdad's streets. For the weapons removal teams, they defused or dismantled what explosives they could to make transporting them less risky. Army trucks carried the stockpiles to safe storage places away from residential areas. Once Iraq had a functioning military again, the U.S. Army would turn the weapons over to Iraqi commanders.

The main unit in charge of the job was the 41st Field Artillery Regiment, known as Task Force Victory Bullet. Soldiers physically removed ammunition and equipment, and they coordinated with the 3rd ID to store and transport the weapons caches. Getting it all out of residential neighborhoods was the priority. Major Kemp Chester, operations officer for the 103rd Military Intelligence Battalion, worked with Victory Bullet personnel to identify the stockpiles that posed the biggest threat to civilians. The 103rd was the 3rd ID unit in charge of the weapons removal effort. Although the goal was to move the dangerous equipment as far from residential areas as possible, some of the caches were so large that it was logistically challenging to move them. Yet they managed to remove thousands of pieces of equipment and munitions. At one Baghdad school, the removal of 3,000 cases of small-arms ammunition allowed the school administrators to start classes again. From April through June, Task Force Victory Bullet moved more than 1,200 truckloads of weapons and ammunition out of Baghdad's neighborhoods. The beige military trucks hauled more than 30 million small-arms rounds, 70,000 rocket-propelled grenades, and thousands of pistols, rifles, bombs, and mortar rounds.[28]

In addition to conventional weapons, 3rd ID soldiers also had to search for weapons of mass destruction in Baghdad. Reports came into Blount's office, and if they seemed to have some credibility, he and a team went out to investigate. On one occasion, Blount went out to a school where neighbors had reported their suspicions about a new basketball court on the playground. Back in December, educators had been told to close their school for a week, and the school was shut down. While they were gone, a construction crew had come in and built the basketball court. The principal told

Blount that school officials had not requested the court. Blount called in some Australians who had ground-penetrating radar, and they searched for 50-gallon drums hidden under the court but found nothing. Another report suggested that Hussein had ordered a canal to be shut down, chemicals buried there, and the canal refilled. But Iraq contained thousands of miles of canals, so searching for something allegedly hidden in a canal would amount to a wild goose chase. An Iraqi general offered to tell a search team an exact location for a million dollars, but the soldiers declined.

Another tip came from a farmer whose land was adjacent to Hussein's motor pool, which included a bullet-ridden Lincoln that Uday Hussein had been driving when would-be assassins opened fire on him. According to the farmer, a crew with earthmovers had arrived at the motor pool and spent a few days digging holes, and then another team of men in hazmat suits showed up and buried items in the holes. Blount called in a U.S. survey team, and about 6 feet down surveyors uncovered containers filled with battery acid, not an ingredient in a WMD. At that point, the survey team moved on to a new site, and Blount let it go. No tip called into Blount's office ever led to a discovery of anything related to WMDs.

Maintaining soldier morale was a concern for commanders as they navigated the security and stability operations, missions for which they had not trained. Palace headquarters and the forward operating bases had satellite television, but through April and May, there were no phones or e-mail for soldiers to contact loved ones back home. Hot meals were still scarce. But care packages arrived from the U.S. in droves, and that helped. The 3rd ID received so many care packages that units began portioning out items that they could give to hospitals and schools. When soldiers went out on patrol and shared items from the care packages, they built friendships with the Iraqis, especially children. Eventually, someone told the kids to stop accepting gifts from Americans.[29]

Part of what made the transition from combat to security difficult for some soldiers was that they never had a "spike-the-ball" moment, that moment where they felt like they had won. 1st Brigade had taken the Baghdad International Airport, but for O'Brien and his soldiers, the complex was so vast and unknown that seizing it felt anticlimactic. "We're here. Now what?" characterized how he and his soldiers perceived the situation. The second thunder run was a spike-the-ball moment for the 3rd ID as a whole, but from that point on, O'Brien's soldiers, and probably many others, were focused on doing what they needed to do to go home. When the redeploy date kept changing, morale plummeted.[30]

Among Blount's concerns about Baghdad's potential for stability once the U.S. left was the police force. He had been told that retired Iraqi officers would take charge of police responsibilities, but no structure was in place for that to happen when the 3rd ID arrived in the city. Since the regular police and firefighters had all abandoned their posts during the war, Blount and his team had to reestablish the city's police department. There had been bad blood between Baghdad citizens and police officers, with citizens viewing the police as corrupt, susceptible to bribery, and loyal to Hussein. Meanwhile, Hussein had emptied Iraq's prisons just before the U.S. invaded, and kidnappings and other crimes left Baghdad citizens feeling unsafe.

To lure city workers back to their jobs, Blount received money from the Commanders Emergency Response Program (CERP), run through the U.S. Defense Department, which gave U.S. military officials access to cash that could be used for local projects. He authorized the payment of $25 stipends, the equivalent of about a month's salary, to every civil servant and government employee. Initially, the funds for the program came from money the Army confiscated during and after the war, but later CERP also received federal funds. Military authorities worked with municipal leaders to determine the community's needs and then fund accordingly. Relationships between U.S. troops and Iraqi local leaders was a vital component of the postwar military mission in Iraq. Leaders served as liaisons between their communities and U.S. personnel, and helped identify community needs while also facilitating the trust-building process between Americans and Iraqis. Together, Iraqis and U.S. personnel established district and neighborhood advisory committees in Baghdad as precursors to the creation of official governing bodies.

Through CERP, the 3rd Infantry Division under Blount's direction paid more than $8 million through Iraq's government ministries to revive the country's economy. Without pay, the employees of civil agencies had little incentive to return to work, and so pumping money into wages was part of the process of building postwar Iraq. Most places took either the dinar or the dollar, so currency made no difference. Some of the funds provided back pay to employees who had not received a paycheck since the war began.[31]

Hussein was still on the loose, and that made some city employees reluctant to return to work. If Hussein managed to seize power again, or if his lackeys still held on, they could come after civil servants who had disobeyed them. But 3rd ID leaders earned their trust and slowly began to get the city moving again. As municipal leaders began to come forward, they asked to take control of the money that was earmarked for city employee salaries, but Blount kept control of it. Centralized distributions emanating from 3rd ID headquarters allowed him to keep track of who got how much money and when. It was a big task, but not one he was willing to delegate to the Iraqis.

Combining community assistance projects with patrols allowed 3rd ID teams to show Baghdad residents that they were there to help, not just brandish weapons. V Corps implemented Task Force Neighborhood to figure out what locals needed in order to improve their communities. Army engineers repaired buildings and installed picnic tables in elementary schoolyards, while in a pop-up dental clinic, Army dentists examined patients' teeth and performed routine dental care – something that some of the citizens who visited the clinic had not previously received. Engineers also built soccer goals for parks within the city. Colonel Greg Martin, commander of V Corps' 130th Engineer Brigade, considered the efforts of Task Force Neighborhood as part of the mission to win the peace after winning the war. From his viewpoint, Baghdad was an engineer's paradise. Neglect and war had left city buildings, schools, water systems, and electrical plants in decay.[32]

Blount wasn't content to stay at his command post at the airport. When he had free time, he took walks through downtown neighborhoods and made use of local services. He usually traveled with an interpreter, as well as his security detail, but he also knew some Arabic from his years living and working in Saudi Arabia, and saying a few Arabic phrases helped break the ice with Baghdad residents. Retired Iraqi generals approached Blount wanting to talk, or they invited him to meet with them. They felt a sense of camaraderie with Blount, and they enjoyed trading war stories. Inside the Palestine Hotel, which sat on the edge of Firdos Square overlooking the Tigris River, a barber cut Blount's hair, and the laundry service washed and pressed his clothes. Doing business at the city's hotels gave Blount a chance to talk with locals. He made it a point to apologize to the manager of the Palestine for American tank fire that hit the hotel during a fight with Iraqi artillery on April 8.

One night after Blount and his commanders had dinner at the Palestine, that same manager took Blount into his office and closed the door behind him. It was a habit; during the Hussein days, Iraqis were afraid to talk near open windows and doors for fear that a spy was listening. People didn't even trust their own children in some cases. The manager told Blount that for the past three years he had photocopied the passports of Russian and Chinese guests who had stayed at the hotel. He knew the U.S. had been looking for weapons of mass destruction, and he wondered if perhaps some of the hotel guests had been involved in weapons development. The manager gave the copies to Blount, who turned them over to the CIA. By going around and talking with locals, Blount built a rapport with Baghdad's citizens that led to instances like the these. Locals were willing to cooperate because Blount took an interest in them.

Traveling with an interpreter and security detail, Blount visited key sites throughout the city. Hospitals were a mixed bag; some had survived the war intact, others needed serious help, and about a third had been shut down. All the hospitals still operating needed security and fuel for their generators. Blount designated the city's hospitals as priority sites for fuel distribution, and he sent mechanics to fix generators that needed repairs. He also stationed Bradleys at each hospital because they were targets for looters.

Most of the medical personnel who worked at Baghdad's hospitals spoke English, but Blount's interpreter helped when hospital staff took him to visit patients. Staff members often escorted him to meet the families of children who had been injured by American cluster bombs. The bombs' red ribbons attracted the attention of unsuspecting children, and as they lay in Baghdad hospitals, disfigured and often missing limbs, staff wanted Blount to see the consequences of American bombing. Mothers fussed at him, and he empathized. It would have been useless to explain to the mother of a wounded child that he had limited the use of cluster bombs but the Air Force had dropped them much more frequently. Those were minor details to a mother whose child would not walk or see again.

Soldiers from the 3rd Brigade and the 30th Medical Brigade, V Corps, distributed medical supplies donated by the Ministry of Kuwait and the government of Australia. Most hospitals had survived the war unscathed, but bombs had targeted one, which had been responsible for treating Hussein and his family. The hospital structure was destroyed, but some equipment survived, and soldiers removed it from the building; another hospital would be able to make use of it. Even though most hospitals escaped war damage, many were chronically undersupplied, and some did not have reliable access to water. Blount met with the staff of Kasmir University Hospital and toured the hospital with Dr. Issim Khuleif in an effort to determine how the 3rd Infantry Division could help. The hospital desperately needed fuel for generators, water, medicines, and supplies, Khuleif told Blount. The general replied that his troops would do all they could to stock the hospital.[33]

The 3rd ID's 11th Engineer Battalion teamed up with Iraqi engineers to rebuild Baghdad's Al-Wasity Hospital, which had been damaged during the war. The team of American and Iraqi engineers examined the hospital's structural, electrical, and mechanical elements to determine repair and reconstruction priorities. Once they established work plans, the engineers hired local construction workers and electricians to carry them out. Hundreds of workers for hire showed up each morning and took on jobs ranging from trash removal to skilled electronic and construction tasks. Their pay came from frozen Iraqi government accounts. Iraqi engineers served as managers for the project because they had both technical expertise and knowledge of Iraq's specific infrastructure and electrical systems. Captain James Lockridge, officer in charge of the engineering team, hoped that the Al-Wasity project would serve as a model for other infrastructure reconstruction projects throughout Baghdad. The team had already worked at the Baghdad College of Pharmacy, restoring power to auditoriums and offices. Restocking hospitals with medicines and other supplies was a crucial part of Task Force Neighborhood. Looters targeted hospitals, leaving some of them ill-equipped to care for patients. To fill in the gaps, military medical units set up temporary clinics in neighborhoods that lacked a functioning hospital.[34] As a contribution to the humanitarian effort, Saudi Arabia provided a modern field hospital to Baghdad. This turned out to come from the Saudi Arabian National Guard modernization program that Blount had managed in Riyadh. Blount knew some of the officers and doctors who came to Baghdad from Saudi Arabia to staff the hospital.

The soldiers of the 3rd ID had not been trained in humanitarianism, nor had they been trained in zookeeping, but 2nd Brigade troops found themselves having to deal with exotic animals in Baghdad. Looters stormed the zoo and stole exotic birds and other animals that didn't pose harm to them. Looters also opened cages, and animals wandered out onto the zoo grounds, and eventually made their way out onto the streets. When 2nd Brigade soldiers discovered the zoo and saw the animals out of their cages, they quickly realized the dire condition the surviving animals were in. The animals had suffered from lack of proper food and medical supplies under the Hussein regime due to UN sanctions, and the war made the animals' plight worse. Iraqi forces had placed a gun battery in the zoo, transforming the animals' home into a military target. As an emaciated lion stumbled near them, they fed him crackers and dried meat from their ration packs, but they knew it wasn't nearly enough.

Adapting on the fly, the soldiers became temporary zookeepers. They found a pen containing goats and slaughtered and fed them to the lions and tigers. They also moved a wolf carcass onto the zoo grounds for the animals to feed. Blount had not restored running water to the city yet when the soldiers arrived at the zoo, so they enlisted the help of Iraqi citizens to truck water in from a nearby lake for the thirsty animals. Army officials contacted zookeepers in Kuwait, and the Kuwaiti government arranged to ship 7 tons of meat, fruit, and vegetables to Baghdad for the animals.[35]

Still, even though the animals were sick and needed help, lions, tigers, bears, and others were still life-threatening to humans. Out of concern for the safety of local residents, soldiers shot a lion that had escaped zoo grounds. Other lions managed to escape, and soldiers of Task Force 1-64 embarked on a mission to corral them, shining headlights at them and shooting into the air. They succeeded in capturing only one lion. To protect the humans in the neighborhood, they shot and killed the other two lions. For weeks after 3rd ID soldiers found the zoo, stray animals continued to turn up in Baghdad. Gazelles ran across the airport tarmac. Riding in a vehicle down a city street, Blount looked out and saw a cheetah running alongside him. Soldiers tracked down a baboon hiding in a theater.[36] When U.S. troops closed in on Baghdad, zookeepers had fled, leaving animals – including bears, monkeys, lions, and camels – without food or water. Some of the animals died in their cages; those who clung to life desperately tried to escape.[37]

Like other city workers, zookeepers hadn't been paid for two months, so they had little incentive to return to work, especially given the dangers that existed at a zoo where starving predators now roamed free. Hisham Mohamad was one of the few Iraqi veterinarians who showed up to work at the zoo after the looters had plundered it, and he worked with 2nd Brigade troops to care for the animals while waiting on international aid.[38] As aid organizations made plans to send food, supplies, and veterinarians to Baghdad for the animals, another complication arose that Blount and his team had to manage. The U.S. Army now controlled Baghdad's runways, but Blount had no mechanism for air traffic control and giving air clearance. Daily city operations that did not enter the minds of most Americans in a normal context were challenges that needed solving in postwar Baghdad.

Some soldiers found animals; others found cash. A team of 2nd Brigade engineers stationed on the palace grounds went looking for tools to move some trees. They found several pump houses that were cemented over. Curious, they smashed one with a sledgehammer, revealing a pile of aluminum cases. The soldiers opened one of the cases and stared astonished at its contents, bundles of $100 bills bearing the seal of the Bank of Jordan. It turned out there was $12 million in the case, and there were 15 or 20 cases in the pumphouse. The soldiers soon realized that there were other pumphouses on the grounds. As they smashed each one open, they found the same contents as they had discovered in the first one. All told, the boxes hidden throughout the palace grounds would contain nearly one billion dollars in U.S. currency.

SJA Lyle Cayce thought the Americans could do a lot for the citizens of Baghdad with that money. Like it or not, international law would designate the U.S. an occupier, allowing Blount and other 3rd ID commanders to use the money for the benefit of Iraqis. But Congressional red tape about appropriations and spending led to arguments about what the Army could spend according to American law. It wasn't the first time Cayce had to argue for the use of Iraqi money to help Iraqis. Soldiers at a checkpoint had found $40,000 in stolen currency on an Iraqi major. When he learned of the money, Cayce got an idea. He had heard there was a water source on one side of a checkpoint, and citizens had to traverse the checkpoint to get to the water. That made for a lot of vehicle traffic, which brought the risk that a vehicle could be carrying a bomb that could kill U.S. troops. Cayce proposed that the U.S. take the $40,000 to pay a contractor to move the water from the source to the other side and deliver it to those who needed it. But legal council said it would be an illegal augmentation of U.S. funds that had been appropriated to the war effort. Cayce was stunned. The division was in the middle of a war, and the rigidity was incompatible with the efforts to bring stability to the area and protect U.S. soldiers. After a few days of arguing, the U.S. government agreed to Cayce's plan.[39]

As they continued to search the palace grounds, the inspectors found that Hussein's henchmen had stashed money away in another shed and cinder blocked the door opening. There was a petting zoo on the grounds, and Hussein's men had placed boxes of cash inside the empty cages and then cemented them shut. Over the course of about three days, U.S. soldiers found nearly one billion dollars. Blount ordered his team to load the aluminum boxes onto a C-130 bound for CFLCC headquarters in Kuwait. It was later infused back into the Iraqi economy. Payments authorized to civil servants, interpreters, street sweepers, and other workers were drawn from the money through CERP.

Like Blount, Wesley believed in the importance of getting to know Iraqis on their terms. Sometimes that meant sitting on the floor in a person's home and eating dinner with their hands from a common plate. Whenever Wesley went to a council meeting or entered a home, he removed his Kevlar and flak vest and set his weapon aside. He was fully exposed, but he did it to create common ground and build trust. Whenever he had the chance, he walked to meetings so that locals would see him out among them. Every time Wesley made himself vulnerable like that, he risked his safety, but he believed it was important to convey to locals that he was on their side.[40]

Reopening Baghdad's main post office symbolized a return to normalcy, as in the everyday tasks that people undertook regardless of who controlled their nation. The Al-Kadhimiya Post Office first opened in 1922, a year after the Kingdom of Iraq was founded under the reign of Faisal I. Post offices did not fare well during the war. Many were located in the same buildings as telecommunications offices, which coalition bombs targeted. Bombing destroyed some of the post office buildings, and postal services found new homes in temporary buildings. Postmaster General Kalid Al-Aziew wore a suit to the ribbon-cutting ceremony at Al-Kadhimiya Post Office. Of Baghdad's 69 post offices, 44 survived the war.

Employment was a goal of the postwar mission in Iraq, and civil affairs committed funding to ensure that all postal workers could return to jobs. Baghdad's post offices employed nearly 2,000 workers, and when the war began, postal workers fled for safety, hunkering down with family at home. In order to encourage them to return to work, the Army's civil affairs office paid each worker $20 and invested money into the postal system so that it could continue to pay workers until it became financially self-sufficient. When word spread that post offices were opening back up, Baghdad residents set out to try to mail letters and packages, seeking a connection with those elsewhere and a return to the ordinary rhythms of everyday life. Until those phone and internet networks were back up and running, postal mail was Iraqis' means of communication. Baghdad's post offices functioned not just as mail delivery but also as a financial center. Ministries that provided benefits, such as the Ministry of Finance, allowed recipients unable to travel to ministry offices to pick up their benefits payments at their local post office.[41]

Close in age to Baghdad's Al-Kadhimiya Post Office was the Iraqi Meteorological Organization. Established in 1923, it was the oldest meteorological society in the Middle East. Before the war, the IMO had operated more than 50 meteorological and four seismological stations through the country. The site at Baghdad International Airport was the first to resume operations after the war. Meteorologists returned to their weather station at the airport on May 24, a crucial component in getting air travel to and from the airport back up and running. International aviation standards required that pilots receive weather reports before flying.[42] Looters had ransacked the airport's weather station, so meteorologists with the U.S. 15th Aviation Support Operations Squadron had installed new equipment there. The stolen equipment was outdated, so the looters inadvertently did the meteorologists a favor.

There were also museums. Iraq's modern history began in the 1920s, but as the cradle of civilization, Iraq was the home of thousands of years of human history. Historians and archeologists have pieced together the worlds of ancient Mesopotamia through the discoveries of artifacts the earlier civilizations left behind. Curators had preserved many such antiquities in the Iraqi National Museum, which housed about 170,000 artifacts, some of which dated back 7,000 years. The museum became a target for looters in the aftermath of the fighting in Baghdad. Thieves stole gold and silver items from ancient tombs, artifacts from Hammurabi's reign, and the gold leaf overlay from Alexander the Great's throne. Looters dumped out a card catalog onto the floor of a museum office and knocked over desks and chairs in their rush to seize antiquities. State Department staff in Baghdad surveyed the damage aghast, and archaeologists overseas demanded to know why the 3rd ID hadn't done a better job of protecting Iraq's history and culture.[43]

Blount understood the distress, but he knew that his troops had not willfully neglected the museum. They'd been fighting a war and trying to secure suspected weapons of mass destruction sites. No doubt that the museum and its contents were valuable, but they didn't register when measured against the bigger picture. The media got ahold of the story, and soon reporters and television cameras were competing for scoops and footage. At first, Blount wasn't even sure if any of the museums were in his sector of the city, as the Marines shared security duties. But watching an ABC report about museum looting, Blount noticed that there were no U.S. troops guarding the building on the screen. That was a bad look, he thought. Where were the Marines? Should he have posted 3rd ID soldiers there? To check, he rummaged through his things until he found a guidebook to Iraq that one of his daughters had given to him for Christmas. Blount thumbed through it and found the museum's address. Turned out it was in the 3rd ID's sector.

Blount called headquarters and ordered a security detail sent to the museum as soon as possible. When he arrived, he made his way through a gauntlet of reporters to meet the museum curator. The curator asked to speak with Blount in private and led him into a room in the interior of the museum. There were secret rooms hidden behind a brick façade that held some of the most valuable antiquities in the museum's collection. Not everything gone off the shelves and walls was lost, the curator told Blount.

The curator asked Blount to drive him to a warehouse where museum staff had hidden more artifacts. The warehouse consisted of five locked bunkers holding the most priceless of the museum's items that staff were able to move. Museum staff had been preparing for the war for a year, the curator told Blount. Long before the 3rd ID reached Baghdad, museum staff had taken items off the walls and put precious statues in secret hiding places. Anticipating tremors caused by bombs, museum staff lined the floors of the storage spaces with mattresses to provide cushioning for artifacts if they fell from the shelves. The curator pointed to one of the bunkers and told Blount that the Queen of Sheba's golden headdress was in it. Then he asked Blount to send troops to guard the warehouse.

That would just draw attention to the hiding place, Blount replied. No one knew to look there for the antiquities, but if U.S. troops showed up, it would tip off the looters that something valuable was there. As things were now, if people thought many of the artifacts were stolen, let them keep thinking that. Meanwhile, 3rd ID soldiers printed fliers asking looters to return museum items, and they recorded a loudspeaker message with the same plea. The message threatened prison if 3rd ID troops found items that weren't returned.

At checkpoints throughout the country, U.S. troops stopped vans and other vehicles only to find smuggled museum goods in boxes hidden under blankets or floor mats. At one checkpoint near the Iran border, Iraqi soldiers stopped a white truck and found an aluminum case filled with ancient parchment scrolls and statuettes. The soldiers confiscated the artifacts and turned them over to the Joint International Agency Cardinal Group, a unit that consisted of FBI, CIA, and U.S. Customs personnel. JIACG was founded after 9/11 to coordinate the sharing of intelligence regarding terrorist activity. In Baghdad, agents investigated various types of criminal activity, including theft. Back during Operation *Desert Storm*, looters had stolen some 2,000 artifacts from the Iraqi National Museum, most of which were never recovered. The job of recovery was complicated. Museum staff, those who were still around, did not have an inventory of what items had been stolen versus what was in storage. Before the war began, some museum staff members had moved artifacts to bomb shelters and bank vaults for safe keeping, but no one had a record of where specifically the items had been hidden. Some of the items were already on the black market. Safety concerns slowed the investigation of the museum. During the war, the Iraqi Republican Guard had set up a fighting position inside the building, and so JIACG agents had to move carefully from room to room in order to avoid tripping any unexploded ordnance.[44]

In the 800s BC, Assyrian King Ashurnasirpal II commissioned the building of his grand palace at Nimrud, an ancient city located near present-day Mosul on the Tigris River. Stone panel carvings depicted the king leading military campaigns, hunting, and performing spiritual rituals. The Assyrian Empire eventually collapsed, and Nimrud was forgotten for centuries until archaeologists discovered remnants of the city in the 1840s. Artifacts included cuneiform tablets depicting some of the earliest known writing. As archaeologists uncovered more ruins, they found the remains of palaces and sculptures, including statues of the Lamassu, a mythical beast with the head of a human, a bull's body, and an eagle's wings. The objects represented Iraq's ancient history and testified to the power of Ashurnasirpal's kingdom.

The Iraqi National Museum eventually gained possession of many of the Nimrud remains. In 2003, when museum staff realized that war was imminent, they moved the most valuable artifacts, including the Nimrud items, to various hiding places throughout Baghdad for safekeeping. In the quick efforts to do so, record-keeping was shoddy, and when the war ended, investigators struggled to determine which museum items were hidden and which had been the victims of looting. In the two months following the siege of Baghdad, a U.S. investigation team searched the city with help from museum staff to try to locate the hidden artifacts. The team retrieved the items in June, finding them in a safe box in a vault deep inside the Central Bank of Iraq. Damage to the building had caused sewage to erupt in the vault and the safe box had been submerged in the filth. When investigators opened the box, they found gold earrings and other rings, necklaces, and dishware embedded with semiprecious stones. The safe box had appeared to protect the relics from water damage. Archaeologists considered the items to be treasures of human history, not just Iraqi history.[45]

Investigators also found other secret vaults in Baghdad buildings that contained museum artifacts. One vault held 179 boxes containing nearly 8,000 items. Before the war, the Iraqi National Museum had held ancient Babylonian, Assyrian, and Sumerian collections, as well as rare Islamic texts. Knowing that looters had absconded with some of the missing relics, the U.S. investigation team issued a "no questions asked" return policy to encourage looters to bring the items back. In some cases, the investigation team raided homes after being tipped off to looters' whereabouts. International outcry had erupted over the looting of the museum, and some angry voices blamed the U.S. military for not doing a better job of protecting the museum. In the aftermath of the conflict, the Coalition Provisional Authority made restoring the museum a priority. Perhaps one day it would tell the story of Saddam Hussein and what became of Iraq after his regime collapsed.

Most Baghdad residents used liquid propane gas for cooking, but none had been available for more than two months, from the time the Americans invaded Iraq to late May. When the Ministry of Oil began distributing propane again, 3rd ID units assisted with crowd control at distribution sites throughout the city. Restless Baghdad residents had not been able to cook normally for more than two months, and the stress of wartime austerity caused crowds to grow unruly as they waited at designated spots to buy propane. It became especially tense when distribution sites ran out of the day's allotment of gas. Residents worried that there wouldn't be any more coming and they'd missed their chance. In order to communicate with locals, each 3rd ID crowd control unit began bringing an interpreter and a psychological operations vehicle equipped with a loudspeaker. Although U.S. troops were visible on site, U.S. authorities wanted Baghdad residents to associate services such as propane distribution with the government, to see it as a normal relationship between a government and its citizens.[46]

Another city service that ceased when the war began was trash collection. Residents in Baghdad's Al Mansur neighborhood took to dumping their garbage in an empty lot that local kids had once used as a playground and soccer field. In another jarring scene revealing the juxtaposition of battle front and home front in an urban war, an Iraqi missile had somehow landed on top of a vehicle in the Al Mansur trash dump. In other parts of the city, residents dumped trash on road medians. As the garbage piled up, the makeshift dumps became breeding grounds for diseases and attracted insects and rodents. As part of U.S. Army clean-up efforts, units went into the neighborhoods with dump trucks to move the garbage to a landfill outside the city. Baghdad residents had done what they could to continue on with their lives despite the interruption of city services due to the war. The removal of mountains of garbage from residential neighborhoods was another effort at a return to normalcy.

In addition to making rounds throughout the city and meeting with local leaders, Blount also checked in with his soldiers, including those who were not part of the 3rd ID but whose units were attached to the division in Iraq. Blount, usually with Birmingham along, would do a morning briefing with his commanders over the radio, and then he'd get in a vehicle and go out to visit with the troops. If it was around mealtime, Blount would sit and eat MREs with the soldiers. He did not stay ensconced at the airport; he got out and tried to make sure that the soldiers knew he supported them.

Conversations with Iraqi POWs and generals enlightened Blount as to the Iraqi Army's struggles during the war as well as to soldiers' motivations for fighting. The Iraqi National Command Authority made most of the tactical decisions for the forces, and that centralized approach prevented commanders from making decisions as conditions changed quickly. Berdy was in on some of the meetings, and he likened the imbalance between the U.S. and Iraq to "one organization fighting in digital and the other organization fighting in analog." Because Iraqi forces had to wait for orders from central command, they were always a few days behind the U.S., which prevented them from doing anything that could significantly disrupt the 3rd ID's advance. Soldier motivation came down to two perspectives. Some, the professional soldiers of the Iraqi Army, fought out of a sense of duty to their nation and a desire to defend their homeland. The other motivation was fear. Some of the generals who spoke with Blount explained that they knew Hussein had ordered the executions of senior leaders he didn't trust, and they feared a similar fate, so they followed his orders. Among the enlisted and Fedayeen, some fought under the threat of harm to their loved ones if they refused. Hussein's henchmen held family members hostage and tortured them, to force men into the regular army and the Fedayeen militias. Those Iraqis faced an impossible choice, and some lost their lives in the war so that Hussein would spare their wife or child or parent.[47]

Rumsfeld made a quick visit to Baghdad at the end of April. Blount welcomed him to the capital and made arrangements for a press conference to be held at the airport. In a speech to Iraqi citizens, Rumsfeld promised that the U.S. would train military and police officers and send contractors to help Iraq rebuild, but then U.S. troops would get out of the way and leave it to Iraqis to craft their new nation as they saw fit. That had been the plan all along, as Blount and other Army leaders understood it. The 3rd ID's mission was to capture Baghdad and remove Hussein and other Ba'ath Party operatives, not to conquer and rebuild Iraq. Contractors and the State Department, not the Army, should remain in-country as needed to help with nation building.

A month into the transition, the looting and the chaos in Baghdad had not subsided. Garner's job was a casualty, and Paul Bremer, a diplomat and counterterrorism expert, replaced him on

May 12. Gone, too, was ORHA, and Bremer would head up the newly established Coalition Provisional Authority (CPA), which was tasked with building democracy in Iraq so that the country would stand as a model for democracy building throughout the Middle East. Pentagon officials had created ORHA assuming that some degree of Iraq's governmental administration would remain in place and the U.S. troop presence would be short-lived. Creation of the CPA indicated a deeper and longer-term commitment the U.S. government was making to rebuilding Iraq.[48]

Bremer's arrival caused a shift in U.S. soldiers' engagement with Iraqis and was a turning point in post-invasion operations. Bremer's strategy for ending looting was to authorize U.S. troops to shoot looters on sight.[49] The order ran counter to Blount's approach to Baghdad, which centered on assessing the needs of the citizens and restoring basic services as quickly as possible. Bremer's and Blount's experiences in the Middle East sharply diverged, with Bremer's amounting to a crash course on Iraqi politics before he arrived in-country. Blount's years in Saudi Arabia had taught him the importance of getting to know local culture and meeting leaders, associates, and citizens on their own terms. Shooting looters amounted to wounding or killing the people the 3rd ID had just fought to liberate. Blount wanted to understand them before making any decision to attack them.

Bremer also proposed a plan to isolate and disenfranchise members of the Ba'ath Party. When he arrived in Baghdad to replace Jay Garner as head of ORHA, Bremer went around and met with all the brigades stationed in the capital city. On the day of his visit with 2nd Brigade in the regime district, Perkins was out on patrol, so Lieutenant Colonel Eric Wesley, 2nd Brigade's executive officer, briefed Bremer about the brigade's activities. Wesley realized that Bremer was far senior to him, but he ended his brief with an opinion anyway. From his perspective on the ground, the U.S. should *not* isolate, cut off, or disenfranchise the Ba'ath Party because it was Iraq's bureaucratic mechanism for governing. If an Iraqi wanted to rise in station by running a business or corporation, or wanted to be in politics or become a general in the army, joining the Ba'ath

Party was required. The narrative coming out of Washington was "Ba'ath Party, bad" because it was Hussein's party, but what Wesley had learned from talking to people in Baghdad was that people joined the party for reasons that had nothing to do with supporting Hussein. Party membership offered the only path for upward mobility.[50]

Armed with that knowledge, Wesley made the case to Bremer that the Americans should vet senior Iraqi Army leadership individually, as opposed to applying a blanket policy of "If you're a Ba'ath Party member, you're castigated." It was naïve, shortsighted, and unwise, Wesley asserted. Bremer looked at Wesley incredulously and said, "I don't get you guys. You fought from Kuwait to Baghdad, and these guys were shooting at you, and you want these senior party leaders to potentially have a role in the rebuilding of Iraq." In that instant, Wesley realized that while Bremer was an accomplished diplomat, he did not understand the profession of arms. Leaders of nations employ armies to protect and defend their sovereignty, and the Iraqi soldiers and officers in Hussein's army had a professional obligation to do their duty to their nation. Wesley understood that concept, and he did not have a personal vendetta against an enemy soldier who might have pulled the trigger on him. Now that the war was over, Wesley explained to Bremer that the better approach to Ba'athists was to interview individuals and judge them one by one rather than make assumptions about them as a whole. At the very least, the Americans needed them to establish a new Iraqi army.[51] Wesley didn't know if Bremer took his argument to heart, but he would learn later that he had not swayed the diplomat.

Like Wesley, Blount disagreed with the conventional wisdom coming from the Bremer camp that the U.S. had to completely purge all Ba'athists from Iraq. He spent much time ruminating on how the balance of power between Shia and Sunni would work in a rebuilt Iraq. Sunni–Shia animosities went back centuries, but the two groups had managed to coexist in Iraq before the U.S. Army arrived. Blount assumed they could handle it better than American advisors understood. He also believed that affiliation with the

Ba'ath Party didn't necessarily mean a person was evil. The highest level Ba'athists who were closest to Hussein no doubt should be removed, but moving beyond Hussein's inner circle, many of Iraq's educated professionals were Ba'athists to some degree, and they were Sunni. Blount advocated for keeping the Sunni-dominated universities and government ministries intact because Iraq needed its technocrats, engineers, doctors, and business leaders to help the country achieve postwar stability.

Given Blount's association with the Saudis, who were Sunni, he didn't have the same knee-jerk negative reaction to Iraqi Sunnis as other Americans did. From a pragmatic perspective, he believed it made sense to keep certain Ba'athists in their positions. Ba'athists had controlled the oil ministry and the food distribution system, and both continued to work well after the war. If the Americans removed every Ba'athist from positions in those institutions, the systems would fall apart. A bigger threat than Ba'athists to security as Blount saw it was the potential for Shia retribution against Sunnis now that Hussein was gone. If Shia individuals or groups were to get power over the Sunnis, Blount worried that they would seek revenge for real and perceived oppression they experienced during the Hussein regime. The way Blount saw it, the Shia were an extension of Iran, a country which had been anti-American since 1979.

Blount and Bremer did not see eye to eye on several issues in Baghdad. One was the entrepreneurialism of some city residents regarding fuel sales. Resuming gasoline services was a major concern for Blount and the 3rd ID. Hussein had shut down Iraq's oil refineries, and it would take weeks to get them running again. Without fuel for cars and propane for cooking, Baghdad would not be able to return to normalcy. Blount put in an emergency call to Kuwait requesting fuel imports. The 3rd ID's equipment ran on JP-8 jet fuel, but the division's vehicles could have run on bourbon if needed. Only the generators needed gasoline, so the division kept just what was needed for the generators. Blount called McKiernan at CFLCC, and soon fuel trucks began making the three-day trek to Baghdad. Meanwhile, Blount met with officials in the Ministry of Oil, one of the few ministries still operating, and made a plan for gasoline distribution. Blount brought along Brigadier General Robert Crear, who had been in charge of keeping Iraq's oil fields open.

At the oil ministry, Blount suggested that the U.S. trucks deliver the gasoline directly to gas stations. But the oil minister refused, telling Blount that his office already had a distribution system in place. His drivers knew where the gas stations were and could get to them quickly. The oil minister suggested that Blount send his 5,000-gallon trucks to transfer their loads to Iraqi trucks for distribution. Blount was skeptical, but he agreed. The point of U.S. occupation was to stabilize Iraq and then leave, so if there were working systems still in place, Blount believed the U.S. should honor them. That didn't stop him from sending security units to each gas station in Baghdad to supervise gasoline distribution.

When word got out that gasoline was available again, cars turned out in droves, sometimes thousands of cars lining up at a gas station to buy fuel. Drivers waited two or three days for gas, knowing that they couldn't go much farther without it. Some drivers didn't have gas to begin with, so they pushed their cars to the nearest fueling station. As it turned out, some motorists waited in vain. Blount learned that the Iraqi fuel trucks weren't arriving as planned, so he had Military Police (MPs) follow some of the trucks to monitor distribution. What he discovered was that the fuel truck drivers had an entrepreneurial spirit. On the way to the gas stations, they stopped and sold gas on side streets, selling a couple hundred of his thousand gallons and pocketing the money before heading to their designated gas stations. The black market extended from there to individual customers who bought gas from the oil ministry's trucks and then siphoned it into gallon jugs and sold it for $1 per liter, when they had bought at 15 cents. Some men brought cars without engines to gas stations just to get the gas that they then sold on the black market.

It wasn't illegal, and Blount tried to explain that to Paul Bremer, who was eager to shut down the black market. The men selling gas that way had already paid for it, and so at that point it was theirs,

Blount reasoned. If a motorist wanted to pay two to three times as much as the going rate at the pump in order to avoid sitting in line for days, that helped U.S. efforts to distribute gas more quickly. Gas distribution was key to the return to normalcy. Blount stood his ground against Bremer's disdain for Baghdadi innovation in gasoline distribution. Bremer eventually saw Blount's point and left it alone.

Another issue on which Blount and Bremer initially disagreed was food distribution. As war planners envisioned what Iraq would look like postwar, they expected to have to feed millions of refugees displaced by the fighting. But Hussein had run the Oil for Food program well since its establishment in 1995, and his government delivered three months' worth of food to cities in March just before the war started. Each citizen had a ration card, and city neighborhoods had food distribution points. Iraqis generally were not starving, and no one asked the U.S. for food because hunger wasn't an issue. Bremer wanted to shut down the existing distribution system and implement a U.S.-controlled process instead, but Blount convinced him to leave it alone. Messing with a working system could result in chaos, Blount reasoned, and he won the argument.

Most significant for Iraq's chance at stability was Bremer's decision to disband the army. From Blount's view, disbanding the Iraqi army played into the developing insurgency. Bremer assumed all Iraqi military personnel were Ba'athist and had to be disarmed as part of broader efforts at de-Ba'athification. Blount reminded Bremer that V Corps had conducted psychological warfare during the drive to Baghdad aimed at convincing Iraqi soldiers to desert. Planes dropped leaflets encouraging soldiers in Arabic to not die for Hussein. U.S. troops conducted the operations daily, coaxing Iraqi soldiers to take off their uniforms and go home; Hussein wasn't worth the fight. Blount believed the psychological operations were successful and that by the time the 3rd ID got to Baghdad, most Iraqi regulars had deserted, leaving only the elite Republican Guard units fighting.

Blount figured that the regulars could eventually be reconstituted into a new Iraqi Army to support the post-Hussein government. But

Bremer had a different mindset which saw anyone associated with Hussein's Iraq as Ba'athist. According to Bremer's order, former Iraqi soldiers were ineligible for the stipend payments that the U.S. had doled out in Baghdad as a way to get citizens back to work. What it meant was that thousands of trained soldiers were sent home to their communities and families with no source of income, no job, and a bleak future. Without an income, the young men couldn't get married because they couldn't support a family. Iraqi soldiers holding the rank of colonel or above were not allowed to work for the new Iraqi government, and they were ineligible for retirement benefits. Disbanding the Iraqi military put approximately 350,000 former soldiers out of work.[52] A whole population of disaffected former soldiers with no money and nothing to do became a source of rebel fighters.

Grimsley was with Lieutenant General David McKiernan when he learned of Bremer's order. McKiernan had come to Baghdad to visit with the 3rd ID, and he was going to walk a patrol with a 1st Brigade unit. Before going out, the men sat and talked in Grimsley's headquarters, and McKiernan told him that an announcement was coming. Bremer was disbanding the Iraqi Army. Grimsley was astonished. The army was supposed to be the local security force. There would have to be some purging of any remaining Hussein loyalists or hardcore Ba'athists, but the army was supposed to be the foundation on which Iraq would build a new stabilizing force.[53] With this disheartening news, it seemed like things were starting to unravel.

Birmingham saw Bremer's decision as the turning point at which the U.S. went from liberator to occupier in the minds of Iraqis, and there was nothing the 3rd ID could do about it. Conspiracy theories swirled through Baghdad neighborhoods suggesting that occupation had been the U.S. goal all along. Birmingham and his public affairs team, as well as Blount and his staff, reached out to local imams and other community leaders, but it was difficult to reach the general population. One of the ways public affairs tried was by publishing a newsletter called *The Liberator*. Birmingham conceived of it as a way to highlight the work 3rd ID soldiers were doing to help Baghdad residents, always with the aim of handing things over to the Iraqis and getting out. *The Liberator* was printed in English and Arabic by a local printing company, meaning that it also helped to stimulate the local economy. Blount managed his budgets from ORHA and the CPA with a focus on patronizing independent businesses in Baghdad. An Army interpreter read over each Arabic version to ensure the translation was correct.[54]

Despite the 3rd ID's attempts to win the hearts and minds of the Iraqis, tension began building the longer American soldiers remained in country. Frisking contributed to the tension between locals and U.S. troops. Frisking was a topic of conversation at Baghdad's cafés and restaurants, where from a table near a window or on the sidewalk, patrons might have been able to see a group of U.S. soldiers patrolling the area. Cultural sensitivities clashed with security efforts when U.S. male troops frisked Iraqi women at checkpoints throughout Baghdad. Traditional Muslim culture forbade men from touching women unrelated to them, and incidents of male soldiers patting down local women sparked outrage throughout the city. If the patrol unit performed random checks on pedestrians, women would be subject to them, and the chador – a long cloak covering the body – could conceal weapons or explosives. Viewed from the soldier on patrol, frisking was part of the job, if an uncomfortable one. From the perspective of a local sitting at a café table watching a security check, an American man frisking an Iraqi woman was an unacceptable violation of cultural norms and a reason to be angry about the continued presence of U.S. troops. Clerics chastised the U.S. practice in their sermons. Sheikh Muhammad Mahmoud al-Samarayee of Baghdad's Imam al-Adham Seminary demanded that Americans station female troops at security checkpoints to frisk women passing through. Members of the al-Rahman mosque staged a protest against the practice of male soldiers frisking Iraqi women. CENTCOM acknowledged the cultural tension and issued a statement requiring patrol units to include, whenever possible, female soldiers who would search local women.[55]

The clash over frisking was part of a vicious cycle that had begun spinning in Baghdad and beyond, threatening to sweep into chaos the work that the 3rd ID had done to rebuild the city and earn the trust of locals after the war. Insurgent attacks on Americans necessitated more security checks, but more security checks meant more close interactions with Americans and Iraqis that violated local social and cultural norms. The violations angered Iraqis and caused them to question the continued foreign occupation. Anger validated insurgency, which motivated U.S. military advisors to increase security efforts.

O'Brien believed relations between Iraqis and U.S. Army troops might have been better had Army units done patrol operations differently. Alpha Company platoons went out in their zone, interacted with locals and gathered information, and then returned to their forward operating base after a couple of hours. As O'Brien reflected on that method, he saw two problems with it. One had to do with soldier morale. It was a strange thing to gear up for patrol, which could be dangerous and could get a soldier killed, go out and do the job, and then go back to the base and watch television. The jarring dichotomy of experiences was difficult for some soldiers to process mentally. The other problem O'Brien recognized was the loss of situational awareness and loss of contacts that occurred every time soldiers went back to the base. While U.S. soldiers were out among the people, those who were willing to cooperate felt protected by the Americans. But when their patrol ended and they left, the Iraqis who had worked with them had to live with the danger of being marked as a collaborator with the enemy. Some stopped talking to O'Brien. He understood the risk of living among the population, but his experiences in Baghdad convinced him that it was the better way.[56]

Overall, the mood in Baghdad shifted as time went on. Interactions between locals and Americans went from calm and friendly to agitated as expectations rose. O'Brien often heard among his Iraqi contacts, "Okay, so what? I'm free but I still have no electricity and no job."[57] One Iraqi friend told Wesley that he had heard McDonald's was coming to Baghdad, just weeks after the war had ended. Wesley understood the expectations, and he had them, too. Iraq had a well-educated population, and Wesley imagined that Iraq could be like Turkey, a developed nation screaming to get out from under a theocratic or political dictator. Iraqi citizens expected money to start flowing into the country as soon as the Americans took control of Baghdad, but they didn't understand that complex bureaucracy that prevented U.S. military officers from paying for things they knew Iraq needed. In the name of anti-corruption, the U.S. government had put so many rules in place for approving contracts and allocating funds that it took weeks for cash to be distributed. Giving a briefcase of cash to every colonel in Baghdad would have resulted in some mismanagement, but it also would have generated more immediate satisfaction that was not possible when a maze of red tape separated a contract from approval. Wesley believed that the benefit of readily available cash for use in Baghdad would outweigh the risk of minor corruption or mismanagement. Instead, the slowness of the American bureaucracy frustrated the Iraqis. At the same time that Wesley saw signs of Iraqi frustration, he also saw signs of insurgency. It was difficult to tell how closely the two were related, but it seemed possible that they fed into each other.

General Jack Keane, Army Vice Chief of Staff and one of Rumsfeld's close advisors, traveled to Baghdad in June and demanded to know why the 3rd ID hadn't gotten the looting under control.[58] Why weren't soldiers arresting more thieves? Was Blount soft on crime in Baghdad? Blount's strategy for managing Baghdad was predicated on the knowledge that the Hussein regime had oppressed Iraqi citizens for decades and what was happening on the streets of Baghdad now that the Ba'athists were gone was akin to a pressure valve being opened. Looting wasn't a constructive way to release pent-up anger and despair, but Blount understood why it occurred. But as his superiors insisted that division security forces arrest more people, Blount wondered if they thought he sympathized with the Arab world too much. Why else would he not order his troops to kick in Iraqi doors and shoot suspected criminals on sight?

Instead of ordering his soldiers to shoot looters, Blount reinforced patrols at hospitals, banks, and power plants to deter potential thieves. But images of a lawless Baghdad appeared in newspapers and on television in the U.S., and some of the blame fell on Blount and the 3rd ID.[59] But the soldiers of the 3rd ID accomplished their mission as they understood it when they took control of Baghdad on April 7. They had done the job of destroying the Hussein regime, and then they had taken on the unexpected mission to win the hearts and minds of Iraqis. For a time, it had seemed as though locals trusted the Americans, but anti-U.S. sentiment grew louder as the summer wore on. Instead of receiving the reward of redeployment, 3rd ID soldiers who had captured Baghdad more swiftly than anyone had expected found themselves with new orders and without a return date. They had not trained for managing postwar urban chaos or handling looters. 3rd ID troops were ready to go home, and their loved ones in the States wanted them back.[60] Frustrated soldiers began venting, sometimes to journalists. Private Matthew C. O'Dell told a *New York Times* reporter, "You call Donald Rumsfeld and tell him our sorry asses are ready to go home."[61]

Back in the U.S., families were aggravated, too. The way they had understood it, brigades would begin returning home after the 3rd ID captured Baghdad. When CENTCOM commanders had addressed the troops in Kuwait before the invasion, they told the soldiers: "Your ticket home is Baghdad." By June it seemed like the 3rd ID would begin redeploying. A brigade of the 1st Armored Division arrived in Iraq, and Blount sent his 3rd Brigade to Kuwait, the first stop toward home. The soldiers turned in their equipment and moved into tents to await transport, but General John Abizaid, who had taken command of CENTCOM, refused to release them. In Washington, Pentagon officials were requesting more troops, so they couldn't send home the ones who were already there without raising Congressional eyebrows. Lawmakers would be skeptical of a request for 50,000 more troops if 20,000 were cycling home. Meanwhile, the 3,000 soldiers sitting idle in Kuwait e-mailed their spouses to explain that they didn't know when they'd be home.

Birmingham rebuked the reporters who seemed to take advantage of distraught soldiers to get a provocative soundbite. He asked one reporter what he would have printed had the soldier been optimistic instead of disgruntled. Would the reporter have written the quote if the soldier had said, "We're here until the mission's complete"? It was in those kinds of moments that Birmingham saw a difference between the journalists who had embedded with the division's forces and been with the troops since training in Kuwait and the "unilateral" journalists who arrived in Baghdad on their own. Some of them seemed to have something to prove and were there merely for a soundbite.[62]

Birmingham wasn't mad at the soldiers who expressed their frustration to reporters. They had thought they'd completed their mission on April 9, and then they accepted the new humanitarian mission and did their jobs. When soldiers heard that they might be going home, only to be told they would have to stay longer, disappointment and anger were normal reactions. Pentagon officials could have helped the situation, Birmingham thought, if they had admitted that it was a mistake to release an early notice of an expected return date only to take it back. To Birmingham, it was cowardly of the Pentagon to not take ownership of that when soldiers started talking.[63]

Conditions on the ground in Iraq gave defense policymakers reason to believe they needed to deploy more troops. Looting had given way to violence that suggested a simmering insurgency. When another brigade of the 1st Armored Division arrived to replace the 3rd ID's 2nd Brigade, this time the 3rd ID troops were not even allowed to go to Kuwait. Blount called Lieutenant General William Wallace, V Corps commander, for an explanation, and Wallace told him that his brigade could go to any of the trouble spots in Iraq, including Fallujah, where clashes between troops of the 82nd Airborne and locals resulted in civilian deaths. The need for more troops in-theater meant the Department of Defense was slow to authorize the rotation of brigades home. Wallace himself was on his way out of V Corps, with Lieutenant General Ricardo Sanchez slated to take command.

Blount wanted to send his soldiers home. But he himself wanted to remain in Baghdad. From what he had observed at ground level, the city wasn't ready to be left alone. If given the choice, Blount wanted to remain in-country with a limited team of officers with whom he worked closely. General Ricardo Sanchez had replaced Wallace at the helm of V Corps, and Blount asked him if he could stay on in Baghdad. Part of what worried Blount was the newness of the men in charge. In addition to Sanchez recently taking control of V Corps, Paul Bremer had replaced Jay Garner as the head of ORHA, and Blount was concerned about how the lack of institutional memory would affect the situation in Baghdad if he left. Hussein was still at large, which was another point of concern. U.S. Special Forces and troops of the 101st Airborne Division assassinated Uday and Qusay Hussein on July 22, 2003, but their father's whereabouts remained unknown. Some U.S. defense officials believed he was in hiding, riding out U.S. occupation, and as soon as the Americans left Iraq, he would return to power.

From the beginning, Blount had understood the 3rd ID's mission to be seizing Baghdad and deposing Hussein. Then the State Department would hire independent contractors to handle the postwar rebuilding and humanitarian efforts. The plan assumed the capture or assassination of Hussein, but as that hadn't happened, the 3rd ID remained in-country longer due to the security threat Hussein posed. When Bremer replaced Garner, U.S. efforts shifted from securing Baghdad and the oil fields to rebuilding the entire country, from infrastructure to political institutions. Blount was confident in his soldiers' ability to handle some of the peacekeeping work, and they had performed well despite having little to no training in that area. But implementing long-term political change was not, in Blount's mind, the job of the 3rd ID or any other military unit.

As Blount and his superiors hashed out the details, June turned into July, and 3rd ID soldiers were still in the Middle East. When families received news that their loved ones would remain in Iraq indefinitely, it hit hard. A group of wives in Hinesville, Georgia, near Fort Stewart, met to vent and commiserate. Several were mothers of small children, and they hadn't seen their deployed fathers for six months to a year – long stretches of time at any age, but especially for the very young. Dominique Marabello's husband, Anthony, was a sergeant in the 3rd ID, and she worried that he would miss their nine-month-old son's first birthday. Sergeant Marabello had already missed other milestones like the baby's first tooth.[64]

Candace Reave, another 3rd ID wife, had bought her husband NASCAR tickets as a welcome home gift, but they sat unused. The race had been on June 5, and Reave bought them believing that her husband, a private first class with the 3rd ID's 315th Scout Headquarters, would be home shortly after the division completed its mission in April. A mother of two who worked at a daycare center, Reave was frustrated by the changing nature of the 3rd ID's mission in Iraq.[65] The way home had been through Baghdad, but now it turned out that getting to the city wasn't enough. Soldiers stayed on to stabilize the city, but that was more difficult than commanders had expected. April, May, and June had passed, and families didn't know if their loved ones would be home before summer ended.

Spouses seeking assistance as they struggled to cope with the indefinite deployment turned to the mental health clinic at Fort Stewart only to be told that no appointments were available before the end of July. First Baptist Church of Hinesville, about a mile away from the base, tried to help, offering a support group for spouses and children of deployed soldiers. Church staff members named the initiative "Operation Enduring Separation," and they hosted activities ranging from beach trips to cooking classes and vehicle maintenance lessons. Some spouses simply asked for prayers. They believed in the 3rd ID's mission, and they were proud of their loved ones, but they wanted them home safe.[66]

Anita Blount understood their worries and their frustrations. She had been an Army wife for more than 30 years by then. As the wife of the division commander, Anita took seriously the responsibility she had as a leader and model for the wives and families waiting at home. After her husband communicated to Fort Stewart families saying that he hoped his soldiers would be home by September, Anita wrote an e-mail to the wives sharing her empathy but also imploring them to not express their disappointment to the press. If the Iraqis learned of their anger, it could embolden them to rise up more violently against U.S. troops and result in an even longer deployment.[67]

The 3rd ID had already suffered 37 casualties since the start of the war, and the uptick in urban violence terrified the families who now knew that their loved ones would remain in Iraq to counter the attacks. Don't let the Iraqis believe that American resolve is weakening, Anita pleaded in her e-mail. The Fort Stewart newspaper *The Frontline* published Anita's letter, and R.L. Brownlee, acting secretary of the Army, thanked her for her words. He hoped her message encouraged 3rd ID spouses to persevere until their soldiers came home.[68]

Brigadier General Bill Weber, the assistant division commander for support, knew another reason 3rd ID soldiers were anxious to go home. The Army's policy was that rotations, or separation assignments, were for one year. Some of the 3rd ID's brigades had rotated to Kuwait months before the invasion and thus had been in Iraq for a year by the time the division completed the attack to Baghdad. About two-thirds of the division had completed their year and were qualified to go home. Not only had the soldiers completed their mission with unprecedented speed, but they had served their time as the Army had dictated.[69]

The soldiers of Charlie Company, 1-64 Armor, were as disappointed and frustrated as their comrades were when they learned of the mission to Fallujah. Jabari Williams thought about his unit, the entire battalion, all that U.S. soldiers had accomplished in a couple of months. He'd rather fight in Iraq than at home, and if taking it to Fallujah was needed to ensure that America's mothers and fathers, sons and daughters, his own young daughter, could live in safety and peace, then he was ready to go. 2nd Brigade had a saying, "Cobras lead the way," and this time, the way was to Fallujah.[70]

9

Fallujah

In late April, in a schoolhouse in Fallujah – a Ba'ath Party and Sunni stronghold about 30 miles west of Baghdad in the "Sunni triangle" – soldiers of the 82nd Airborne Division's Charlie Company had set up their headquarters. They also settled into Dreamland, a former Ba'ath Party vacation resort. Fallujah had been fairly quiet despite its pro-Saddam leanings. Fallujah's new mayor, Taha Bedawi Hamed, was known to be pro-American, as were members of the city council, and incidences of looting had been few. So U.S. military leaders decided to send only a small number of troops to conduct peacekeeping operations. But the 82nd Airborne's presence in Fallujah fanned the flames of anti-American sentiment.

Mayor Taha Bedawi Hamed thought it would be better if U.S. troops established their office on the outskirts of the city to avoid the look of an occupation. City officials had already gotten municipal offices running again, and imams urged their faithful to respect law and order. Leaders were open to working with the Americans, but they preferred U.S. assistance to be behind the scenes. Americans thought differently. Lieutenant Colonel Eric Nantz, 1st Battalion commander, 325th Airborne Infantry Regiment of the 82nd Airborne, believed proximity to the people would allow his soldiers to better understand the needs of the community and communicate with locals. Nantz also knew that the Iraqi Army had stockpiled weapons in schools elsewhere in the country, and using the al-Qaid school as a headquarters would give his troops a chance to search it for arms.[1]

Residents of Fallujah didn't like seeing foreign troops in the school. U.S. security patrols as well as rumors that American soldiers used their night vision goggles to spy on local women exacerbated their frustration with the U.S. presence in their city. Increasingly Nantz realized that Charlie Company's use of the school was hindering his soldiers' efforts to generate goodwill among Fallujah residents, and he requested permission to move to a different location. The troops packed up and prepared to leave, but on April 28, the day before their departure, angry citizens launched a protest of what they considered to be a U.S. occupation of their city. The date was significant – it was Saddam Hussein's birthday.[2]

Around 6:30pm, about 150 protesters gathered at the former Ba'ath Party headquarters in the city center and marched to the al-Qaid school. As the crowd neared the school, its number grew to about 250. It was dark by then, and armed soldiers in the school took positions near the second-floor windows and on the roof of the school. Demonstrators demanded that the Americans leave so that the city could use the school for its intended purpose. Some protesters threw rocks at the school while others shouted angrily in Arabic. Hoping to disperse the crowd, a soldier threw a smoke canister out onto the street, but the protesters remained unfazed.[3]

Shortly after the marchers arrived at the school, shots rang out. Soldiers of the 82nd Airborne returned fire, killing 17 civilians and wounding 70 more. Among the dead were three boys no older than ten. Outrage among Fallujah citizens snowballed, and another protest two days later ended in more violence. A crowd of about 1,000 demonstrators, mostly men, marched on the Ba'ath Party headquarters, nearly breaching the sandbag barrier separating them from the U.S. soldiers on the other side. A few of the protesters carried a banner with the words "Sooner or later, U.S. killers, we'll kill you" written in English on it. Someone in the crowd fired shots, and U.S. soldiers fired back, killing three protesters.[4]

In the aftermath, Taha Bedawi Hamed implored leaders of the 82nd Airborne to launch an investigation into the shooting and pay the families of the deceased. The 82nd Airborne's civil affairs officers refused to pay blood money and replied that the shooting was justified in self-defense. Payment of blood money was customary in Iraqi society, and refusal to do so was a cultural affront that intensified the animosity Fallujah citizens felt toward U.S. troops. In the city's mosques, imams encouraged worshipers to fight Americans. Conversations in the city's market invariably turned to anger at what appeared to be an American occupation.[5] After a series of riots and attacks on U.S. troops, commanders decided to send the 3rd ID's 2nd Brigade to Fallujah. Having completed the daring thunder runs into Baghdad, the soldiers of the 2nd Brigade had the combat experience that commanders hoped would allow them to do damage control and stabilize the situation in Fallujah.[6]

In June, Perkins got a call to go out to 3rd ID headquarters at Baghdad International Airport. He arrived to see a group of generals – Blount, Austin, and John Abizaid, the incoming CENTCOM commander – having a meeting, so he hung back until Blount approached him with some news. Instead of returning to Kuwait, 2nd Brigade was going to Fallujah. "Fallu*what*?" Perkins asked in surprise. Blount explained that there were some problems in the city in Al Anbar Province, west of Baghdad, and he wanted Perkins, Wesley, and a few other 2nd Brigade staff members to ride out to Fallujah and get a feel for the city before bringing the entire brigade in. They took a small armored convoy out, and they immediately picked up a "Wild West" vibe. Fallujah had been an unruly city for decades, a Sunni stronghold subject to repeated Shia insurgencies. Not even Hussein had been able to control Fallujah.

There wasn't a need for another thunder run type of mission because Americans already had access to Fallujah, and in any case, Fallujah was different from Baghdad. There were no Republican Guard troops defending the city; the problems there involved factionalism and insurgency controlled by sheiks and other local leaders. The tensions in Fallujah were personality driven, and Perkins and Wesley realized that they had to get to know who was in charge and what the politics were. They also had to find a place to set up headquarters for the brigade, which would not be an easy feat. Some 5,000 soldiers and nearly as many armored vehicles needed space.

Someone suggested that Perkins try the MEK compound on the outskirts of Fallujah. MEK was the Mujahedin-e-Khalq, an Iranian dissident group that had taken refuge in Iraq after protesting the government of Ayatollah Khomeini in the early 1980s. Founded in the 1960s by leftist Iranian students opposed to Shah Rezi Pahlavi, MEK had participated in the 1979 Iranian Revolution and was placed on the U.S. terrorist list after members were implicated in the murders of U.S. military personnel and civilian contractors working in Iran. Khomeini's crackdowns on civil rights in the aftermath of the Iranian Revolution caused the secular MEK to flee to Iraq, where members fought in the Iran–Iraq War on Iraq's side. MEK leaders eventually established a headquarters in Paris but maintained the large compound in Fallujah. Among MEK's central tenets was gender equality in response to the Khomeini regime's oppression of women, and MEK's military arm boasted a commander corps dominated by women.[7]

Because MEK was on the U.S. terrorist list, its compound in Fallujah had been a bombing target during the invasion of Iraq. But after taking MEK members prisoner, U.S. intelligence agents saw them as sources of information about Iran, and the Americans made peace with MEK. The group's compound had the kind of space needed to house a brigade, and its location on the edge of Fallujah allowed the Americans to avoid moving tanks and Bradleys into the city and angering locals who were already suspicious of, if not hostile to, U.S. troops. Accompanied by a few armored Humvees, Perkins took his M113 up to the compound's entrance gate and introduced himself. A female commander introduced as Madame Parzai met him and ushered his convoy through the checkpoint. The commander offered Perkins and his team tomatoes from the compound garden, and it was the first real food, not MREs, the soldiers had eaten in months. In that moment, it was the best tomato Perkins had ever tasted.[8]

As they toured the compound, Perkins learned that men and women were housed separately to prevent fraternization. MEK was in a state of war, and love and lust would only get in the way of the mission. The place had a Jonestown vibe to Perkins, with founders Massoud and Maryam Rajavi at the center of what seemed to be a cult as much as a dissident group. Perkins didn't know that the compound had been bombed until he entered an auditorium and saw a crater in the center of it, courtesy of a U.S. JDAM missile. Madame Parzai told Perkins it was too bad; the auditorium would have made a great command center. She'd have to take it up with the Air Force, Perkins replied, and in any case, he needed a place to house his brigade. Parzai agreed to allow it, and soon after that, soldiers and their tanks, Bradleys, Humvees, and jeeps made the trek west to Fallujah.[9]

Blount wanted Perkins to connect with locals in Fallujah as soon as possible. His experience building relationships across cultures in Saudi Arabia taught him that his soldiers needed to meet Fallujah residents on their terms if the 3rd ID was going to make things right. Blount planned to make a full-court press to win Fallujah with the hope that then he could finally send his soldiers home. Once 2nd Brigade was settled, Perkins and Wesley went out to meet with Mayor Taha Bedawi Hamed and local clerics and tribal leaders. They sat on couches in Hamed's office and spent three hours discussing the situation in Fallujah and the citizens' needs. The mayor was a Western-educated doctor whose impeccable English made communication easy.

The Fallujans' initial response was that they wanted the Americans out. Perkins made it clear that that was not an option, so the clerics and tribal chiefs tried some different requests. They asked that U.S. soldiers not drive their tanks through the city's neighborhoods in the middle of the night when people were sleeping. They pointed out that it was culturally offensive to Iraqis when a man searched a woman at a security checkpoint. And they explained that the 82nd Airborne won no friends by assuming guilt every time they searched a house, kicking in the door and dragging residents out in handcuffs.

Wesley thought about it from the perspective of the soldiers in the replacement units. Like the soldiers of the 3rd ID, they had trained for war; it was the profession they had chosen. Yet when they arrived in Iraq, instead of performing the duties they had trained for, they policed the recovery. It was part of the broader problems related to rotating units. There was an inherent lack of coherence and evolutionary growth in the rotation of troops. It wouldn't be fair to burden one unit with a deployment that could last years, but rotations made it difficult to create a culture of building up rather than one focused on isolating and leaving. He also understood that insurgency was a real danger by the time the later replacements arrived, especially in places like Fallujah, and that made relationships and trust-building more difficult.[10]

Wesley realized that no one before had bothered to ask the imams' and sheiks' opinions on what the Army could do for the city. Captain John Ives, a military intelligence officer and liaison between the 2nd Brigade and local leaders, agreed that the 3rd ID could meet most of the requests, but there would need to be some give and take. It was on the local officials to make sure women didn't hide weapons under their clothes and suspects didn't resist arrest.[11] Everyone agreed that Fallujah's primary need was law and order, and Perkins agreed to assign platoons to run patrols and train local police. Residents didn't like the patrols coming through the crowded areas of the city like the markets, so Perkins made a deal with the mayor. He agreed to not send patrols into the markets unless there was another attack. If an attack occurred in any of the markets, Perkins would send the tanks and Bradleys back into those areas. It was up to the mayor to keep the insurgents out of the markets if he didn't want 2nd Brigade patrolling there, and while Perkins didn't know what the mayor said to the insurgents, it worked for the rest of the time 2nd Brigade was in Fallujah.[12]

The city's leaders were receptive to Perkins and Wesley, but the broader public in Fallujah was more difficult to bring around. Fallujah was a rough town, a dark town. Driving down the street, Wesley was taken aback by scowls on the faces of locals that sent chills up his spine. English was not widely spoken in Fallujah, and

2nd Brigade relied on locals for hire to be their interpreters. In order to determine an interpreter's trustworthiness, Wesley tried to build friendship first so that the trust would be mutual. He also kept the brigade's linguists nearby so they could pay attention to the translations and check them for accuracy based on their linguistic expertise. If there were other speakers present, he asked them privately what they heard from the conversation, and if the response was consistent with the initial translation, then he figured he could trust the interpreter. Wesley also considered the level of risk an interpreter engaged in when judging loyalty. The general population considered interpreters turncoats, and the pay that interpreters brought home bred jealousy among those who already distrusted them.[13]

For the soldiers of 2nd Brigade, going to Fallujah was not the order they were hoping for. 2nd Brigade had been in-theater since September 2002 when the units deployed to Kuwait. The fight for Baghdad had been emotionally and physically draining, and soldiers and commanders alike thought they'd be going home in May. For Hilms' Alpha Company, the loss of Staff Sergeant Stevon Booker compounded the emotional strain of combat. Any time senior leaders came to speak with the units, the question on every mind was, when are we going home? Hilms knew that Blount was trying to send his division home, and around Memorial Day, word came down that 1st Armored Division was coming from Germany to relieve the 3rd ID. For Hilms and his soldiers, it felt like time to celebrate, and everyone was excited. But then Fallujah began making its way into conversations. There were reports about a unit from the 3rd Armored Cavalry Regiment that had been involved in a firefight, and some soldiers had been killed. One of the medevac helicopters that was trying to evacuate wounded soldiers crashed. It sounded bad all around. Soon 2nd Brigade received the order to go to Fallujah. The soldiers were crestfallen. It was as though they'd had their return ticket snatched out of their hands. Summer 2003 turned out to be the hardest period in Hilms' two decades in the Army, and probably the hardest summer of his life.[14]

As soon as Hilms arrived in Fallujah, he knew it was nothing like Baghdad. It was a desolate, windblown place. The buildings that served as 2nd Brigade's headquarters had been heavily looted and had no windows or electricity. Most striking for Hilms was the atmosphere. Locals were resentful and angry and did not want American occupiers in their country. When Alpha Company went out on patrol, residents stopped and took their shoes off and held the soles of the shoes toward the soldiers, a major insult in Iraqi culture. Hilms had a bad feeling about Fallujah.[15]

The 2nd Brigade's twofold mission to conduct combat operations against insurgents and administer humanitarian aid to Fallujah and surrounding towns was part of a broader effort by Combined Joint Task Force 7 in Iraq in mid to late June called Operation *Desert Scorpion*. The purpose of this operation was to eliminate remaining Ba'athists and anti-coalition insurgents and provide humanitarian aid aimed at helping cities and towns get back up and running again with some degree of normalcy. Locating and seizing hidden weapons caches was a key goal of Operation *Desert Scorpion*. Fallujah was an important site in the operation because of its pro-Saddam sentiment, and the 2nd Brigade called its particular mission Operation *Spartan Scorpion* after the brigade's nickname, "Spartan." The battle-tested soldiers of Spartan Brigade went to Fallujah to test the hearts and minds counterinsurgency concept in Iraq.

Staff Sergeant Jabari Williams of Charlie Company, 1-64 Armor, could feel that the air was thick with hostility when his unit arrived in Fallujah. Locals eyed the troops with suspicion and anger. No one welcomed the Americans as Baghdad's residents had. Charlie Company's tanks and Bradleys did not impress the residents of Fallujah. The only thing they wanted to know was when the Americans were going to leave.[16]

Although Taha Bedawi Hamed and his municipal government had the city under relative control, there still were needs that had not been met since the war for Baghdad ended. The 2nd Brigade developed a plan to help with those needs. Knowing that soccer was the favorite sport of many Iraqis, 2nd Brigade soldiers also repaired soccer fields and handed out hundreds of soccer balls to would-be players hoping to get back out on the pitch. Units distributed gasoline to citizens, while other teams of soldiers cleaned up trash. All of it was aimed at winning hearts and minds, that stalwart philosophy embedded in U.S. counterinsurgency strategy since the Vietnam War.[17]

The 2nd Brigade's efforts didn't ingratiate Fallujah residents to the Americans overnight. Animosity remained, and it manifested in different ways. Sometimes children threw rocks at U.S. soldiers; other times, insurgents shot at them. Perkins met with the mayor daily, and Blount made a trip to Fallujah from Baghdad once a week to meet with city officials. Taha Bedawi Hamed told them it all went back to the blood money. The relatives of those who died in the skirmishes with the 82nd Airborne expected the customary payment.

Blount asked Hamed if payment would stop the residents from shooting at his soldiers, and the mayor replied that he thought it would. Hamed suggested a payment of about $1,500 per deceased victim and $500 for the wounded. The Coalition Provisional Authority had a budget for all things related to stability and security in Iraq, and Blount believed that this qualified. He arranged for the payments to be made to the families, and he continued having weekly meetings with Hamed and the city council to assess the impact of the 2nd Brigade's work in Fallujah. He also met with local imams, who were in tune with the residents and had the power to sway public opinion.

It hadn't helped that the 3rd ID's predecessors in Fallujah had not shown much cultural awareness or sensitivity to the locals. On his first trip to the city, Blount observed a checkpoint where soldiers in body armor and brandishing M16s stopped a family in a van. They motioned everyone out of the vehicle and put the male driver on the ground. The soldiers patted him down and searched the van but found nothing suspicious, so they ordered the family back into the van and waved them on with their rifles. As security personnel at a checkpoint, what they did was acceptable as part of their job. But it revealed to Blount how disconnected those soldiers were from the citizens. He saw anger in the man's eyes and knew the man was lost to anti-Americanism after that. According to Iraqi custom, it was taboo to embarrass a father in front of his family, which is what the soldiers did when they pushed the van driver to the ground. Iraqi social norms also expected a greeting between two interacting parties, but there was no hello or acknowledgment before the soldiers began their search. It was a complicated balance. Had the van been loaded with explosives, pleasantries would have been a waste of time. Yet respect for local customs went a long way in relationship building.

He used that knowledge to handle a situation that had bothered Fallujah residents since the 82nd Airborne arrived. As in Baghdad, citizens had complained about male soldiers searching women at checkpoints. At one checkpoint that Blount observed, female MPs conducted the searches, but because of their uniform and protective gear, the Iraqis couldn't decipher their gender. Blount noticed the locals getting agitated as women passed through the checkpoints, and he realized it was because they couldn't tell that the guard was female. They thought a male guard was patting down local women. Blount told the female MPs to let their ponytails show out of their helmets, and it worked. It was a small thing, but it lessened the animosity the citizens of Fallujah showed toward U.S. soldiers.

In other cases, the tension between Americans and locals in Fallujah resulted in violence that demonstrated how difficult it was for U.S. soldiers and Iraqi citizens to trust each other. One incident occurred during a house-to-house search a team of 2nd Brigade soldiers conducted. A group of soldiers stood watch on a street corner when a white pickup truck pulled up about a block away. Three men jumped out of the back and appeared to be holding something in their hands. One of the soldiers thought the men held rifles, and he fired on them, hitting the truck and killing a seven-year-old child he hadn't seen in the front seat.

The men did have something in their hands. They had been out chopping wood for their mothers to use to heat their stoves for cooking because propane was unavailable. What they had in their hands were their axes and the wood they had just chopped. After the incident, Blount told the battalion commander, a lieutenant colonel who had done a tour in Saudi Arabia and understood local Arab customs, to go meet with the child's father and the tribal chief, express condolences, and pay the blood money. A few days later, Blount learned that the tribal chief offered his support to U.S. troops because of their show of respect for local customs.[18]

Working with Fallujah's mayor and city council, 2nd Brigade commanders and soldiers learned that hospitals needed repairs and electricity, including air conditioning, schools needed repairs and supplies, local police needed training and equipment, and citizens needed medical care and propane for cooking. Captain John Ives was the brigade's government support team leader, and he spent his days in the mayor's office, talking with Hamed and other municipal officials about Fallujah residents' needs. The 3rd ID's efforts in Fallujah were meant to be a partnership with local leaders because the soldiers' presence was meant to be temporary. Ives' team of 15 soldiers went out into the city's neighborhoods to assess infrastructure and interact with locals. Soldier and civilian alike hoped that the troop patrols and U.S. military presence would eventually disappear from Fallujah's landscape.

Police training was one of the initiatives aimed at taking over security duties so that U.S. troops could go home. Elements of the 3rd Military Police Company and the 411th Civil Affairs Battalion taught classes to Fallujah's officers on basic law and order techniques. Working with an interpreter, Staff Sergeant Sean Sullivan led morning classes at the main police station in Fallujah, and he found that many of the officers knew little about policing techniques and most had never seen a pair of handcuffs. Sullivan hoped that his lessons would instill confidence in Fallujah's police officers, and they would be more proactive in their jobs because of it. His interpreter, Fallujah Police First Lieutenant Saad Abdalkareed, believed that his men could do the things Sullivan taught them.[19]

Soldiers of the 382nd Military Police Detachment, an Army Reserve unit out of San Diego, deployed to Fallujah in late July to provide additional policing classes for Fallujah's officers. The new classes focused on human rights issues, including gender discrimination. When Sergeant Emily Frasca walked in to teach a class, shocked Fallujah police stared at her uncomfortably. But they eventually seemed to accept her, which Frasca hoped would translate to acceptance of Iraqi women in positions of authority. Corporal James Martinez taught a class about freedom of expression, which drifted into sensitive territory given local cultural norms. Showing the soles of one's feet was considered rude in Iraqi society, but it shouldn't be an arrestable offense, Martinez told his class of officers. As his students murmured their surprise at his answer, Martinez insisted that he wasn't trying to change local ways, just open minds.[20]

Medical aid was another critical component of the 2nd Brigade's counterinsurgency mission. In Fallujah and in nearby cities and towns, teams of soldiers examined patients, handed out medicines, and worked to improve hospital and clinic buildings. In Habbaniyah, a town west of Fallujah in Al Anbar Province, medics and other soldiers of the 4th Battalion, 64th Armor Regiment – nicknamed "Tuskers" – served eight clinics in their month-long assignment there. Looters had stripped some of the clinics of equipment, supplies, and medicine, so the Tuskers provided half-a-million dollars' worth of replacements. Some of the looters were Hussein's people, which the Tuskers realized when they discovered a stockpile of supplies and pharmaceuticals in one of the dictator's former private hospitals.[21]

It wasn't just looting that kept medical equipment and medicine from the doctors and patients who needed them. There were no coordinated networks between cities or between suppliers and hospitals. Tusker soldiers found a warehouse in Baghdad that had enough supplies to stock Habbaniyah's eight clinics for a year, but no one was making deliveries. Soldiers loaded trucks with supplies and drove them out to the town.[22] Much of the Tuskers' assignment relied on spontaneity. Soldiers stumbled upon the warehouses and stockpiles and made decisions in the moment on where they needed to go and how to get there. Planning ahead was not an option.

First Lieutenant Monica Casmaer, a physician assistant with C Company, was one of the soldiers who cared for patients in

Habbaniyah. It frustrated her to know that the medicines and equipment patients needed existed in Iraq, sometimes in bountiful supply, yet the citizens of Habbaniyah had been without medical care since the war began. The arrival of the Tuskers remedied those problems but also created a new one. Patients only wanted to see the American doctors and medical personnel, thinking they were better than Iraqi doctors. Casmaer knew the myth wasn't true, and she also knew that it would hinder her unit's efforts to turn medical care back over to local doctors and nurses.[23]

To fix the problem, Casmaer and her medics changed how they administered physical exams. They continued delivering supplies to hospitals, but they offered examinations unannounced on neighborhood streets instead of in the clinics. Casmaer hoped the move encouraged patients to see the doctors on staff at the clinics while her medics delivered simple healthcare on the streets. In the evenings, medical teams went with an interpreter into neighborhoods, approached groups on the sidewalk or in a park, and offered medical care. Yet even that approach was not clandestine. As soon as word got out that American medics were offering exams, residents lined up. The Tuskers saw patients until the sun began to set, and then the danger of an ambush became too great for them to risk staying any longer. The soldiers packed up and headed back to headquarters, leaving locals to hope that they would return the next day.[24]

Soldiers of the 1st Battalion, 64th Armor, patrolled near the main hospital in Fallujah and stopped one day to inquire about the hospital's need for equipment and medicine. Based on their assessment, Iraq's reorganized Ministry of Health donated 10 tons of medical supplies to the hospital. Battalions of the 2nd Brigade delivered the shipment to the hospital under the supervision of Rashid Assamarajee, a local Iraqi orthopedic surgeon. Hospital employees and their children helped the soldiers unload the equipment, and they tried out their English on the Americans as they worked. The soldiers did the same with their broken Arabic. Soldiers installed an X-ray machine and a refrigerator for blood storage. Meanwhile, engineers from the 890th Engineer Battalion repaired the hospital's plumbing, electrical, and air conditioning systems. Assamarajee appreciated their work and also hoped that there would be a time in the future where the Americans who came to Fallujah were civilians coming to collaborate on medical issues rather than a military force fighting a war.[25]

For some of the medics, the chance to treat children was especially rewarding. Calm engagements with children offered respite from the chaos and fear that came with the job of combat medics who worked in the midst of battle. In Fallujah, a physician's assistant and a team of medics from 1st Battalion, 9th Field Artillery, as well as a pediatrician from the 26th Forward Support Battalion, set up a temporary clinic for local kids. It was mostly mothers who brought the children to the clinic, and an interpreter explained to them the diagnoses and treatment options. Medics treated more than 200 patients for ailments ranging from dehydration to more serious conditions such as thyroid disease and neurological problems that required referrals to the local hospital. Children played with the soldiers while they waited to be called for their exams.[26]

Task Force 1-64 Armor set out to do some goodwill projects and decided to focus on Fallujah's schools. Williams had attended meetings with local sheiks and municipal leaders about the schools, and he hoped that his unit could help. Hilms and other commanders contacted teachers and principals, but they were reluctant to talk with the Americans. They weren't unfriendly, but they also weren't welcoming. But the task force personnel persisted, and eventually some of the teachers told them that they needed chalkboards for their classrooms. The Americans submitted requests for chalkboards and other school supplies, assuming the materials fell under the category of humanitarian aid. But Hilms heard that the purchasing authority denied the requests, stating that the U.S. occupation wouldn't last much longer and the government was trying to keep costs down. So they never got the chalkboards. The soldiers tried to improvise, and some engineers sanded down a large piece of wood, spray-painted it black, and framed it so that it looked fairly close to a chalkboard. When they brought it to one of the local schools, the teachers were unimpressed. Alpha Company and Task Force 1-64

Armor struggled throughout June and July to make headway with the locals.[27]

Part of the problem was that Fallujans tended to avoid interacting with the Americans. In Baghdad, Hilms usually could find a resident willing to help him, and many spoke English. The Army hired interpreters and contracted with Iraqis for various other services and paid local employees in cash. 2nd Brigade had contracted with a local Iraqi internet service provider to install a Wi-Fi system in the brigade's convention center headquarters. In Fallujah, Hilms struggled to hire interpreters because no one wanted the job. There weren't as many English speakers in Fallujah, but even if someone wanted to do business with the Americans, they were afraid of getting attacked or killed for being seen with the foreign occupiers.[28]

There wasn't much for the soldiers to do in Fallujah to relax, but they found ways to get creative. Task Force 1-64 headquarters had a projector, and one of Hilms' lieutenants would steal it from the office for Alpha Company movie nights. Another lieutenant had brought a stash of DVDs, and the soldiers used the projector to play movies on a wall in the courtyard of company headquarters. Everyone who wasn't on guard duty came out and sat in the courtyard to watch whatever movie the lieutenant had chosen for that night. Even if just for a couple of hours, A Company's movie nights eased the tension that was so palpable in Fallujah.[29]

After the war, U.S. military leaders prioritized electrifying Iraq again. V Corps issued a directive to secure all power stations. In Fallujah, Perkins stationed two Bradleys outside the city's power plant, but the vehicles soon became targets for insurgents. Every couple of days, rebels fired on the Bradleys. One day, Blount went out to visit the power plant, and upon meeting the Iraqi plant manager, he remarked that the manager must feel secure with two U.S. armored vehicles guarding the facility. The plant manager replied that the Bradleys had the opposite effect. Insurgents shot at the Americans, not the power plant or the Iraqis working there. Their purpose was to attack U.S. troops, the manager explained. If the Bradleys went away, the rebels would stop shooting at the power plant. Blount appreciated the manager's perspective, and he ordered the Bradleys to move out. After that, the shootings stopped.[30]

Addressing the need for cooking fuel was another project the soldiers of the 2nd Brigade managed in Fallujah. Although Iraq sat on one of the largest oil reserves in the world, cooking gas was in short supply for a variety of reasons related to the war. Looters attacked and sabotaged the country's oil fields, and bombs took out the high-voltage transmission lines needed to power the refineries. UN sanctions dating back to the first Gulf War also limited Iraq's oil-refining capabilities. Frustration among locals unable to fuel their stoves generated rumors that gas station owners and U.S. troops were stealing fuel.[31]

In order to get propane into Iraqi kitchens, U.S. and Iraqi authorities contracted with the governments of Turkey, Jordan, and Kuwait to import propane tanks into the country. There was no missing the irony in the shipments coming from Kuwait. Iraq's invasion of its oil-rich neighbor in 1990 had set in motion the course of events that led to Iraq's predicament in 2003. The Ministry of Oil coordinated the distribution of propane to cities and towns throughout the country. Soldiers of the 2nd Brigade provided security at the distribution sites in Fallujah and nearby towns.

Knowing some imams in Fallujah preached anti-Americanism in their sermons, Blount ordered his soldiers to make sure they delivered some of the propane shipments directly to the mosques. If the imams associated the desperately needed propane with U.S. troops, maybe they would soften their views on Americans. Initially, a few imams turned the soldiers and their propane tanks away. But the troops persisted, and eventually the clerics relented and took the fuel to distribute to their congregations. Theirs were some of the hardest hearts to win, but Blount's troops had managed to coax some of them over to the American side.

Black-market trade in propane had grown lucrative, with a tank of propane going for 3,000 dinar, more than $9,000, in some cases. Once the Ministry of Oil began importing fuel and established a national distribution system, the cost of a tank dropped to about 250 dinar. Platoons of 1st Battalion, 9th Field Artillery provided security at the distribution sites. When the distribution sites initially opened, chaos ensued as residents desperate for cooking fuel rushed to the sites. Some customers waited as many as three hours to purchase two tanks, the maximum allowed by the ministry. Troops developed an orderly distribution process and worked with an interpreter to talk with residents waiting in line about their community's concerns and needs.[32]

While the troops of the 1-9 Field Artillery helped citizens of the Fallujah area get the propane they needed for cooking, soldiers of Task Force 3-15 Infantry, 1-64 Armor, and 4-64 Armor, along with their interpreters, delivered chickens and canned meat to mosques in and around Fallujah. Not all imams welcomed the soldiers or accepted the donations. When Sergeant Jason McGinn of the 346th Psychological Operations Company and his interpreter arrived at a mosque with a box of frozen chicken, the imam who greeted him declared that his people would rather eat rocks. Meanwhile, groups of young children threw rocks at soldiers driving by. Other imams were polite but still refused the food. McGinn talked with his interpreter about other ways to get the food to the people, and they decided interpreters should go alone with the deliveries. The presence of U.S. troops still angered Fallujah residents, and even food for the needy did not easily win their hearts and minds.[33]

Within a month of the U.S. seizing Baghdad, evidence of a possible insurgency began to emerge. Lack of planning for postwar control of Iraq left a power vacuum in Hussein's wake, and the looting that occurred in the aftermath of major combat bred resentment in Iraqis who expected U.S. troops to do something about the chaos. When Bremer disbanded the Iraqi military, he put more than 300,000 former soldiers out of work. Bremer also banned former soldiers with the rank of colonel or above from serving in the new Iraqi government, and they did not receive retirement pay or benefits, all of this contributing to a rising sense of disaffection among Iraqi citizens.[34] Postwar disillusionment combined with existing sectarian tensions between Sunni and Shia

Muslims in Iraq due to Hussein's discrimination against Shiites. In May 2003, insurgents armed with grenades and guns launched attacks on U.S. troops in Baghdad, Fallujah, and Tikrit, all part of a region known as the "Sunni triangle."[35]

Combat operations occurred concurrently with the humanitarian mission. Soldiers used information about where they had been fired on to determine insurgents' possible hideouts. Commanders chose to initiate raids in the early morning hours when few people were awake and out so as to minimize civilian casualties and disruption to daily life. Reconnaissance conducted before the raids established four objectives in and around Fallujah. Intelligence units had found what they believed to be a Fedayeen training facility, Fedayeen headquarters, a safe house hiding insurgency leaders, and a possible weapons stockpile.[36]

Insurgents fought back, firing on U.S. soldiers from inside houses and yards. Others were positioned on rooftops. The shooting clued troops in to where the insurgents were located, and the soldiers entered the homes to make arrests. At some homes, they also found weapons, sometimes in crates inside the house, other times buried in the yard. Tank heat rounds, sticks of dynamite, AK-47s, rocket-propelled grenades, and flare guns were among the munitions U.S. soldiers found during the early morning raids. At one house, a Bruce Lee poster hung on the wall of a bedroom where soldiers found rifles, knives, and a camouflage jacket. A teenaged boy had tried to flee the scene, but soldiers captured him.[37]

After the 2nd Brigade completed their raids, Fallujah eased into a relative calm. International media outlets still portrayed it as a dangerous city, which perplexed some locals. Cattle farmer Maher Sahdoun stood on his land and looked out onto the Euphrates River, thinking that reporters were conflating Sunni with pro-Hussein. What outsiders didn't understand was that the city's devout Sunni tribes had always opposed the secular, socialist Ba'ath Party. Some Hussein loyalists had fled to Fallujah from Baghdad as the capital city fell, but city leaders had cooperated with 2nd Brigade personnel to identify Ba'athist holdouts. Alaa Hussein Hummadi, a young man who worked at a tire shop on Fallujah's bustling main drag, wondered why the media still called his city a violent place. No one had defaced Fallujah's buildings with anti-American sayings as they had in the fundamentalist Shiite cities to the south. Markets stayed open into the night without any problems. Sheik Hasna al Bouaifan, chief of one of the largest tribes in Fallujah, believed that the Americans had kept their promises to respect locals' mores.[38]

In July, the combination of humanitarian aid and combat action had seemed to diminish the chance that an insurgency might occur in Fallujah. Blount surveyed the city and deemed it a success story for the 3rd ID and America. Schools were open and classes were in session, water and electricity were reaching homes and businesses, soccer matches took place on new fields, and the municipal police force was trained and had the necessary equipment. Children no longer threw rocks at U.S. soldiers. The 3rd ID's engineers had handed over contracting responsibility to Iraqi engineers, putting reconstruction and infrastructure improvements in local hands. Mayor Taha Bedawi Hamed selected three engineers to oversee contracting in the city. During the Hussein era, the Baghdad government funneled infrastructure appropriations directly to contractors, cutting out local leaders' control over which projects got funded.[39]

Fallujah police also took control of their operations from 2nd Brigade troops. Officers took the initiative, gathering outside the mayor's office and requesting autonomy from the U.S. military. Brigadier General Riyadh Abbas Karbool spoke for the group through an interpreter and asked for a chance to prove that Fallujah's police officers could do their jobs without American supervision. They were trained, equipped, and uniformed, and they believed that self-sufficiency was the point of the U.S. mission in Fallujah. Karbool insisted that the officers' desire for independence was not anti-American but rather the desired outcome of U.S. aid to the city.[40]

In July, Blount took the evidence of the 2nd Brigade's success in Fallujah to Lieutenant General Ricardo Sanchez, then commander of V Corps, to show that the 3rd ID had done its job. Fallujah was the poster child for a success story, Blount told Sanchez. The city's police controlled law and order, allowing the brigade to cut their combat patrols by 80 percent. Blount used an example involving a Ba'athist demonstration to show that Fallujah police could handle municipal security. A group of Ba'athists had gathered in the city square and began burning barrels and shooting off rifles. The brigade advisor to the chief of police offered to send in American tanks to shut the protest down, but the police chief took control. He sent some officers, and told the Americans that if things got out of hand, he'd call for backup. American MPs stood ready to provide assistance, but local officers quelled the protest without incident.

This instilled confidence in Blount that Fallujah was ready to operate with minimal U.S. intervention. In mid-July, 2nd Brigade units began leaving the 22 sites around Fallujah where they had been stationed. U.S. soldiers continued to patrol the city, but they had handed over the bulk of the security duties to local police and a militia run out of the mayor's office. Colonel Joseph DiSalvo, the new commander of 2nd Brigade, established the militia, called the Fallujah Protection Force, to augment the city's police department. Mayor Hamed selected the militiamen from Fallujah's largest tribes, and Captain John Ives organized the training program for the recruits.[41] There were other signs of success, too. Imam Mekki Hussein Kubeisi had once regularly denounced the U.S. military to the faithful who prayed at the Abdelaziz Samarrai mosque, but he had softened his tone after observing the work of the 3rd ID. He admonished worshipers to not tolerate violence in Fallujah. Mayor Hamed heard from citizens who were happy to see fewer U.S. troops and military vehicles on the city's streets.[42]

As they spent more time in Fallujah, 2nd Brigade commanders realized that the anti-Americanism on display earlier wasn't primarily coming from Hussein loyalists. That element existed, but most of the animosity stemmed from perceived cultural slights. Attacks against U.S. soldiers had plummeted, not because brigade troops had taken out Ba'athists but because they had made an effort to understand local customs. That was a testament to Blount's leadership. Meeting Iraqis on their terms when appropriate was not idealistic but pragmatic. It was a method for achieving stability in Fallujah by recognizing that the point of America's continued presence in Iraq was to bring order and, hopefully, a lasting peace.

Blount suggested to Sanchez that the Army leave a civil affairs team and an engineering unit in the city to assist as needed, but the 2nd Brigade could finally go home. The mayor was in charge, and he had Fallujah running smoothly. Let Fallujah show the world that the U.S. was in Iraq to help temporarily, not to occupy, Blount told Sanchez. Combat troops were no longer needed in Fallujah, which had been a hotbed of pro-Saddam sentiment. The city's residents had settled into a cautious tranquility.

Sanchez was skeptical. He wanted to leave a combat force in Fallujah. Blount reminded him of the violence that occurred when the 82nd Airborne was there, but despite the bad blood, it was the 505th Parachute Infantry Regiment of the 82nd, as well as elements from the division's headquarters, that relieved the 3rd ID troops leaving Iraq in September.[43] Violence erupted not long after the troops arrived. On September 12, as Fallujah police chased a car carrying suspected insurgents, the chase sped past the 82nd Airborne's base. Troops opened fire, killing eight Iraqi policemen and a Jordanian guard while shooting up the police cars the U.S. had provided to Fallujah's force under the 3rd ID's supervision. Since the fallen Fallujah officers were on the Americans' side, it was the worst friendly fire incident since May 1.[44] Meanwhile in Baghdad, a suicide bomber drove a truck loaded with explosives into the Canal Hotel building and killed 22 people, most of them UN employees and representatives, including Sergio Vieira de Mello, head of the UN mission in Iraq. In the aftermath of the bombing, the UN withdrew most of its 600 staff members from Iraq.[45]

More violence between 82nd Airborne troops and Fallujah civilians occurred at the end of September. A pickup truck driving toward a security checkpoint near Fallujah slowed as it approached. Believing they were under attack, soldiers fired on the truck, killing four civilians including two women.[46] Troops struggled to maintain control of the city as more insurgents poured in from the west, and

Mayor Taha Bedawi Hamed and the city's chief of police resigned amidst the unrest. In February 2004, the 1st Marine Division arrived to replace the 82nd Airborne. Fallujah once again became a site of major anti-American and anti-coalition sentiment, and the Marines fought in some of the heaviest urban combat there since the Tet Offensive fighting in Hue during the Vietnam War.

Bremer's decision to disband the Iraqi Army fed into the insurgency. Resistance leaders, including Ba'athists, former Republican Guardsmen and Fedayeen soldiers, and foreigners linked to Al-Qaeda, found the idle young men lingering at a café or sitting around playing cards and offered them money to shoot Americans. The insurgents provided the weapons and the cash; for the former soldiers, it was income. As ex-servicemen, they knew how to operate the guns. 3rd ID troops captured some of them, and they shared their stories during questioning. U.S. policy toward the Iraqi Army was shortsighted in its view of the regulars, but had a long-term impact on Iraqi society as it contributed to the instability that lasted for nearly a decade after the U.S. had toppled Hussein's regime.

Conclusion

Captain Andrew Hilms worried about his soldiers the whole time they were in Fallujah. They had accomplished their mission to Baghdad better than anyone could have imagined, and they had been so proud of that. But all they had been through to get there had left the soldiers emotionally and physically exhausted. Then the Army sent them to Fallujah, and to Hilms, it felt like being forgotten. Hilms felt on edge in Fallujah, and his soldiers did, too. The residents were inhospitable, and the way they looked at the soldiers as they passed by on the streets unnerved Hilms. His guard was always up. He never felt sure that the suspicious glances and angry looks wouldn't become attacks.

Making it worse was a lack of communication with loved ones at home. There was no phone or internet service available to the soldiers in Fallujah. Hilms didn't talk to his wife the entire time he was there. In the midst of it all, changes of command occurred, upending the continuity within the brigade. 1-64 Armor battalion's command sergeant major, Colonel David Perkins, was promoted to brigade sergeant major. Perkins, who had led 2nd Brigade from Kuwait through the thunder runs, had been reassigned to a job at the Pentagon. Hilms was supposed to change out his command in May, but he implored his superiors to let him finish out Alpha Company's tour with his soldiers. He wanted to see them home.[1]

And Hilms did. In early August, 2nd Brigade commanders got word that they would depart Fallujah en route to Fort Stewart. Heavy equipment transporter systems arrived in Fallujah, and the soldiers had 24 hours to load up and get ready to go. When the plans were made for the return trip to Kuwait, someone mentioned IEDs, improvised explosive devices, a new form of weaponry that had begun to materialize in-theater. Most soldiers didn't know what they were or how they worked, and that made it even more crucial that drivers exercise caution on the road to Kuwait. Commanders decided that crews would ride in their vehicles on the Heavy Equipment Transporter System (HETS). For the entire 350-mile trip, tank crews stayed in their positions – driver, commander, gunner, loader. As they made the two-and-a-half-day trip, no one knew that IEDs would define the next decade for U.S. soldiers stationed in Iraq.[2]

2nd Brigade set out from Fallujah early in the morning and made it to An Nasiriyah that night. They set up camp and stretched out, relieved after an entire day inside their tanks. Everyone was thirsty because they had run out of cold water on the trip. But they lay down and slept, and the next morning, the soldiers rose with the sun and made the trek all the way to Kuwait. And then they were back at Fort Stewart, after almost 11 months in the Middle East.[3]

When the soldiers were preparing to leave Fallujah, a group from V Corps came to the city and spoke to the master gunners and other soldiers about their experiences in the fight for Baghdad. They asked about the equipment and how it operated, if they'd had any trouble, what they found to be most effective. Staff Sergeant Jabari Williams was one of the master gunners they spoke with, and he learned later that the Army made changes based on the conversations in Fallujah. To Williams, it meant that the American soldiers who died in battle did not die in vain. Army leaders were using everything that happened in Operation *Iraqi Freedom* and using it to learn and develop more effective strategies and tactics. Williams was proud not just of Charlie Company but of the entire 1-64 Armor battalion. The Army began teaching thunder-run tactics at the sergeant major academy, and that was all Task Force 1-64.[4]

Captain Charles O'Brien ended up changing command while his Alpha Company, 3-69 Armor, was still in Baghdad. He hated to leave his soldiers, but he was ordered out so that another captain could get combat experience. After saying goodbye to his company, O'Brien got a ride to Baghdad International Airport and hopped on a C-130 to Kuwait City. From there, he bummed a ride with the Marines and landed stateside at the Marine Corps Air Station in Cherry Point, North Carolina, about 24 hours after leaving Baghdad. O'Brien hadn't talked to his wife since early February, just after she had given birth to their first child, a girl. The last time he had seen her, she was pregnant and standing in their driveway, waving goodbye to him.[5]

His wife was a high school teacher, and O'Brien had wanted to surprise her with their own *An Officer and a Gentleman* moment in which he would walk into her classroom and carry her away à la Richard Gere and Debra Winger, but as he stood there in Cherry Point, he knew he just needed to talk to her, so he called her and told her he was home. When O'Brien finally walked through the door, hugged his wife, and held his infant daughter for the first time, he decided he would never leave his family again. After 14 years in the Army, he wrote his resignation letter. Then he reconsidered. O'Brien believed in God, and he believed God would continue to take care of him, so he ended up staying in.[6]

Reflecting back on his interactions with the Iraqis in Baghdad, O'Brien realized that the Americans had not understood that the impact of sanctions, the embargo, and no-fly zones in the decade leading up to Operation *Iraqi Freedom* had affected Iraqis' views of the U.S. He wished the Army had included cultural awareness on nationalism, tribal communities, the differences between Sunni and Shia from a religious standpoint, the different factions among Iraqi Christians, and other aspects of Iraqi culture in the pre-war training.[7] If nation building was to be part of U.S. military interventions, then soldiers needed opportunities to learn about the people with whom they would interact. In the case of Operation *Iraqi Freedom*, they needed to understand Iraq's recent history to make sense of why locals viewed them with suspicion. Many Iraqi citizens likely perceived 3rd ID soldiers as detached occupying troops on patrol, not allies there to help Iraq achieve political stability. Of course, there was the larger question of whether military troops, or the

U.S. government, should embark on nation-building projects at all. The U.S. invasion of Iraq in 2003 definitively showed the superiority, professionalism, and confidence of the U.S. military in war fighting. The quagmire that Iraq became for the U.S. after the defeat of Saddam Hussein illustrated how disorganized, vague, and insecure U.S. policymakers are regarding nation building.

As Birmingham prepared to leave, he didn't have a good feeling about Iraq's potential stability. He believed in the American soldier and in the U.S. military, and he still marveled at how swiftly and decisively the 3rd ID had charged to Baghdad. Division forces had seized bridges and kept them intact, they seized Tallil Air Base and Baghdad International Airport and kept both intact, and they seized downtown Baghdad and kept it intact, in no small measure due to Blount's gamble on the thunder runs. He'd had high hopes for Iraq's future in the first month after the 3rd ID had arrived in the capital city. At that time, it had seemed like Americans were on the right track for turning control over to the Iraqis sooner rather than later. When Bremer arrived and insisted upon hardcore de-Ba'athification at the expense of the trust building that Blount and his division had done, the CPA sowed the seeds of insurgency.[8]

Brigadier General Bill Weber flew back to the United States on July 19, 2003, a day after his 50th birthday. In the weeks and months that passed, Weber found himself thinking with profound respect about what the 3rd ID had accomplished in Iraq. The division had lost 44 soldiers and about 300 were wounded, which was tragic for the loved ones of each individual numbered among the casualties. Yet it was phenomenal how small the numbers of dead and wounded were considering the division started with 20,000 soldiers who fought in intense combat every day for 21 days. The soldiers didn't have a day off in those three weeks, and Weber felt deeply proud and grateful whenever he thought of the servicemen and women of the 3rd ID. They reflected their leaders well, and Weber was also grateful for the commanders with whom he served in Operation *Iraqi Freedom*. They had trust and confidence in each other and in their soldiers, who did everything their commanders asked of them and more, in Weber's estimation.

As the years went by after the invasion, Weber watched with dismay as the insurgency overshadowed the 3rd ID's work.[9]

The insurgency that had been responsible for alarming attacks, including the bombing of the Canal Hotel in August, continued to grow. As Blount and other 3rd ID leaders had suspected, disaffected Sunnis who had been forced out of the military or marked due to their Ba'athist allegiance had joined the insurrection that included Syrians and other foreigners who had arrived in Iraq to fight the Americans that spring. On October 26, the first day of Ramadan, as motorists and pedestrians clogged Baghdad's streets in the morning rush, five suicide car bombs exploded in the city within an hour of each other. The terrorists hit the office of the International Red Cross, three police stations, and the health ministry, killing 42 people.

The attack followed a rocket strike on the al-Rashid Hotel in Baghdad's green zone, an area that was assumed to be secure, around six o'clock the previous morning. Deputy Secretary of Defense Paul Wolfowitz was staying there and survived the attack, but Lieutenant Colonel Charles H. Buehring was killed, and 15 others were wounded. Buehring was from North Carolina, a husband and father of two young boys and a Boy Scouts leader in his spare time when not deployed. A career officer with 18 years in the Army, Buehring had been serving as the chief of the military information support team with the Coalition Provisional Authority when he was killed.[10] The attacks continued into November 2003, when a suicide bomber in a tanker truck exploded at the Italian military police headquarters in An Nasiriyah and killed 28 people. Later that month, insurgents used Strela missile launchers, likely purchased on the black market, to down three U.S. Black Hawk helicopters and one Chinook, killing 39 soldiers and injuring 31. With the attacks, the insurgents made clear that they were targeting Americans and coalition forces and Iraqi police and government officials who had been cooperating with them. The attacks came to be known as the Ramadan Offensive.

In response to the growing insurgency, the U.S. called in air strikes targeting suspected ambush sites and mortar launching positions. The year ended with U.S. forces capturing Hussein, who had been hiding out in a hole on a farm near Tikrit, his hometown. American soldiers had killed Uday and Qusay in Mosul back in July. Things were quieter at the beginning of 2004, but in February, suicide bombers attacked the headquarters of Kurdistan Democratic Party and the Patriotic Union of Kurdistan, killing 70 people. The following month, terrorists killed 140 Shia worshippers observing the Ashura holiday in Baghdad and Karbala. The prime suspect was Abu Musab al-Zarqawi, a Jordanian-born jihadist who had orchestrated the attack on the Canal Hotel in August 2003. Al-Zarqawi struck again in May 2004, when his organization assassinated Ezzedine Salim, leader of the Iraqi governing council. Al-Zarqawi later pledged his allegiance to Osama bin Laden, and his group became known as Al-Qaeda in Iraq.[11]

U.S. forces fought two battles in Fallujah in 2004. The first, in April, was a response to the murder of four Blackwater employees who were delivering food to a private food service company. After killing the four contractors, insurgents burned their bodies and dragged them through the streets of Fallujah before hanging the bodies from a bridge over the Euphrates River. The photographs that were sent to international media looked like Mogadishu. Americans and coalition forces fought the Second Battle of Fallujah in November to wrest control of the city from Al-Qaeda in Iraq. Al-Zarqawi and some of his associates fled Fallujah during the fighting, but the city remained an insurgent stronghold in Anbar province.

Although the entire 3rd ID had returned home by September 2003, it wasn't the end of the division's engagement with Iraq. In January 2005, the 3rd ID became the first U.S. Army division to serve a second tour there. The units returned to Baghdad, and soldiers conducted security and humanitarian missions while also fighting against insurgents. January 2005 was an important month in Iraq's post-Hussein history because citizens voted in their first election since the war. The election filled the 275 seats in Iraq's Transitional National Assembly, a council tasked with selecting a prime minister and writing a new constitution.[12] Iraqis voted along sectarian lines, and a conservative and religious Shiite coalition assembled by Ayatollah Ali al-Sistani won control of the government. Sunni voter turnout was low, in part because Sunni leaders encouraged their followers to boycott the election and in part due to heavy violence in Sunni areas. The election of a majority Shia government intensified Sunni resentment and fueled the insurgency.[13]

During the 3rd ID's second tour, the division lost 103 soldiers killed in action. After completing a yearlong deployment, the 3rd ID handed responsibilities over to the 4th ID and went home in January 2006. After the division's second tour, the Army reorganized the 3rd ID to include a fourth brigade and transformed the brigades into self-sustaining brigade combat teams that could operate separately from the full division. In January 2007, 1st Brigade Combat Team deployed to Iraq with Multinational Forces Iraq-West in Anbar Province under the command of the 1st Marine Division, making it the first Army unit to serve three terms in Iraq. As part of "the surge" of 2007, 3rd Brigade deployed to the areas surrounding Baghdad in March, and 2nd Brigade deployed to the region southeast of Baghdad in May.

Some 3rd ID soldiers who had been part of the 2003 invasion with Blount ended up going back to Iraq. About a year after returning to Fort Stewart, Captain Alexis Perez-Cruz of 2-69 Armor received orders that his unit was going back to help build a new Iraqi Army. Paul Bremer had disbanded Hussein's army, so there was no nationwide security force. Without security, it would be difficult, if not impossible, to establish a stable government. Perez-Cruz had come home in August 2003, and the Army sent him to the Maneuver Captain's Career Course, from which he graduated in 2004. He deployed to Iraq with 2-69 Armor's Security Forces Training Team as the executive officer in Baqubah, north of Baghdad in Diyala Province, where he led training exercises and conducted operations with an Iraqi Army battalion.[14]

Perez-Cruz found it ironic that he was training the Iraqi soldiers, officers, and battalion commanders who had fought against him in his previous deployment. Yet over time he developed friendships with many of the Iraqi soldiers and officers he worked with, and he became very close with some of them. His job was to train them, and he wanted them to be successful. They lived together and ate meals together; and they cried together when they lost one of their own. One of the company commanders received a phone call in which the person on the other end told him to meet Perez-Cruz at a certain location, and when the company commander arrived, he walked right into a booby trap that mortally wounded him. Perez-Cruz watched him die on the operating table.[15]

Baqubah was known for its orange groves along the Diyala River, and insurgents used them as hideouts. When Perez-Cruz's Iraqi battalion went into the groves to clear them out, he went with them. He'd carry rounds of explosives out of the groves and think to himself that it probably wasn't the smartest thing to do, but he did it because he wanted to be there for his men. That's what they had become to him. They were his soldiers. But being in an insurgency meant that there were people who looked like his soldiers but who wanted to kill him and incapacitate the new Iraqi army. It was exhausting mentally as well as physically.[16]

Perez-Cruz eventually went home again, but he returned to Iraq for a third tour, this time as a company commander assigned to Baghdad. By that point, locals recognized Perez-Cruz. A cousin of someone he had trained would come up to him on the street and say they remembered him from when he was in their town. Baghdad was a city of millions, but the Americans stood out, especially those who kept coming back. He thought about how to measure the Army's success in Iraq. The 3rd ID had done its job beyond expectation, but Perez-Cruz likened it to what international relations experts called a catastrophic success. The U.S. Army was successful in its short-term mission to capture Baghdad and depose Hussein, but it was catastrophic in the long term. Having toppled Iraq's government and disbanded its military, the Americans had to take charge of civil affairs and security until they could turn those operations over to Iraqis.[17]

Williams returned to Iraq with the U.S. Army three more times – in 2005, 2007, and 2009. In 2005, he deployed as a platoon sergeant with Charlie Company, 3-15 Infantry to deal with violence in Sadr City, a suburb of Baghdad. Like Perez-Cruz, he also trained Iraqi soldiers, focusing specifically on non-commissioned officers. As one himself, Williams stood as an example of what a non-commissioned officer could accomplish. He had enlisted in the Army right out of high school at age 18, distinguished himself as a leader and a master gunner, and earned bachelor's and master's degrees along the way. Establishing a stable non-commissioned officer track in the Iraqi Army could give young Iraqi men the chance at the kind of future Williams had achieved.

Each time he went back, Williams saw the gains and the losses. Shopkeepers opened their stores every day and served their customers. Markets were full of merchants selling their goods to support their families. American soldiers handed out humanitarian aid, but it didn't mean that the recipients liked them. Sometimes, the same people accepting aid during the day were the ones shooting at U.S. troops at night. Williams and his soldiers grappled with the difficulty in distinguishing between friend and foe in Iraq. Some of the insurgents were foreign fighters from Syria, but they knew how to blend in with the populace. The Americans even had to be careful with the Iraqi soldiers they trained. "Blue on green" killings were ones in which an Iraqi soldier in a U.S. training program turned on his American mentor.[18]

It was the knowledge of those kinds of incidents that left Williams pondering the purpose of U.S. military efforts in Iraq. Without a doubt, he believed in service to his country, and he impressed upon his soldiers the magnitude of their commitment. If not for love of country and comrades, then why join? Why fight? But when they did their jobs with honor, when they worked to train Iraqi soldiers to fight for their own freedom, and those soldiers turned around and shot at them, how could the American troops be expected to keep going? Williams saw and was himself among America's sons and daughters sent to a foreign country with the expectation that the people they were helping appreciated the aid that American soldiers rendered.[19] It was a reasonable expectation, yet it seemed increasingly out of reach as more time passed since the 3rd ID demolished Hussein's regime.

In 2008, William Grimsley returned to Iraq for his second tour, this time with Multi-National Division Baghdad. His office had received a tip from local police about the location of an IED on the north side of Sadr City, and Grimsley went out with a company to try and clear it. They spotted it and got out of their vehicle to see if they could disable it, but the IED went off. Grimsley happened to be standing closest to it, and the blast shattered his ear drum and shrapnel tore up his face. Luck was on Grimsley's side that day, and his injuries required only some stitches.[20] Grimsley recognized his good fortune and also pondered an IED's ability to harm soldiers and civilians.

After the 2003 invasion of Iraq, Perkins did two more tours in-country, the third as commander of the 4th Infantry Division, and was the last division commander to pull out of Iraq in December 2011. As Perkins reflected on Operation *Iraqi Freedom*, he realized that U.S. policymakers, military leaders, and troops didn't really know what they were getting into when they decided to invade Iraq. A question Perkins often pondered was, "Did Iraq make Saddam, or did Saddam make Iraq?" He learned that leaving a country was much more difficult than invading one. The Americans had been so focused on Hussein as a threat to Kuwait and Saudi Arabia that they did not pay enough attention to Iraq's internal dynamics that played into how Hussein maintained and exercised power. The animosity between Sunni and Shia that had been building for generations was an internal security threat that Hussein had to suppress, and for that reason, perhaps the bellicosity about weapons of mass destruction was aimed not at the U.S. but at Shia Iraqis and their Iranian allies.[21]

Part of the problem for Americans, as Perkins saw it, was their inability to accept that things were done differently in other parts of the world. The engineers who went out to try to restore electricity in Baghdad after U.S. forces captured the city were baffled by the convoluted control systems that made it easy to turn on power in some neighborhoods, yet more complicated for other neighborhoods. It was because Hussein used electricity and other municipal services to control the masses. The Sunni Mansour district got power quickly, but in Shia-dominated Sadr City, engineers had to go to multiple switching stations before they could restore power there. The engineers complained to Perkins about the inefficiency of the system, but efficiency wasn't the point for Hussein. Control was. It was as though Hussein knew insurgency and sectarian violence was just under the surface, and if he relinquished control, the tension would explode into an uprising. Perkins likened it to a nuclear reactor: Rods inside the reactor control nuclear fission, but if the rods are pulled, nuclear meltdown occurs. In Iraq, it was as though Americans pulled out all the control rods, and the tensions that had always been there burst through the surface.[22]

Perkins had seen similar situations elsewhere during his career with the Army. He had served 14 years in Europe, including as a battalion commander with 1-63 Armor in Macedonia and deputy chief of staff for General John Abizaid when he commanded the 1st Infantry Division in Kosovo. The initial problem had been Serbians committing genocide, but after the Americans arrived, Albanians used their presence to justify attacking Serbians. Josip Broz Tito had been the strongman in Yugoslavia, but once he was gone, the tensions frozen beneath the surface thawed and erupted. U.S. forces didn't create the conflicts or insurgencies, but they removed the controls that had suppressed them.[23]

When Perkins was battalion commander in Macedonia, he was part of a UN mission patrolling the border between Serbia and Macedonia, a breathtaking outpost in the mountains. One day, he received a call in the command center from one of the patrol units that had met some Macedonian village women who told them that the Serbs had killed all their military-aged men and kidnapped all their boys. Another genocide, Perkins thought with dismay. He mobilized a quick reaction force and boarded a helicopter to head to the village. Meanwhile, a lieutenant on the ground had a translator with him, and he began talking to more of the women, who talked aggressively about all the bad things Serbians had done to their village. But as the lieutenant looked around, he saw no sign of conflict or destruction. Buildings were intact, nothing appeared to have been burned or ransacked. He asked the women when the Serbian attack had occurred. One hundred years ago, they replied. Villagers had been waiting for the Americans to show up and help them get revenge on the Serbs. It didn't matter that the bloodshed had happened a century ago; the villagers believed they deserved retribution, and they believed that the Americans were on their side. Perkins saw similar dynamics in Iraq, where Shia and others who had been oppressed by the Ba'athists saw their chance for revenge when the Americans arrived and blew the lid off the powder keg.[24]

Upon returning from Iraq, General Blount was assigned to a position at the Pentagon. His Middle East experience was invaluable to the commanders and war planners who determined what was needed on the ground in Iraq and Afghanistan. Blount had envisioned the possibility of a three-star promotion, but such opportunities depend on numerous alignments, some of which were out of his control. Getting a three-star appointment required a ranking position to open up. There had been speculation that McKiernan was going to be moved to another position, opening up the Third Army commander position, which was a three-star assignment. But McKiernan ended up staying at the helm of Third Army as Blount was returning from Iraq.

Blount was hoping for a three-star Corps command but was told there were only two, and they were already slated. If he was going to stay in the Army, Blount wanted to command troops. He loved working with soldiers and didn't want to give up what was one of the most rewarding aspects of his career. He talked with Anita about his options; they made every decision about their lives as a team. She wasn't ready to have her husband deployed to the Middle East again and was ready for a forever home. In Anita's mind, 33 years was enough to give to the Army, and she told him so. Blount retired as a two-star general, the commander who had taken the 3rd ID into the heart of Baghdad more quickly and decisively than anyone had thought possible.

Blount remained engaged in defense issues in his retirement, working as a lobbyist and forming a consulting company. He and Anita settled in Hattiesburg, Mississippi, building a home that they designed together modeled after the architecture they loved in Saudi Arabia. Blount made regular trips to Washington, DC, for work, and on one of them, a friend invited him to lunch with a Kurdish-American real estate developer. Intrigued, Blount accepted the invitation. When he arrived at the restaurant, he and the Kurd looked at each other as they shook hands and said, "I know you."

In the days following the 3rd ID's triumphant arrival in Baghdad, ORHA head Jay Garner had brought some Kurdish associates into the capital city to discuss ways to involve northern Iraq's Kurds in rebuilding the nation. One evening, a unit of 3rd ID soldiers out on patrol stopped a group of Iraqi men standing outside a house holding AK-47s. The rifles, the enemy's weapon, were banned in Baghdad. As the soldiers questioned the men, several others came out of the house, also carrying AK-47s. No shots were fired, but the U.S. troops confiscated the weapons and went inside to search the premises. They found a suitcase full of money and more rifles, which they confiscated, and then went back outside and arrested the men.

The next morning, Garner called Blount about the incident. It turned out that the armed men were security guards for a Kurdish-American businessman who was in Baghdad to advise the Americans on integrating the Kurds into Iraq's political life so they wouldn't try to break away and form an independent Kurdish state. The businessman, Rubar Sandi, was the son of a Kurdish tribal chief who had been tortured by Hussein's henchmen after they confiscated his property. Hussein's troops had also tortured and killed Sandi's mother and sister. Garner told Blount to return the money and weapons and apologize.

Not knowing what to expect, Blount dressed in his battle gear and rounded up a couple of MPs to ride with him to the Kurdish headquarters in Baghdad. The general walked in, introduced himself to Sandi, and began to apologize for the previous night's incident. In perfect English, Sandi told him not to worry. He understood the job of a warrior, especially in Iraq. He himself had been fighting Hussein for years. Blount thanked Sandi for understanding, returned the money and rifles, and said goodbye.

It was the last they saw of each other until their chance meeting at lunch in Washington. As they ate and talked, Sandi told Blount his story. When he was a teenager in 1976, he had been part of a militia that fought against Hussein and the Ba'ath regime. Hussein's soldiers raided Sandi's village and captured some of his relatives, but he escaped to Iran. Sandi sought asylum in the U.S. and wound up in Maryland where he got jobs cleaning hotel rooms and working at a 7-Eleven. A coworker told him that computers were all the rage, so Sandi bought a book about computers and read it as he worked the counter at 7-Eleven. A customer noticed the book and told Sandi that there was an IBM office just down the road.

All the little moments were opportunities that Sandi seized. He sent an application to IBM but got no response, so he went directly to the office and asked to see the president. When the secretary told him absolutely not, Sandi sat down in the waiting area and waited until the president came out of his office to leave for the day. The president was startled and called security, but he let Sandi talk. In the end, the president gave Sandi a job in the mailroom. Three years later, Sandi was a division chief in charge of establishing IBM in Saudi Arabia.

While in Saudi Arabia, Sandi's father contacted him and told him to return to Iraq to help fight Hussein. He did as his father asked and spent a year fighting the Ba'athist military. CIA agents took note of Sandi, and when U.S. policymakers began planning for war in Iraq, they contacted Sandi for a Kurdish perspective. President Bush hosted Sandi at the White House, and Sandi wrote a paper called "The Phoenix Plan" which outlined his thoughts for what the U.S. needed to do to be successful in Iraq. It would be a difficult project at every level. Sandi warned the Americans to take democracy building slowly. Iraq was a pressure cooker under Hussein's control for so long, and ripping the lid off would have disastrous consequences, Sandi asserted.

Sandi suggested replacing Hussein with a benevolent dictator who would have control of the country but also had the best interests of the citizenry in mind at all times. Restarting the economy would have to be the first priority, starting with giving every young man a job. State Department officials invited Sandi to join their Iraq working groups, and Pentagon staffers pored over his pages. But then Chalabi came around and insisted that Sandi was wrong. Chalabi's Free Iraqi Forces could handle it. All the Americans needed to do was get rid of Saddam and send money, and Chalabi and his people would do the rest. It was more in line with what Bush and Rumsfeld wanted to hear, so they shelved Sandi's report.

By that time, Sandi had gotten rich through real estate investments, banking, and defense contracting. He remained engaged in post-Hussein Iraq by funding the development of hotels, a security guard service, a convention center in Baghdad, and telecommunications infrastructure through his company, the Sandi Group. Sandi regularly traveled to Baghdad where he reveled in the Wild West atmosphere. Men carrying briefcases full of cash met in hotel lobbies to make deals. Armed guards wearing sunglasses and Kevlar vests stood watch. Baghdad's streets bustled with workers and shoppers and traffic. Stores and cafés were open again. But rumors floated over tea and coffee that Syrians were smuggling weapons into the country, and sometimes exploding bombs interrupted the conversations.

After reconnecting with Blount in Washington, Sandi asked him to join forces on a construction company in Saudi Arabia. Blount agreed, and the venture began a partnership that took the American and the Kurd to many parts of the globe together where security consultants were needed. They traveled to Malaysia and Moscow, where a Russian mogul wanted to upgrade the security at his aluminum factories. Former KGB agents had been doing the job, but they were old and didn't seem to put in much effort. When Blount and Sandi arrived at the mogul's office, two security guards armed with Uzis escorted them to an elevator, and a guard bearing a machine gun took them up to the office.

Inside the office, Blount and Sandi found the mogul sitting at his desk looking dejected. He motioned for them to sit, and then he confided that he wasn't happy. He felt constantly threatened; he had too many enemies. But he hadn't meant for the meeting to be a therapy session. He needed security at his mining operations in Guinea. The Russian mogul owned three bauxite mines, two towns, two railroads, and a port in Guinea, and the locals were starting to rebel. The mayor of one of the towns threatened to take over the mine.

The Russian asked Blount and Sandi to fly to Guinea, assess the situation, and then give him a proposal. They needed to go immediately, and the Russian would have offered his private jet if he wasn't already scheduled to fly to Hong Kong for business. He thought for a second, and then he picked up the phone and dialed his friend, Vladimir Putin. Next thing they knew, Blount and Sandi were boarding one of the Russian presidential aircraft. The plane's cockpit and communications room were off limits to Blount and Sandi, but the vodka flowed freely into their glasses as the plane transported the men to Africa.

Sandi also took Blount to Erbil, Iraq, where his brother owned a hotel, and then they went to Sandi's hometown. He had invested in building an orphanage and a hospital there, and the town residents welcomed Sandi back as a hero. He introduced Blount as the general who ousted Hussein, and that made the general very popular. An elderly Kurdish man approached Blount, hugged and kissed him, and thanked him. The man broke down in tears as he told Blount that he had spent 20 years battling Hussein, and had lost seven sons in the fight.

For Grimsley, one of the biggest mistakes Americans made in trying to plan for involvement in postwar Iraq was clinging to the idea that Iraq could become a democracy that looked like the U.S. Iraq, with its educated populace and abundance of wealth-producing natural resources, had the potential to be a stable nation. Under the control of a dictator, the intelligentsia and professional classes had little to no control over the affairs of the state, but freed from his grip, Iraqi educated elites might have been able to build a secure nation on their own terms. It might not have been in the image of the U.S., but in Grimsley's mind, that didn't matter. He had no love for Shia cleric and politician

Muqtada al-Sadr, but he respected al-Sadr's willingness to tell the Americans to step aside and let Iraqis take full control of their own nation-building.[25]

From Perkins' perspective, Americans were hamstrung in part by their fear of being seen as conquerors. He recognized that in Iraq, the Middle East, and other parts of the world, the U.S. *was* the conqueror. When an armored column rolls into a capital city and takes down a regime, it's hard to see the owner of that army as anything but a conqueror. It was up to the conqueror to fix what was broken, but in Iraq, Americans didn't want to be seen as an occupier or conqueror, so they focused on turning control over to Iraqis more quickly than was prudent. Perkins believed a better approach would have been to treat Iraq as the U.S. had treated Germany and Japan after World War II, where the U.S. had committed large occupying forces for the purpose of rebuilding the defeated nations. Instead, the Americans took the lid off of several centuries of animosity and expected the Iraqis to sort it out.[26]

The Iraqis understood this better than the Americans did. On one of his tours of duty in Iraq, Perkins was responsible for negotiating a status of forces agreement, and during an exchange with a senior Iraqi military official, Perkins threatened that U.S. troops would leave if the Iraqis didn't sign the agreement. The Iraqi general, who happened to be Shia, called his bluff and advised Perkins that U.S. forces should leave and try again – but next time, come in and really take control. Occupy the country and commit to fixing it rather than blowing everything to chaos and then leaving. Perkins appreciated the general's response. It was not humane or helpful to remove control from a volatile situation and then step back and allow mayhem to take over. In a regime change mission, the conqueror sometimes must become the regime for a while, but U.S. policymakers could not come to grips with that vis-à-vis Iraq.[27]

Perkins believed the U.S. had two options for handling Iraq, neither of which policymakers chose. One was to invade, take out the Hussein regime, and then set parameters for Iraqi independence without U.S. involvement. Iraqis would be free to set up whatever government they wanted and conduct their affairs however they saw fit as long as they didn't support terrorism or threaten neighboring countries. If Iraqis crossed either of those lines, then the U.S. military would return with full force. The second option was to take out Hussein and then stay and not worry whether the world saw the Americans as liberators or occupiers or imperialists. U.S. troops had fought a war and won, and the subsequent mission involved taking control of Iraq's oilfields, electricity grids, government system, and economy – not to steal, but to get the country back up and running. It would likely take several years, and during that time, the Americans would call the shots. When the country was stable by all possible measures, the Americans would turn control over to the Iraqis. U.S. policymakers decided on a third option, which was to take out the Hussein regime, decapitate the security apparatus, and then sit back and watch from the sidelines, wondering why the whole thing didn't work out so well.[28]

During the planning stage for the war in Iraq, Secretary Rumsfeld pushed a proposal involving fewer troops fighting a quick mission and then returning home. General Shinseki told the Bush administration that the fight in Iraq would take more than what Rumsfeld had proposed, and Perkins agreed. Perkins said to Wesley one day, "I wish the administration would let us do the war thing. We've got the war thing down. What we need the administration to focus on is the transition."[29] The political and strategic leaders needed to figure out how to leverage the momentum and decisive performance of the U.S. military to move into a transition phase where building a new nation was possible. As the 3rd ID left Iraq, Wesley looked back and saw the insurgency, and he thought about how a decisive military victory gave way to an ambiguous transition performance. He couldn't help but feel discouraged, and his disillusionment grew in the subsequent months because the insurgency got worse.[30]

Wesley thought about how well the troops had done in the kinetic campaign. It was an unprecedented armored land movement in terms of distance and speed, and it was decisive. He thought about the soldiers and how well they adapted to the changing environments, from flat desert in Kuwait and southern Iraq, to agricultural lands and villages, to the major metropolis of Baghdad. Wesley was proud of all that the soldiers had achieved based on wisdom and independent decision-making. Not he, nor Perkins, nor any other commander could take credit for what individual soldiers achieved in the moment. Their precise application of power would make any American cry because it was so well adjudicated. The insurgencies and complex problems that followed stole some of the luster from the soldiers' accomplishments during the drive to Baghdad, and that bothered Wesley long after he had returned home.

There were glimmers of light every now and then. When Wesley was in Fallujah in the summer of 2003, he befriended the executive to the mayor, who also served as an interpreter for 2nd Brigade. In 2005, Wesley returned to Fallujah as a battalion commander, and he found his Iraqi friend. Their young daughters had become pen pals in the years between Wesley's deployments. It was an example of the goodness in human connection that popped up every once in a while in the midst of strife.

Like Perkins, he thought about post-World War II Germany and Japan and the effectiveness of the U.S. occupations of those countries. There were lessons from those operations that strategists and policymakers needed to learn or relearn, but in Iraq, they allowed the insurgency to distract them. Politicians tended to think of transition as an afterthought, but reflecting on his time in Iraq, Wesley concluded that transition needed to be a primary thought for war planners.[31]

Yet Germany and Japan after World War II were unique in that both were vanquished nations. It wasn't just that their armies were defeated, but the entire society accepted the defeat culturally and politically. Devastating bombing campaigns that killed civilians vanquished the two countries, but 21st-century military technology made it easier for Americans to attack enemy troops without harming civilians. Without a doubt, limiting civilian casualties is a positive development in war fighting. But with precise application of force comes fewer wars that result in a vanquished enemy. As the

Americans advanced to Baghdad, Iraqi civilians retreated to their homes and watched the war play out from their windows. U.S. missiles were not aimed at civilian targets, and the war produced fewer civilian casualties than World War II did. But it also did not result in a vanquished Iraq, and an unvanquished citizenry might be less willing to comply with the demands of a foreign power. Wesley didn't know how to solve this conundrum, and the solution was not to return to a method of war fighting that caused more civilian casualties, but he wondered how policymakers might handle postwar transition if they considered the perspectives of an unvanquished enemy.[32]

In Wesley's mind, part of what made it difficult for policymakers to prioritize transition was the concern over whether the Iraqis and the rest of the world would see the Americans as liberators or occupiers. To liberate is to empower, to free, to grant independence. The way Wesley saw it, as soon as the Americans decided that everyone and everything associated with the Ba'ath Party was bad, they made themselves occupiers. In the literal sense, to liberate the Iraqis meant to let them decide which political party was legitimate, but the American way, at least in the last half-century or so, aimed to eradicate institutions and rebuild them in the image of the U.S. That's what an occupier does.

General David Petraeus, who had commanded the 101st Airborne Division during the 2003 invasion of Iraq, now commanded coalition forces. In the interim, Petraeus had used what he had learned in Iraq in 2003 to revise the Army's counterinsurgency manual, and an updated edition was published in 2006. The new manual emphasized a "hearts and minds" approach to counterinsurgency, and understanding local culture was key. Petraeus wrote that excessive force had the potential to be counterproductive, while economic security and "restored hope" were some of the strongest counterinsurgency weapons. When it came to responding to unrest, sometimes the best course of action was to do nothing rather than overreact.[33] Former enemies also had a role to play in counterinsurgency, a theory Petraeus put into practice when he approved a plan to recruit Sunnis into militias to protect central Iraq from Shiite militias, including those loyal to Shiite cleric Muqtada al-Sadr.[34] Sometimes counterinsurgency meant getting out of the way and letting locals handle things.

Blount and the 3rd ID had done or advocated for all of those things in the spring and summer of 2003. One of Blount's top priorities had been to pay all the municipal employees so that they would return to work. Another priority had been restoring electricity. Division engineers reestablished power in Baghdad's neighbors, sometimes after going house to house and knocking on doors to find the man with the key to the local power plant. 3rd ID troops were visible in Baghdad. Company commanders met with principals and teachers to determine how the division could help their schools, and then soldiers arrived to make repairs and deliver supplies. Blount toured hospitals and spoke with doctors about medical needs. In Fallujah, Perkins and Wesley worked closely with municipal leaders and imams to address citizens' needs and concerns. 2nd Brigade had done so well to calm the city that Blount had held up Fallujah as an example of a successful security and stability mission.

When Bremer arrived to lead the Coalition Provisional Authority, replacing ORHA and Jay Garner in May 2003, Blount tried to convince him that the division's approach to the situation in Baghdad was the right one. Bremer questioned the systems in place for fuel and food distribution, but Blount emphasized that the Americans didn't need to mess with what Baghdad citizens already had in place because it was working. Although Bremer was intent on disbanding the Iraqi army and shunning Ba'athists, Blount argued that it would be better to use the soldiers' and officers' skills and knowledge to create a new Iraqi army. In any case, Blount reasoned, turning loose 350,000 men who knew how to fire a weapon and leaving them with no income and no job prospects guaranteed that at least some of them would join the growing insurgency. To combat looting, Bremer ordered troops to shoot looters. Blount took flak from General Jack Keane, the Army's vice chief of staff, for ordering the opposite. But Blount wanted his soldiers to understand why Iraqi citizens were looting. For decades they had been trapped under the heavy hand of Hussein and the Ba'ath Party, and they saw the riches Hussein and his associates enjoyed. Meanwhile, the lights didn't always come on in some neighborhoods. Now that Hussein was gone, looting was a release of the pent-up frustrations that Iraqis could not express during his reign lest they be targeted for harassment, arrest, torture, or even death. Shooting an Iraqi for stealing a fancy sofa from Hussein's palace would serve only to show that Americans were out of touch with the Iraqis and would breed resentment towards U.S. troops. All of the recommendations published in the 2006 version of the Army's counterinsurgency field manual the 3rd ID had been doing since 2003.

Yet by the time the hearts and minds concept was codified in the new field manual, the insurgency had ravaged Iraq for three years. Sectarian violence and jihadism had exploded and was the main cause of turmoil in the country. Bombings killed Sunni and Shia, and reprisals created a vicious cycle of violence and death. Terrorism made Iraq even bloodier. The Islamic State in Iraq (ISI), an offshoot of al-Zarqawi's AQI, used car bombs and suicide bombers to kill hundreds of people. To counter the jihadists, the U.S. Army began recruiting and arming Sunnis to fight the terrorists. Some of the recruits had worked with Al-Qaeda but left disillusioned by the indiscriminate killing of Iraqis. There was no guarantee that the Sunni fighters wouldn't turn their American guns on the people who armed them or use them against their Shia adversaries. The commanders involved suspected some of the Sunnis of having attacked U.S. troops in the past. But the Army, including 3rd ID units, had built relationships with Sunnis in Anbar province since 2003, and commanders hoped they would have the same success here. By the end of 2007, violence had decreased due to the troop surge, but the human cost for the Americans was nearly 900 soldiers killed. The death toll made 2007 the deadliest year for the U.S. in Iraq.

Americans began turning over control to Iraqis the following year. In February 2009, President Barack Obama announced that the U.S. would begin withdrawing troops and end combat missions by August 2010. He made good on that promise, and the last U.S.

combat troops left Iraq on August 19, 2010. In December 2011, the remaining U.S. military advisors and personnel withdrew, officially ending the U.S. military intervention in Iraq. ISI's bombings had become routine in Baghdad and other cities, and Sunni insurgents repeatedly protested the government of Prime Minister Nouri al-Maliki, a Shiite. In 2013, ISI merged with a Syrian jihadist group to form ISIS, the Islamic State in Iraq and Syria. Six more years of fighting saw ISIS gain and then lose swaths of territory across the two countries. As recent as 2022, CENTCOM conducted missions with Iraqi and Syrian security forces to find and arrest ISIS holdouts.

In September 2003, about a month after 2nd Brigade had returned to Fort Stewart, Hilms hosted Alpha Company at his house for a cookout. As the men stood in a circle drinking beer and reminiscing about Iraq, Hilms overheard Ronald Gaines talking to another platoon sergeant about the April 5 thunder run. Gaines had been in the tank ahead of Hilms, and Hilms was leaning out of his turret and fighting. If the captain was out fighting, then the sergeants and everyone else had to be out fighting, Gaines reasoned, but damn, it was bad out there. Each time Gaines looked back, he hoped Hilms would have dropped into his hatch so he could do the same and not feel like he was being a coward. Hilms laughed and replied that the reason *he* had kept fighting was because his soldiers were fighting. The courage of men like Gaines inspired him to stay up in his turret despite the danger. Hilms knew that soldiers drew courage from their leaders, but he also knew from experience that leaders were inspired by and drew courage from their soldiers. His soldiers' courage had made Hilms a better leader.[35]

Courage flowed both ways between soldiers and commanders when they trusted each other. In 21 days, the 3rd Infantry Division accomplished a feat no one had expected. Pentagon officials estimated that the trek to Baghdad would take months, but the 3rd ID completed it in three weeks. The division lost 33 soldiers in its first Iraq tour, each loss huge for the loved ones of the deceased, but a small total number of casualties. Courage and trust at all levels of command fueled the division's soldiers and officers during those 21 days and the days that followed. It required courage in soldiers and battalion and brigade commanders to lead an armored charge into a metropolis, and it required the trust of division and corps commanders to let it happen. Courage was dodging fires to move fuel trucks lest they explode. Trust was giving the go ahead to an idea that sounded crazy. Hearts and minds counterinsurgency required courage and trust, and the 3rd ID as a division embodied both qualities.

With the creation of the Coalition Provisional Authority, trust ceased to be a central operating force in how the Americans conducted the transition. Shoot looters. Ostracize former Iraqi soldiers and officers. Orders such as these were rooted in suspicion, of Iraqis but also of Blount, who advocated for completely opposite approaches. He was the Arabist, and the CPA did not appreciate Blount's insistence on looking at things from the Iraqi point of view. To do so was a risk; it required courage and trust. Absent both, nation building becomes a military occupation with a purpose or an end. From SJA Lyle Cayce's view, Blount's decision making was not insubordination, it was innovation. It was audacity.[36] The 3rd ID made history when it completed its mission in only 21 days. It was the fastest armored advance the world had ever seen, surpassing what had previously been the most impressive armored drive, that of General George Patton's Third Army in World War II. Patton's troops fought from the Falaise Gap to the Rhine River, but it took them four months to cover a distance that the 3rd ID traversed in two weeks.[37] But Pentagon officials and policymakers in Washington were not prepared for what came next, and there was no postwar plan for what the Americans would do in Iraq after the 3rd ID and other military units completed their mission of capturing Baghdad. The blunders of the CPA dragged the U.S. into a quagmire in Iraq that lasted seven years and inflamed the terrorists that formed the Islamic State. For SJA Lyle Cayce, and likely for others too, this was the biggest sin of the war.

Appendix: Third Infantry Division Order of Battle, Iraq 2003

V Corps
- 1st Brigade
  - 2nd Battalion, 7th Infantry Regiment (Mech)
  - 3rd Battalion, 7th Infantry Regiment (Mech)
  - 3rd Battalion, 69th Armor Regiment
  - 1st Battalion, 41st Field Artillery Regiment (155SP)
- 2nd Brigade
  - 3rd Battalion, 15th Infantry Regiment (Mech)
  - 1st Battalion, 64th Armor Regiment
  - 4th Battalion, 64th Armor Regiment (Tuskers)
  - 1st Battalion, 9th Field Artillery Regiment (155SP)
- 3rd Brigade
  - 203rd FSB 3rd Brigade Combat Team (Mech)
  - 1st Battalion, 15th Infantry Regiment (Mech)
  - 1st Battalion, 30th Infantry Regiment (Mech)
  - 2nd Battalion, 69th Armor Regiment
  - 1st Battalion, 10th Field Artillery Regiment (155SP)
  - 1st Battalion, 39th Field Artillery Regiment, 3rd ID DIVARTY
- 3rd Squadron, 7th Cavalry Regiment

Acronyms

ARAMCO	Arabian American Oil Company
ARCENT	U.S. Army Central
CENTCOM	United States Central Command
CERP	Commander's Emergency Response Program
CFLCC	Combined Forces Land Component Command
CPA	Coalition Provisional Authority
CSG	Corps Support Group
DARCOM	Department of Army Materiel Development and Readiness Command
DIA	Defense Intelligence Agency
FSB	Forward Support Battalion
GCC	Gulf Cooperation Counci
HEMTT	Heavy Expanded Mobility Tactical Tanker
IED	Improvised Explosive Device
INC	raqi National Congress
JIACG	Joint International Agency Cardinal Group
JSM	al-Jamaa al-Salafiya al-Muhtasiba
KDP	Kurdish Democratic Party
LAV	Light Armored Vehicle

LSA	Logistics Support Area
MEK	Mujahedin-e-Khalq (Iranian dissident group)
MOOTW	Military Operations Other Than War
MOPP	Mission-oriented Protective Posture
MP	Military Police
MRE	Meal-Ready-to-Eat
NIC	National Intelligence Council
NSC	U.S. National Security Council
NTC	National Training Center
OPEC	Organization of Petroleum Exporting Countries
OPM-SANG	U.S. Army Office of the Program Manager–Saudi Arabian National Guard
ORHA	Organization for Reconstruction and Humanitarian Assistance
PUK	Patriotic Union of Kurdistan
RPG	Rocket-propelled Grenade
SCIRI	Supreme Council for the Islamic Revolution in Iraq
TEC	TeleEngineering Kit
TOC	Tactical Operations Center
WMD	Weapons of Mass Destruction

Notes

INTRODUCTION

1 Interview with General Buford "Buff" Blount, July 2022, Bassfield, MS. Unless otherwise noted, all interviews were conducted by the author.

CHAPTER 1

1 Details about the Blount family history come from the research of Ms. Lisa Blount, sister of General Buford Blount.
2 Duplin County, NC – Warren Blount, Petition – Revolutionary Service. Delamar Abstracts, pp. 1–200. Legislative Papers Relating to Revolutionary Service, NC Archives.
3 Family history conducted by Lisa Blount.
4 Family history conducted by Lisa Blount.
5 "David Blount killed, wife critically hurt," *Hattiesburg American*, October 28, 1972, A1.

CHAPTER 2

1 Louisa Dris-Ait-Hamadouche and Yahia H. Zoubir, "The U.S.–Saudi Relationship and the Iraq War: The Dialectics of a Dependent Alliance," *Journal of Third World Studies*, Spring 2007, Vol. 24, No. 1, p. 109.
2 Michael T. Klare, "Political Economy of U.S. Arms Sales," *Social Scientist*, June 1976, Vol. 4, No. 11, p. 4.
3 Hannu Kyrolainen, "An Analysis of New Trends in the U.S. Military Training and Technical Assistance in the Third World," *Instant Research on Peace and Violence*, 1977, Vol. 4, No. 3/4, p. 175.
4 Klare, "Political Economy of U.S. Arms Sales," p. 14.
5 Vinnell Corporation advertisement, *Defense Transportation Journal*, Oct. 1982, Vol. 38, No. 5, Forum Issue, p. 17.
6 Lincoln P. Bloomfield, Jr., "Saudi Arabia Faces the 1980s: Saudi Security Problems and American Interests," *The Fletcher Forum*, Summer 1981, Vol. 5, No. 2, p. 262.

7   Kyrolainen, "An Analysis of New Trends in the U.S. Military Training," p. 172.

8   Edward M. Kennedy, "The Persian Gulf: Arms Race or Arms Control?" *Foreign Affairs*, October 1975, Vol. 54, No. 1, p. 4.

9   Kennedy, "The Persian Gulf: Arms Race or Arms Control?" p. 26.

10 Eli Melki, "Mecca 1979: The mosque siege that changed the course of Saudi history," BBC News, December 27, 2019, https://www.bbc.com/news/stories-50852379

11 Melki, "Mecca 1979."

12 Melki, "Mecca 1979."

13 Lincoln P. Bloomfield, Jr., "Saudi Arabia Faces the 1980s," p. 250.

14 Mansoor Akbar Kundi, "Security Integration Under the Gulf Cooperation Council," *Pakistan Horizon*, January 1989, Vol. 42, No. 1, pp. 93–99.

15 Scott Anderson, "The True Story of Lawrence of Arabia," *Smithsonian Magazine*, July 2014, https://www.smithsonianmag.com/history/true-story-lawrence-arabia-180951857/

16 Anderson, "The True Story of Lawrence of Arabia."

17 "CENTCOM's Saudi Security Fixes Were Geared Toward Too Small a Threat," *Inside the Pentagon*, July 11, 1996, Vol. 12, No. 28, pp. 4–5.

18 "CENTCOM's Saudi Security Fixes."

CHAPTER 3

1   Justin Marozzi, *Baghdad: City of Peace, City of Blood. A History in Thirteen Centuries* (Boston: Da Capo Press, 2014), pp. 1–5.

2   Marozzi, *Baghdad*, p. 244.

3   Marozzi, *Baghdad*, pp. 294–298.

4   Marozzi, *Baghdad*, p. 298.

5   Marozzi, *Baghdad*, p. 313.

6   Marozzi, *Baghdad*, p. 333.

7   Marozzi, *Baghdad*, pp. 342–352.

8   William K. Polk, *Understanding Iraq* (New York: Harper Perennial, 2005), p. 128.

9   Polk, *Understanding Iraq*, p. 129.

10 Pierre Razoux, *The Iran-Iraq War* (Cambridge, MA: Belknap Press of Harvard University Press, 2015), p. 495.

11 Polk, *Understanding Iraq*, p. 130.

12 John Robertson, *Iraq: A History* (London: Oneworld Publications, 2015), p. 299.

13 Robertson, *Iraq*, pp. 300–301.

14 Razoux, *The Iran-Iraq War*, p. 510.

15 U.S. Department of State, Office of the Historian, "The Gulf War, 1991," https://history.state.gov/milestones/1989-1992/gulf-war.

16 U.S. Department of State, "The Gulf War, 1991."

17 U.S. Department of State, "The Gulf War, 1991."

18 Catherine Dale, *Congressional Research Service Report for Congress: Operation Iraqi Freedom: Strategies, Approaches, Results, and Issues for Congress*. Foreign Affairs, Defense, and Trade Division, March 28, 2008, p. 6.

19 Dale, *Service Report*, p. 12.

20 Dale, *Service Report*, p. 13.

21 Dale, *Service Report*, p. 14.

22 Ahmed Chalabi obituary, The *Guardian*, November 4, 2015, https://www.theguardian.com/world/2015/nov/04/ahmed-chalabi

23 *Report of the Select Committee on Intelligence on the Use by the Intelligence Community of Information Provided by the Iraqi National Congress* (Washington, DC: U.S. Government Printing Office, 2006), p. 6.

24 *Report of the Select Committee on Intelligence*, p. 7.

25 *Report of the Select Committee on Intelligence*, p. 10.

26 *Report of the Select Committee on Intelligence*, p. 12.

27 *Report of the Select Committee on Intelligence*, pp. 14–15.

28 *Report of the Select Committee on Intelligence*, pp. 16–17.

29 *Report of the Select Committee on Intelligence*, p. 18.

30 *Report of the Select Committee on Intelligence*, p. 25.

31 *Report of the Select Committee on Intelligence*, pp. 30–34.

32 Richard Hanania, "Ahmad Chalabi and the Great Man Theory of History," *War on the Rocks*, December 17, 2018, https://warontherocks.com/2018/12/ahmad-chalabi-and-the-great-man-theory-of-history/.

33 Dale, *Service Report*, p. 16.

34 "Interview: Lieutenant General William Scott Wallace," PBS *Frontline*, February 26, 2004, https://www.pbs.org/wgbh/pages/frontline/shows/invasion/interviews/wallace.html

35 Wallace PBS *Frontline* interview.

36 Dale, *Service Report*, p. 15.

37 Dale, *Service Report*, p. 17.

38 Memo from Assistant Secretary of Defense Philip Rodman to Secretary of Defense Donald Rumsfeld, August 15, 2002, Subject: "Who Will Govern Iraq"? National Security Archive, George Washington University, https://nsarchive2.gwu.edu/NSAEBB/NSAEBB328/II-Doc18.pdf

39 Kevin Whitelaw, "After the Fall," *US News and World Report*, December 2, 2002. From Gen. Blount's personal archive.

40 Whitelaw, "After the Fall."

41 Dale, *Service Report*, p. 19.

42 Whitelaw, "After the Fall."

43 State Department cable, "Future of Iraq Expert Working Groups," July 8, 2002, https://nsarchive2.gwu.edu/NSAEBB/NSAEBB163/index.htm.

44 Dale, *Service Report*, p. 2.
45 Nora Bensahel, Olga Oliker, Keith Crane, et al., *After Saddam: Prewar Planning and the Occupation of Iraq*, 1st ed, RAND Corporation, 2008, http://www.jstor.org/stable/10.7249/mg642a.
46 Dale, *Service Report*, p. 21.
47 State Department memorandum, February 7, 2003. To: Undersecretary Dobriansky, From: Craner, Dewey, Simons. Subject: Iraq Contingency Planning, National Security Archive, George Washington University, https://nsarchive2.gwu.edu/NSAEBB/NSAEBB163/index.htm.
48 Stanford Center for International Security and Cooperation, Mapping Militants Organizations, "Ansar al-Islam," Stanford University, https://cisac.fsi.stanford.edu/mappingmilitants/profiles/ansar-al-islam
49 U.S. Senate Select Committee on Intelligence, *Report on Prewar Intelligence Assessments About Postwar Iraq* (Washington, DC: U.S. Government Printing Office, 2007), pp. 2–3.
50 U.S. Senate Select Committee on Intelligence, *Report on Prewar Intelligence* Assessments, p. 6.
51 U.S. Senate Select Committee on Intelligence, *Report on Prewar Intelligence* Assessments, pp. 7–8.
52 U.S. Senate Select Committee on Intelligence, *Report on Prewar Intelligence* Assessments, p. 9.
53 U.S. Senate Select Committee on Intelligence, *Report on Prewar Intelligence* Assessments, pp. 11–12.
54 U.S. Senate Select Committee on Intelligence, *Report on Prewar Intelligence* Assessments, pp. 17–22.

CHAPTER 4

1 Interview with General David Perkins, Jan. 5, 2023.
2 Interview with General David Perkins, Jan. 5, 2023.
3 Col. Gregory Fontenot, *On Point: The United States Army in Operation Iraqi Freedom* (Fort Leavenworth, KS: Combat Studies Institute Press, 2004), p. 29.
4 Interview with General Bill Weber, May 19, 2023.
5 Interview with Maj. Erik Berdy, Operation Leadership Experiences Project, Combat Studies Institute, digital recording, January 20, 2006. Fort Leavenworth, Kansas. Interviewed by John H. McCool. (Digital recording stored on CD-ROM at Combined Arms Research Library, Fort Leavenworth, Kansas.) https://cgsc.contentdm.oclc.org/digital/collection/p4013coll13/id/226/
6 Interview with Maj. Erik Berdy, Operation Leadership Experiences Project, January 20, 2006.

7   Interview with Maj. Erik Berdy, Operation Leadership Experiences Project, January 20, 2006.

8   Interview with Col. Roberta A. Woods, Operational Leadership Experiences Project, Combat Studies Institute, digital recording, May 18, 2006. Fort Leavenworth, Kansas. Interviewed by Lynne Chandler Garcia. (Digital recording stored on CD-ROM at Combined Arms Research Library, Fort Leavenworth, Kansas.) https://cgsc.contentdm.oclc.org/digital/collection/p4013coll13/id/531

9   Interview with General Bill Weber, May 19, 2023.

10   Interview with General Bill Weber, May 19, 2023.

11   Interview with General Bill Weber, May 19, 2023.

12   Interview with General Bill Weber, May 19, 2023.

13   Interview with General Bill Weber, May 19, 2023.

14   Interview with Colonel Andrew Hilms, Fort Stewart, Georgia, June 2019.

15   Interview with Lieutenant Colonel Alexis Perez-Cruz, Fort Stewart, Georgia, June 2019.

16   Interview with Colonel Andrew Hilms, Fort Stewart, Georgia, June 2019.

17   Interview with Lieutenant Colonel Alexis Perez-Cruz, Fort Stewart, Georgia, June 2019.

18   Interview with Lieutenant Colonel Alexis Perez-Cruz, Fort Stewart, Georgia, June 2019.

19   Interview with Command Sergeant Major Jabari Williams, Fort Stewart, Georgia, June 2019.

20   Interview with Command Sergeant Major Jabari Williams, Fort Stewart, Georgia, June 2019.

21   Fontenot, *On Point*, p. 76.

22   Interview with Maj. Charles O'Brien, Operational Leadership Experiences Project, Combat Studies Institute, digital recording, February 24, 2005. Fort Leavenworth, Kansas. Interviewed by Maj. Kent Strader. (Digital recording stored on CD-ROM at Combined Arms Research Library, Fort Leavenworth, Kansas.) https://cgsc.contentdm.oclc.org/digital/collection/p4013coll13/id/90/rec/3

23   Interview with Colonel Mike Birmingham, December 12, 2022.

24   Interview with Colonel Mike Birmingham, December 12, 2022.

25   Interview with Colonel Mike Birmingham, December 12, 2022.

26   Interview with Colonel Mike Birmingham, December 12, 2022.

27   Interview with Colonel Mike Birmingham, December 12, 2022.

28   Interview with General David Perkins, January 5, 2023.

29   Fontenot, *On Point*, pp. 48–49.

30   Fontenot, *On Point*, p. 49.

31 Fontenot, *On Point*, p. 50.
32 Interview with General William Grimsley, April 2023.
33 Interview with Colonel Lyle Cayce, March 2023.
34 Interview with Colonel Lyle Cayce, March 2023.
35 Robert Burns, "War's Opening: Air assault to open way for ground attack," *Associated Press*, undated. From General Blount's personal archive.
36 David Espo, "Bush to Saddam: Leave Iraq or Else," *Associated Press*, undated. From Gen. Blount's personal archive.
37 Richard Wolffe and Michael Hirsh, "War and Consequences," *Newsweek*, February 2, 2003. From Gen. Blount's personal archive.
38 Espo, "Bush to Saddam: Leave Iraq or Else."
39 Christopher Dickey, "Perils of Victory," *Newsweek*, February 2, 2003. From Gen. Blount's personal archive.
40 Evan Thomas, "Fear at the Front," *U.S. News and World Report*, February 3, 2003, p. 34.
41 Interview with Command Sergeant Major Jabari Williams, Fort Stewart, Georgia, June 2019.

CHAPTER 5

1   Fontenot, *On Point*, p. 86.
2   Interview with General Blount, February 15, 2019.
3   Interview with General Blount, February 15, 2019.
4   Interview with General Blount, February 15, 2019. ·
5   "Interview: Lieutenant General William Scott Wallace," PBS *Frontline*, https://www.pbs.org/wgbh/pages/frontline/shows/invasion/interviews/wallace.html
6   Interview with General Blount, February 15, 2019.
7   Robert Hodlerne, "Into the Fight," *Army Times*, March 31, 2003, pp. 4–7. From Gen. Blount's personal archive.
8   Interview with Lieutenant Colonel Alexis Perez-Cruz, Fort Stewart, Georgia, June 2019.
9   Interview with Lieutenant Colonel Alexis Perez-Cruz, Fort Stewart, Georgia, June 2019.
10 Interview with Command Sergeant Major Jabari Williams, Fort Stewart, Georgia, June 2019.
11 Interview with Maj. Charles O'Brien, Operational Leadership Experiences Project, February 24, 2005.
12 Interview with Colonel William Grimsley, April 17, 2023.
13 Robert Hodlerne, "Into the Fight," *Army Times*, March 31, 2003, pp. 4–7, from Gen. Blount's personal archive.
14 Fontenot, *On Point*, p. 115.

15 Vince Crawley, "A different kind of war," *Army Times*, March 31, 2003, pp. 5–7. From Gen. Blount's personal archive.

16 Crawley, "A different kind of war," pp. 5–7.

17 Interview with Col. Roberta A. Woods, Operation Leadership Experiences Project, May 18, 2006.

18 Interview with Col. Roberta A. Woods, Operation Leadership Experiences Project, May 18, 2006.

19 Fontenot, *On Point*, p. 120.

20 Fontenot, *On Point*, p. 120.

21 Steve Liewer, "On the Road to Baghdad," *Stars and Stripes*, March 30, 2003, pp. 4, 12. From Gen. Blount's personal archive.

22 "With the 3rd Infantry," *Washington Post*, March 26, 2003, p. A23. From Gen. Blount's personal archive.

23 "With the 3rd Infantry." *Washington Post*.

24 George Wright, "US forces battle elite troops," The *Guardian*, March 27, 2003. https://www.theguardian.com/world/2003/mar/27/iraq.georgewright

25 Joseph Giordono, "Iraqi forces put up tough fight in As Samawah," *Stars and Stripes*, March 29, 2003, p. 4.

26 Giordono, "Iraqi forces put up tough fight in As Samawah."

27 *OIF: The Fight for Baghdad* (film), Army University Press, 2020, https://www.youtube.com/watch?v=d8uaFZAxzpw

28 Interview with General Blount, February 15, 2019.

29 Interview with Col. Roberta A. Woods, Operation Leadership Experiences Project, May 18, 2006.

30 Interview with Colonel Lyle Cayce, March 2023.

31 Interview with Colonel Lyle Cayce, March 2023.

32 Fontenot, *On Point*, pp. 165–167.

33 Fontenot, *On Point*, pp. 195–196.

34 Interview with General David Perkins, Jan. 5, 2023.

35 Interview with General David Perkins, Jan. 5, 2023.

36 Interview with General David Perkins, Jan. 5, 2023.

37 Interview with General David Perkins, Jan. 5, 2023.

38 Interview with General David Perkins, Jan. 5, 2023.

39 Interview with General David Perkins, Jan. 5, 2023.

40 Interview with Colonel Andrew Hilms, Fort Stewart, Georgia, June 2019.

41 Interview with Colonel Andrew Hilms, Fort Stewart, Georgia, June 2019.

42 Interview with Colonel Andrew Hilms, Fort Stewart, Georgia, June 2019.

43 Fontenot, *On Point*, p. 203.

44 Mark Fritz, "Sandstorm slows advance," *The Courier-Journal*, March 26, 2003, A1.

45 Ray Quintanilla and Michael Kilian, "Sandstorm lashes allies," *Chicago Tribune*, March 26, 2003, A1.

46 Interview with Colonel Andrew Hilms, Fort Stewart, Georgia, June 2019.

47 James G. Lacey, *Takedown: The Third Infantry Division's Twenty-One Day Assault on Baghdad* (Annapolis, MD: Naval Institute Press, 2007), Chapter 14.

48 Interview with Colonel Mike Birmingham, December 12, 2022.

49 Interview with Col. Roberta A. Woods, Operation Leadership Experiences Project, May 18, 2006.

50 Fontenot, *On Point*, p. 168.

51 Fontenot, *On Point*, p. 169.

52 Interview with Colonel Andrew Hilms, Fort Stewart, Georgia, June 2019.

53 Interview with Colonel Andrew Hilms, Fort Stewart, Georgia, June 2019.

54 Fontenot, *On Point*, p. 209.

55 Interview with General William Grimsley, April 17, 2023.

56 Sgt. Craig Zentkovich, "Raiders secure foothold in Kifl," unknown publication. From Gen. Blount's personal archive.

57 Fontenot, *On Point*, p. 206.

58 Zentkovich, "Raiders secure foothold in Kifl."

59 Interview with General William Grimsley, April 17, 2023.

60 Zentkovich, "Raiders secure foothold in Kifl."

61 William Branigin, "Army Marks a Vigilant Pause in Desert," *Washington Post*, March 28, 2003. From Gen. Blount's personal archive.

62 Branigin, "Army Marks a Vigilant Pause in Desert."

63 "Honor the Fallen" database, *Military Times*, https://thefallen.militarytimes.com/army-sgt-eugene-williams/256553, https://thefallen.militarytimes.com/army-pfc-michael-r-creighton-weldon/256587, https://thefallen.militarytimes.com/army-cpl-michael-edward-curtin/256585, https://thefallen.militarytimes.com/army-pfc-diego-fernando-rincon/256549

64 From "Honor the Fallen" database, *Military Times*.

65 Interview with General William Grimsley, April 17, 2023.

66 Interview with General William Grimsley, April 17, 2023.

67 Col. Joel D. Rayburn, et al., *The U.S. Army in the Iraq War, Volume 1: Invasion, Insurgency, Civil War, 2003–2006* (Carlisle Barracks, PA: U.S. Army War College Press, 2019), p. 93.

CHAPTER 6

1 Fontenot, *On Point*, p. 246.

2 Fontenot, *On Point*, pp. 244–245.

3 *OIF: The Fight for Baghdad* (film).

4 Nicholas Wade, "A Nation at War: Iraqi Defenses," *New York Times*, March 21, 2003, https://www.nytimes.com/2003/03/21/world/nation -war-iraqi-defenses-biological-chemical-weapons-would-be-likely-slow -but.html

5 Wade, "A Nation at War: Iraqi Defenses."

6 Wade, "A Nation at War: Iraqi Defenses."

7 Fontenot, *On Point*, p. 282.

8 Interview with Lieutenant Colonel Alexis Perez-Cruz, Fort Stewart, Georgia, June 2019.

9 "Interview: Lieutenant General William Scott Wallace," PBS *Frontline*, https://www.pbs.org/wgbh/pages/frontline/shows/invasion/interviews/ wallace.html

10 Rayburn et al., *The U.S. Army in the Iraq War, Volume 1*, p. 93.

11 Noelle Phillips, "Night trip starts with confusion," *Savannah Morning News,* April 3, 2003. From Gen. Blount's personal archive.

12 "Interview: Lieutenant General Raad Al Hamdani," PBS *Frontline*, February 26, 2004: https://www.pbs.org/wgbh/pages/frontline/shows/ invasion/interviews/raad.html

13 Al-Hamdani PBS *Frontline* interview.

14 Al-Hamdani PBS *Frontline* interview.

15 Al-Hamdani PBS *Frontline* interview.

16 Fontenot, *On Point*, p. 288.

17 Fontenot, *On Point*, p. 289.

18 Fontenot, *On Point*, p. 290.

19 "Interview: Lieutenant Colonel Ernest 'Rock' Marcone," PBS *Frontline*, February 26, 2004: https://www.pbs.org/wgbh/pages/frontline/shows/ invasion/interviews/marcone.html

20 Interview with Maj. Charles O'Brien, Operational Leadership Experiences Project, February 24, 2005.

21 Fontenot, *On Point*, p. 292.

22 Interview with Maj. Charles O'Brien, Operational Leadership Experiences Project, February 24, 2005.

23 Interview with Colonel Andrew Hilms, Fort Stewart, Georgia, June 2019.

24 Interview with Colonel Andrew Hilms, Fort Stewart, Georgia, June 2019.

25 Interview with Colonel Andrew Hilms, Fort Stewart, Georgia, June 2019.

26 Interview with Colonel Andrew Hilms, Fort Stewart, Georgia, June 2019.

27 Interview with Colonel Andrew Hilms, Fort Stewart, Georgia, June 2019.

28 Interview with Colonel Andrew Hilms, Fort Stewart, Georgia, June 2019.

29 Marcone PBS *Frontline* interview.

30 Marcone PBS *Frontline* interview.

31 Marcone PBS *Frontline* interview.

32 Richard J. Newman, "Ambush at Najaf," *Air Force Magazine*, October 1, 2003, https://www.airforcemag.com/article/1003najaf/

33 Fontenot, *On Point*, p. 301.

34 Fontenot, *On Point*, p. 301.

35 John F. Burns, "Baghdad Empties of People, but It Fills with Foreboding," *New York Times*, March 26, 2003. From Gen. Blount's personal archive.

CHAPTER 7

1   Interview with General William Grimsley, April 17, 2023.

2   Interview with General William Grimsley, April 17, 2023.

3   Interview with General William Grimsley, April 17, 2023.

4   Interview with General William Grimsley, April 17, 2023.

5   Marcone PBS *Frontline* interview.

6   Interview with General William Grimsley, April 17, 2023.

7   Marcone PBS *Frontline* interview.

8   Marcone PBS *Frontline* interview.

9   Fontenot, *On Point*, p. 306.

10 Fontenot, *On Point*, p. 304.

11 Fontenot, *On Point*, p. 308.

12 "Honor the Fallen" database, *Military Times*, https://thefallen .militarytimes.com/army-sgt-1st-class-paul-r-smith/256561

13 Interview with Colonel Lyle Cayce, March 2023.

14 Interview with Colonel Lyle Cayce, March 2023.

15 Fontenot, *On Point*, p. 340.

16 Interview with General David Perkins, Jan. 5, 2023.

17 Interview with Colonel Andrew Hilms, Fort Stewart, Georgia, June 2019.

18 Interview with Col. Eric Schwartz, Operational Leadership Experiences Project, Combat Studies Institute, digital recording, April 21, 2007. Fort Leavenworth, Kansas. Interviewed by Robert Cameron. (Digital recording stored on CD-ROM at Combined Arms Research Library, Fort Leavenworth, Kansas.) https://cgsc.contentdm.oclc.org/digital/collection/ p4013coll13/id/822

19 Interview with Col. Eric Schwartz, Operation Leadership Experiences Project, April 21, 2007.

20 Interview with Col. Eric Schwartz, Operation Leadership Experiences Project, April 21, 2007.

21 Interview with General David Perkins, January 5, 2023.

22 Interview with Colonel Andrew Hilms, Fort Stewart, Georgia, June 2019.

23 Interview with Colonel Andrew Hilms, Fort Stewart, Georgia, June 2019.

24 Interview with SFC Ronald Gaines, Operational Leadership Experiences Project, Combat Studies Institute, digital recording, April 21, 2007.

Fort Leavenworth, Kansas. Interviewed by Dr. Robert Cameron, Armor Branch Historian. (Digital recording stored on CD-ROM at Combined Arms Research Library, Fort Leavenworth, Kansas.) https://cgsc .contentdm.oclc.org/digital/collection/p4013coll13/id/662/

25 Fontenot, *On Point*, p. 344.

26 Fontenot, *On Point*, p. 345.

27 "Stevon A. Booker," *The Hall of Valor Project*, https://valor.militarytimes .com/hero/69218

28 Dan Lewerenz, "Two Pennsylvania soldiers die in action," *The Morning Call* (Allentown, PA), April 8, 2003, A4.

29 Fontenot, *On Point*, p. 346.

30 Interview with Colonel Andrew Hilms, Fort Stewart, Georgia, June 2019.

31 Interview with General David Perkins, Jan. 5, 2023

32 Wallace PBS *Frontline* interview.

33 Interview with General David Perkins, Jan. 5, 2023

34 Interview with General David Perkins, Jan. 5, 2023

35 *OIF: The Fight for Baghdad* (film).

36 Interview with General David Perkins, Jan. 5, 2023.

37 Interview with General David Perkins, Jan. 5, 2023.

38 Interview with General David Perkins, Jan. 5, 2023.

39 Interview with General David Perkins, Jan. 5, 2023.

40 Interview with General David Perkins, Jan. 5, 2023.

41 Interview with Lieutenant General Eric Wesley, Jan. 13, 2023.

42 Fontenot, *On Point*, p. 361.

43 Fontenot, *On Point*, p. 362.

44 *OIF: The Fight for Baghdad* (film).

45 Interview with Col. Eric Schwartz, Operation Leadership Experiences Project, April 21, 2007.

46 *OIF: The Fight for Baghdad* (film).

47 William Branigin, "Three Key Battles Turned Tide of Invasion," *Washington Post*, April 20, 2003, https://www.washingtonpost.com /archive/politics/2003/04/20/3-key-battles-turned-tide-of-invasion/ f2129759-7057-425d-82ce-6a8614f83d2a/

48 Interview with Col. Eric Schwartz, Operation Leadership Experiences Project, April 21, 2007.

49 Interview with Col. Eric Schwartz, Operation Leadership Experiences Project, April 21, 2007.

50 Interview with Colonel Andrew Hilms, Fort Stewart, Georgia, June 2019.

51 Fontenot, *On Point*, p. 352.

52 Wallace PBS *Frontline* interview.

53 Interview with Col. Eric Schwartz, Operation Leadership Experiences Project, April 21, 2007.

54 Branigin, "Three Key Battles Turned Tide of Invasion."
55 Interview with General David Perkins, January 5, 2023.
56 Interview with General David Perkins, January 5, 2023.
57 Interview with General David Perkins, January 5, 2023.
58 Interview with General David Perkins, January 5, 2023.
59 Interview with General David Perkins, January 5, 2023.
60 Interview with General David Perkins, January 5, 2023.
61 Interview with Command Sergeant Major Jabari Williams, Fort Stewart, Georgia, June 2019.
62 Interview with General David Perkins, January 5, 2023.
63 Interview with General David Perkins, January 5, 2023.
64 Interview with General David Perkins, January 5, 2023.
65 Interview with General David Perkins, January 5, 2023.
66 Interview with General David Perkins, January 5, 2023.
67 Fontenot, *On Point*, p. 367.
68 Fontenot, *On Point*, p. 364.
69 Fontenot, *On Point*, p. 369.
70 Branigin, "Three Key Battles Turned Tide of Invasion."
71 Fontenot, *On Point*, p. 371.
72 Interview with Lieutenant General Eric Wesley, January 13, 2023.
73 Fontenot, *On Point*, p. 355.
74 Interview with Lieutenant General Eric Wesley, January 13, 2023.
75 Fontenot, *On Point*, p. 357.
76 Interview with Lieutenant General Eric Wesley, January 13, 2023.
77 Interview with Lieutenant General Eric Wesley, January 13, 2023.
78 Interview with Lieutenant General Eric Wesley, January 13, 2023.
79 Interview with Lieutenant General Eric Wesley, January 13, 2023.
80 Interview with Lieutenant General Eric Wesley, January 13, 2023.
81 Interview with Lieutenant General Eric Wesley, January 13, 2023.
82 Interview with Colonel Andrew Hilms, Fort Stewart, Georgia, June 2019.
83 Interview with Colonel Andrew Hilms, Fort Stewart, Georgia, June 2019.
84 "Interview: Colonel David Perkins," PBS *Frontline*, February 26, 2004, https://www.pbs.org/wgbh/pages/frontline/shows/invasion/interviews/perkins.html
85 Wallace PBS *Frontline* interview.

CHAPTER 8

1 Fontenot, *On Point*, p. 427.
2 Donald P. Wright et al., *On Point II: Transition to the New Campaign: The United States Army in Operation Iraqi Freedom, May 2003–January 2005* (Fort Leavenworth, KS: Combat Studies Institute Press, 2008), p. 71.

3 Wright et al., *On Point II*, p. 65.
4 Wright et al., *On Point II*, p. 56.
5 Wright et al., *On Point II*, p. 57.
6 Wright et al., *On Point II*, p. 58.
7 Wright et al., *On Point II*, p. 59.
8 Wright et al., *On Point II*, p. 70.
9 Rayburn et al., *The U.S. Army in the Iraq War, Volume 1*, p. 111.
10 Rayburn et al., *The U.S. Army in the Iraq War, Volume 1*, p. 47.
11 Interview with Maj. Erik Berdy, Operation Leadership Experiences Project, January 20, 2006.
12 Interview with Lieutenant General Eric Wesley, January 13, 2023.
13 Interview with General William Grimsley, April 17, 2023.
14 Interview with Maj. Charles O'Brien, Operational Leadership Experiences Project, February 24, 2005.
15 Interview with Maj. Charles O'Brien, Operational Leadership Experiences Project, February 24, 2005.
16 Interview with Colonel Lyle Cayce, March 2023.
17 Interview with Colonel Mike Birmingham, December 12, 2022.
18 Interview with Command Sergeant Major Jabari Williams, Fort Stewart, Georgia, June 2019.
19 Interview with Col. Roberta A. Woods, Operation Leadership Experiences Project, May 18, 2006.
20 Interview with Command Sergeant Major Jabari Williams, Fort Stewart, Georgia, June 2019.
21 "Anarchy: Garbage trucks, city buses part of theft spree," *The Sacramento Bee*, April 12, 2003, p. 14.
22 *The Liberator*, May 28, 2003, Issue 1, Vol. 1, p. 10.
23 *The Liberator*, May 28, 2003, Issue 1, Vol. 1, p. 6.
24 Interview with Lieutenant General Eric Wesley, Jan. 13, 2023.
25 "Anarchy: Garbage trucks, city buses part of theft spree," p. 14.
26 *The Liberator*, May 28, 2003, Issue 1, Vol. 1, p. 12.
27 *The Liberator*, June 6, 2003, Issue 2, Vol. 1, p. 6.
28 *The Liberator*, June 6, 2003, Issue 2, Vol. 1, p. 6.
29 Interview with Maj. Charles O'Brien, Operational Leadership Experiences Project, February 24, 2005.
30 Interview with Maj. Charles O'Brien, Operational Leadership Experiences Project, February 24, 2005.
31 *The Liberator*, May 28, 2003, Issue 1, Vol. 1, p. 7.
32 *The Liberator*, May 28, 2003, Issue 1, Vol. 1, p. 4.
33 *The Liberator*, May 28, 2003, Issue 1, Vol. 1, p. 5.
34 *The Liberator*, June 6, 2003, Issue 2, Vol. 1, p. 5.

35   Patrick McDowell, "Food sent to starving zoo animals," *Des Moines Register*, April 19, 2003, 2A.

36   Carol Morello, "Baghdad Bears Don't Have Bare Necessities," *Hartford Courant*, April 30, 2003, A12.

37   McDowell, "Food sent to starving zoo animals," 2A.

38   Philip Sherwell, "Zoo lions war's latest victims," *The Vancouver Sun*, April 21, 2003, A5.

39   Interview with Colonel Lyle Cayce, March 2023.

40   Interview with LTG Eric Wesley, January 13, 2023.

41   *The Liberator*, May 28, 2003, Issue 1, Vol. 1, p. 6.

42   *The Liberator*, June 6, 2003, Issue 2, Vol. 1, p. 10.

43   Aaron Davis, "Museums' priceless riches carried away," *The Sacramento Bee*, April 12, 2003, A17.

44   *The Liberator*, June 6, 2003, Issue 2, Vol. 1, p. 7.

45   *The Liberator*, June 6, 2003, Issue 2, Vol. 1, p. 14.

46   *The Liberator*, June 6, 2003, Issue 2, Vol. 1, p. 7.

47   Interview with Maj. Erik Berdy, Operation Leadership Experiences Project, January 20, 2006.

48   James Dobbins, et al., *Occupying Iraq: A History of the Coalition Provisional Authority* (Santa Monica, CA: RAND Corporation, 2009), pp. xiii–xv, https://www.rand.org/content/dam/rand/pubs/monographs/2009/RAND_MG847.pdf

49   "U.S. troops free to shoot looters," *Baltimore Sun*, May 13, 2003, https://www.baltimoresun.com/news/bs-xpm-2003-05-14-0305140220-story.html. See also David Paul Brown, "Bush administration is messing up postwar Iraq," *Paradise Post* (Paradise, CA), May 22, 2003, A9.

50   Interview with Lieutenant General Eric Wesley, January 13, 2023.

51   Interview with Lieutenant General Eric Wesley, January 13, 2023.

52   "Iraq Timeline: Since the 2003 War," United States Institute of Peace, May 29, 2020, https://www.usip.org/iraq-timeline-2003-war#textonly

53   Interview with General William Grimsley, April 17, 2023.

54   Interview with Colonel Mike Birmingham, December 12, 2022.

55   *The Liberator*, June 27, 2003, Issue 5, Vol. 1, p. 14.

56   Interview with Maj. Charles O'Brien, Operational Leadership Experiences Project, February 24, 2005.

57   Interview with Maj. Charles O'Brien, Operational Leadership Experiences Project, February 24, 2005.

58   Peter J. Boyer, "Downfall: How Donald Rumsfeld reformed the Army and lost Iraq," *The New Yorker*, November 12, 2006, https://www.newyorker.com/magazine/2006/11/20/downfall

59   Boyer, "Downfall."

60   Rayburn et al., *The U.S. Army in the Iraq War, Volume 1*, p. 111.

61 Boyer, "Downfall."
62 Interview with Colonel Mike Birmingham, December 12, 2022.
63 Interview with Colonel Mike Birmingham, December 12, 2022.
64 John-Thor Dahlberg, "Army Town is at a Loss Over Troops' Delay in Iraq," *Los Angeles Times*, July 16, 2003, A9.
65 Dahlberg, "Army Town is at a Loss."
66 Dahlberg, "Army Town is at a Loss."
67 Richard Sisk, "Troop homecoming KO'd," *New York Daily News*, July 16, 2003, 5.
68 "Wife's worried e-mail brings informal rebuke," *Tampa Bay Times*, July 28, 2003, A3.
69 Interview with General Bill Weber, May 19, 2023.
70 Interview with Command Sergeant Major Jabari Williams, Fort Stewart, Georgia, June 2019.

CHAPTER 9

1   "Violent Response: The U.S. Army in al-Falluja," June 16, 2003. https://www.hrw.org/report/2003/06/16/violent-response/us-army-al-falluja#_ftn8
2   "Violent Response: The U.S. Army in al-Falluja."
3   "Violent Response: The U.S. Army in al-Falluja."
4   "Rumsfeld tours Baghdad, but anger brews," *Louisville Courier-Journal*, May 1, 2003, A1–A2.
5   Rajiv Chandrasekaran, "U.S. makes unusual move, backing down in Fallujah," *Fort Worth Star-Telegram*, August 3, 2003, 31A.
6   Chris Tomlinson, "U.S. steps up military presence west of Baghdad," *Louisville Courier-Journal*, June 5, 2003, A14.
7   Elizabeth Rubin, "The Cult of Rajavi," *New York Times*, July 13, 2003, https://www.nytimes.com/2003/07/13/magazine/the-cult-of-rajavi.html
8   Interview with General David Perkins, January 5, 2023.
9   Interview with General David Perkins, January 5, 2023.
10 Interview with LTG Eric Wesley, January 13, 2023.
11 Chandrasekaran, "U.S. makes unusual move."
12 Interview with General David Perkins, January 5, 2023.
13 Interview with LTG Eric Wesley, January 13, 2023.
14 Interview with Colonel Andrew Hilms, Fort Stewart, Georgia, June 2019.
15 Interview with Colonel Andrew Hilms, Fort Stewart, Georgia, June 2019.
16 Interview with Command Sergeant Major Jabari Williams, Fort Stewart, Georgia, June 2019.
17 Spc. Mason T. Lowery, "Spartan raids yield humanitarian efforts," *The Liberator*, Vol. 1, Issue 5, June 27, 2003, p. 2.

18 Interview with General Buford "Buff" Blount," July 20, 2022, Bassfield, MS.

19 Spc. Katherine Robinson, "Reservist helps train Fallujah police," *The Liberator*, Vol. 1, Issue 5, June 27, 2003, p. 4.

20 Sgt. Mark S. Rickert, "MPs teach Iraqis how to be police officers," *The Liberator*, Vol. 1, Issue 9, July 25, 2003, p. 7.

21 Spc. Mason T. Lowery, "Tusker medics treat Habbaniyah citizens," *The Liberator*, Vol. 1, Issue 9, July 25, 2003, p. 6.

22 Lowery, "Tusker medics treat Habbaniyah citizens."

23 Lowery, "Tusker medics treat Habbaniyah citizens."

24 Lowery, "Tusker medics treat Habbaniyah citizens."

25 Spc. Mason T. Lowery, "Rogues, Kings deliver supplies to the hospital," *The Liberator*, Vol. 1, Issue 5, June 27, 2003, p. 6.

26 Spc. Katherine Robinson, "1-9 FA treats children near Fallujah," *The Liberator*, Vol. 1, Issue 9, July 25, 2003, p. 6.

27 Interview with Colonel Andrew Hilms, Fort Stewart, Georgia, June 2019.

28 Interview with General Buford "Buff" Blount," July 20, 2022, Bassfield, MS.

29 Interview with Colonel Andrew Hilms, Fort Stewart, Georgia, June 2019.

30 Interview with General Buford "Buff" Blount," July 20, 2022, Bassfield, MS.

31 "To cope with shortages, Iraq to import gasoline, cooking gas," *Sarasota Herald-Tribune*, May 7, 2005, 3A.

32 Sgt. Craig Zentkovich, "1-9 FA provides security for propane distribution," *The Liberator*, Vol. 1, Issue 5, June 27, 2003, p. 5.

33 Spc. Katherine Robinson, "2nd BCT soldiers set out to feed Fallujah's needy," *The Liberator*, Vol. 1, Issue 9, July 25, 2003, p. 3.

34 "Iraq Timeline: Since the 2003 War," United States Institute of Peace, May 29, 2020, https://www.usip.org/iraq-timeline-2003-war#textonly

35 Alice Hills, "Fear and Loathing in Falluja," *Armed Forces & Society* 32, no. 4, 2006, pp. 623–639, https://www.jstor.org/stable/48608734

36 Spc. Mason T. Lowery, "Spartan raids yield humanitarian efforts," *The Liberator*, Vol. 1, Issue 5, June 27, 2003, p. 2.

37 Sgt. Craig Zentkovich, "TF Enforcer strikes in Habbinyah," *The Liberator*, Vol. 1, Issue 5, June 27, 2003, p. 3.

38 "Fallujah an oasis of relative calm in Iraq," *Billings Gazette*, June 22, 2003, 6A.

39 Spc. Jacob Boyer, "DIVENG turns contracting over to Iraqis," *The Liberator*, Vol. 1, Issue 9, July 25, 2003, p. 5.

40 Spc. Katherine Robinson, "Fallujah police request independence," *The Liberator*, Vol. 1, Issue 9, July 25, 2003, p. 5.

41 Chandrasekaran, "U.S. makes unusual move."

42 Chandrasekaran, "U.S. makes unusual move."

43 "82nd Airborne Division," CNN, https://www.cnn.com/SPECIALS/2003/iraq/forces/coalition/deployment/army/82nd.airborne.division.html

44 "82nd expected back by March," *Charlotte Observer*, September 29, 2003, 4A.

45 Kim Ghattas, "Mixed feelings over UN Iraq role," BBC News, August 11, 2007, http://news.bbc.co.uk/2/hi/middle_east/6941560.stm

46 Charles Hanley, "In Baghdad, US compound fired upon," *Austin American-Statesman*, Sept. 28, 2003, A4.

CONCLUSION

1 Interview with Colonel Andrew Hilms, Fort Stewart, Georgia, June 2019.

2 Interview with Colonel Andrew Hilms, Fort Stewart, Georgia, June 2019.

3 Interview with Colonel Andrew Hilms, Fort Stewart, Georgia, June 2019.

4 Interview with Command Sergeant Major Jabari Williams, Fort Stewart, Georgia, June 2019.

5 Interview with Maj. Charles O'Brien, Operational Leadership Experiences Project, February 24, 2005.

6 Interview with Maj. Charles O'Brien, Operational Leadership Experiences Project, February 24, 2005.

7 Interview with Maj. Charles O'Brien, Operational Leadership Experiences Project, February 24, 2005.

8 Interview with Colonel Mike Birmingham, December 12, 2022.

9 Interview with General Bill Weber, May 19, 2023.

10 "Honor the Fallen" database, *Military Times*, https://thefallen.militarytimes.com/army-lt-col-charles-h-buehring/256871

11 "Iraq Timeline: Since the 2003 War," United States Institute of Peace, May 29, 2020, https://www.usip.org/iraq-timeline-2003-war#textonly

12 "Iraqi Election," *BBC*, February 13, 2005, http://news.bbc.co.uk/2/hi/middle_east/3971635.stm

13 "Overview: The Iraq War," *New York Times*, February 15, 2008, https://archive.nytimes.com/www.nytimes.com/ref/timestopics/topics_iraq.html

14 Interview with Lieutenant Colonel Alexis Perez-Cruz, Fort Stewart, Georgia, June 2019.

15 Interview with Lieutenant Colonel Alexis Perez-Cruz, Fort Stewart, Georgia, June 2019.

16 Interview with Lieutenant Colonel Alexis Perez-Cruz, Fort Stewart, Georgia, June 2019.

17 Interview with Lieutenant Colonel Alexis Perez-Cruz, Fort Stewart, Georgia, June 2019.

18 Interview with Command Sergeant Major Jabari Williams, Fort Stewart, Georgia, June 2019.

19 Interview with Command Sergeant Major Jabari Williams, Fort Stewart, Georgia, June 2019.

20 Interview with General William Grimsley, April 17, 2023.

21 Interview with General David Perkins, January 5, 2023.

22 Interview with General David Perkins, January 5, 2023.

23 Interview with General David Perkins, January 5, 2023.

24 Interview with General David Perkins, January 5, 2023.

25 Interview with General William Grimsley, April 17, 2023.

26 Interview with General David Perkins, January 5, 2023.

27 Interview with General David Perkins, January 5, 2023.

28 Interview with General David Perkins, January 5, 2023.

29 Interview with LTG Eric Wesley, January 13, 2023.

30 Interview with LTG Eric Wesley, January 13, 2023.

31 Interview with LTG Eric Wesley, January 13, 2023.

32 Interview with LTG Eric Wesley, January 13, 2023.

33 Department of the Army, *Counterinsurgency*, FM 3–24, December 15, 2006, 1–27.

34 "US uses Sunnis to patrol streets," *The Age*, August 20, 2007, https://www.theage.com.au/world/us-uses-sunnis-to-patrol-streets-20070820-ge5mgp.html

35 Interview with Colonel Andrew Hilms, Fort Stewart, Georgia, June 2019.

36 Interview with Colonel Lyle Cayce, March 2023.

37 Jack Kelly, "How the bold run to Baghdad paid off," *Pittsburgh Post-Gazette*, April 13, 2003, http://old.post-gazette.com/world/20030413warspeedwp4.asp

Selected Bibliography

PRIMARY SOURCES

Author Interviews
Colonel Michael Birmingham
General Buford "Buff" Blount
Lisa Blount
Colonel Lyle Cayce
General William Grimsley
Brigadier General Andrew Hilms
Colonel Alexis Perez-Cruz
General David Perkins
Brigadier General Bill Weber
Lieutenant General Eric Wesley
Command Sergeant Major Jabari Williams

Oral History Collections and Published Interviews
Operational Leadership Experiences Project, Combat Studies Institute, Fort Leavenworth, KS

Berdy, Major Erik. 2006. Interview by Operational Leadership Experiences Project team with Combat Studies Institute, digital recording, January 20. Fort Leavenworth, Kansas. Interviewed by John H. McCool. (Digital recording stored on CD-ROM at Combined Arms Research Library, Fort Leavenworth, Kansas.) https://cgsc.contentdm.oclc.org/digital/collection/p4013coll13/id/226/

Gaines, SFC Ronald. 2007. Interview by Operational Leadership Experiences Project team with Combat Studies Institute, digital recording, April 21. Fort Leavenworth, Kansas. Interviewed by Dr. Robert Cameron, Armor Branch Historian. (Digital recording stored on CD-ROM at Combined Arms

Research Library, Fort Leavenworth, Kansas.) https://cgsc.contentdm.oclc
.org/digital/collection/p4013coll13/id/662/

O'Brien, Major Charles. 2005. Interview by Operational Leadership
Experiences Project team with Combat Studies Institute, digital recording,
February 24. Fort Leavenworth, Kansas. Interviewed by Maj. Kent Strader.
(Digital recording stored on CD-ROM at Combined Arms Research
Library, Fort Leavenworth, Kansas.) https://cgsc.contentdm.oclc.org/digital/
collection/p4013coll13/id/90/rec/3

Schwartz, Colonel Eric. 2007. Interview by Operational Leadership
Experiences Project team with Combat Studies Institute, digital recording,
April 21. Fort Leavenworth, Kansas. Interviewed by Robert Cameron.
(Digital recording stored on CD-ROM at Combined Arms Research
Library, Fort Leavenworth, Kansas.) https://cgsc.contentdm.oclc.org/digital/
collection/p4013coll13/id/822

Woods, Colonel Roberta A. 2006. Interview by Operational Leadership
Experiences Project team with Combat Studies Institute, digital recording,
May 18. Fort Leavenworth, Kansas. Interviewed by Lynne Chandler Garcia.
(Digital recording stored on CD-ROM at Combined Arms Research
Library, Fort Leavenworth, Kansas.) https://cgsc.contentdm.oclc.org/digital/
collection/p4013coll13/id/531

PBS Frontline
"Interview: Lt. Col. Ernest 'Rock' Marcone," PBS *Frontline*, posted Feb. 26,
2004: https://www.pbs.org/wgbh/pages/frontline/shows/invasion/interviews
/marcone.html
"Interview: Lt. Gen. Raad Al-Hamdani," PBS *Frontline*, posted Feb. 26, 2004:
https://www.pbs.org/wgbh/pages/frontline/shows/invasion/interviews/raad
.html
"Interview: Lieutenant General William Scott Wallace," PBS *Frontline*, posted
Feb. 26, 2004: https://www.pbs.org/wgbh/pages/frontline/shows/invasion/
interviews/wallace.html

Government Reports, Newspaper and Magazine Articles
"Anarchy: Garbage trucks, city buses part of theft spree," *The Sacramento Bee*,
April 12, 2003
Anderson, Scott, "The True Story of Lawrence of Arabia," *Smithsonian
Magazine*, July 2014, https://www.smithsonianmag.com/history/true-story
-lawrence-arabia-180951857/
Boyer, Peter J., "Downfall: How Donald Rumsfeld reformed the Army and
lost Iraq," *The New Yorker*, Nov. 12, 2006, https://www.newyorker.com/
magazine/2006/11/20/downfall

Branigin, William, "Army Marks a Vigilant Pause in Desert," *Washington Post*, March 28, 2003. From Gen. Blount's personal archive

Branigin, William, "In Tight Quarters, the Buddy System Rules, Like It or Not," *Washington Post*, March 26, 2003. From Gen. Blount's personal archive

Branigin, William, "Three Key Battles Turned Tide of Invasion," *Washington Post*, April 20, 2003, https://www.washingtonpost.com/archive/politics /2003/04/20/3-key-battles-turned-tide-of-invasion/f2129759-7057-425d -82ce-6a8614f83d2a/

Brown, David Paul, "Bush administration is messing up postwar Iraq," *Paradise Post* (Paradise, CA), May 22, 2003, A9

Burns, John F., "Baghdad Empties of People, but it Fills with Foreboding," *New York Times*, March 26, 2003. From Gen. Blount's personal archive

Burns, Robert, "War's Opening: Air assault to open way for ground attack," *Associated Press*, undated. From Gen. Blount's personal archive

"CENTCOM's Saudi Security Fixes Were Geared Toward Too Small a Threat," *Inside the Pentagon*, July 11, 1996, Vol. 12, No. 28

Chandrasekaran, Rajiv, "U.S. makes unusual move, backing down in Fallujah," *Fort Worth Star-Telegram*, August 3, 2003, 31A

Crawley, Vince, "A different kind of war," *Army Times*, March 31, 2003. From Gen. Blount's personal archive

Dahlberg, John-Thor, "Army Town is at a Loss Over Troops' Delay in Iraq," *Los Angeles Times*, July 16, 2003, A9

"David Blount killed, wife critically hurt," *Hattiesburg American*, October 28, 1972, A1

Davis, Aaron, "Museums' priceless riches carried away," *The Sacramento Bee*, April 12, 2003, A17

Dickey, Christopher, "Perils of Victory," *Newsweek*, February 2, 2003, from General Blount's personal archive

Espo, David, "Bush to Saddam: Leave Iraq or Else," *Associated Press*, undated. From Gen. Blount's personal archive

"Fallujah an oasis of relative calm in Iraq," *Billings Gazette*, June 22, 2003, 6A

Fritz, Mark, "Sandstorm slows advance," *The Courier-Journal*, March 26, 2003, A1

Giordono, Joseph, "Iraqi forces put up tough fight in As Samawah," *Stars and Stripes*, March 29, 2003

Hanania, Richard, "Ahmad Chalabi and the Great Man Theory of History," *War on the Rocks*, December 17, 2018, https://warontherocks.com/2018/12/ ahmad-chalabi-and-the-great-man-theory-of-history/

Hanley, Charles, "In Baghdad, US compound fired upon," *Austin American-Statesman*, September 28, 2003, A4

Hills, Alice, "Fear and Loathing in Falluja," *Armed Forces & Society* 32, no. 4, 2006, https://www.jstor.org/stable/48608734

Hodlerne, Robert, "Into the Fight," *Army Times*, March 31, 2003. From Gen. Blount's personal archive

"Honor the Fallen" database, *Military Times*, https://thefallen.militarytimes.com/

Kelly, Jack, "How the bold run to Baghdad paid off," *Pittsburgh Post-Gazette*, April 13, 2003, http://old.post-gazette.com/world/20030413warspeedwp4.asp

Kennedy, Edward M., "The Persian Gulf: Arms Race or Arms Control?" *Foreign Affairs*, October 1975, Vol. 54, No. 1

Kundi, Mansoor Akbar, "Security Integration Under the Gulf Cooperation Council," *Pakistan Horizon*, January 1989, Vol. 42, No. 1

Lewerenz, Dan, "Two Pennsylvania soldiers die in action," *The Morning Call* (Allentown, PA), April 8, 2003, A4

Liewer, Steve, "On the Road to Baghdad," *Stars and Stripes*, March 30, 2003. From Gen. Blount's personal archive

McDowell, Patrick, "Food sent to starving zoo animals," *Des Moines Register*, April 19, 2003, 2A.

Melki, Eli, "Mecca 1979: The mosque siege that changed the course of Saudi history," BBC News, December 27, 2019, https://www.bbc.com/news/stories-50852379

Memo from Assistant Secretary of Defense Philip Rodman to Secretary of Defense Donald Rumsfeld, August 15, 2002, Subject: "Who Will Govern Iraq"? National Security Archive, George Washington University, https://nsarchive2.gwu.edu/NSAEBB/NSAEBB328/II-Doc18.pdf

Morello, Carol, "Baghdad Bears Don't Have Bare Necessities," *Hartford Courant*, April 30, 2003, A12

Newman, Richard J., "Ambush at Najaf," *Air Force Magazine*, October 1, 2003, https://www.airforcemag.com/article/1003najaf/

OIF: The Fight for Baghdad (film), Army University Press, 2020, https://www.youtube.com/watch?v=d8uaFZAxzpw

Phillips, Noelle, "Night trip starts with confusion," *Savannah Morning News*, April 3, 2003. From Gen. Blount's personal archive

Quintanilla, Ray and Michael Kilian, "Sandstorm lashes allies," *Chicago Tribune*, March 26, 2003, A1

Report of the Select Committee on Intelligence on the Use by the Intelligence Community of Information Provided by the Iraqi National Congress (Washington, DC: U.S. Government Printing Office, 2006)

Rubin, Elizabeth, "The Cult of Rajavi," *New York Times*, July 13, 2003, https://www.nytimes.com/2003/07/13/magazine/the-cult-of-rajavi.html

"Rumsfeld tours Baghdad, but anger brews," *Louisville Courier-Journal*, May 1, 2003, A1–A2

Sherwell, Philip, "Zoo lions war's latest victims," *The Vancouver Sun*, April 21, 2003, A5

Sisk, Richard, "Troop homecoming KO'd," *New York Daily News*, July 16, 2003, 5

Stanford Center for International Security and Cooperation, Mapping Militants Organizations, "Ansar al-Islam," Stanford University, https://cisac.fsi.stanford.edu/mappingmilitants/profiles/ansar-al-islam

State Department cable, "Future of Iraq Expert Working Groups," July 8, 2002, https://nsarchive2.gwu.edu/NSAEBB/NSAEBB163/index.htm

State Department memorandum, February 7, 2003, To: Undersecretary Dobriansky, From: Craner, Dewey, Simons. Subject: Iraq Contingency Planning, National Security Archive, George Washington University, https://nsarchive2.gwu.edu/NSAEBB/NSAEBB163/index.htm

Thomas, Evan, "Fear at the Front," *U.S. News and World Report*, February 3, 2003

"To cope with shortages, Iraq to import gasoline, cooking gas," *Sarasota Herald-Tribune*, May 7, 2005, 3A

Tomlinson, Chris, "U.S. steps up military presence west of Baghdad," *Louisville Courier-Journal*, June 5, 2003, A14

U.S. Senate Select Committee on Intelligence, *Report on Prewar Intelligence Assessments about Postwar Iraq* (Washington, DC: U.S. Government Printing Office, 2007)

"U.S. troops free to shoot looters," *Baltimore Sun*, May 13, 2003, https://www.baltimoresun.com/news/bs-xpm-2003-05-14-0305140220-story.html.

"US uses Sunnis to patrol streets," *The Age*, August 20, 2007, https://www.theage.com.au/world/us-uses-sunnis-to-patrol-streets-20070820-ge5mgp.html

Wade, Nicholas, "A Nation at War: Iraqi Defenses," *New York Times*, March 21, 2003, https://www.nytimes.com/2003/03/21/world/nation-war-iraqi-defenses-biological-chemical-weapons-would-be-likely-slow-but.html

Whitelaw, Kevin, "After the Fall," *US News and World Report*, December 2, 2002. From Gen. Blount's personal archive

"Wife's worried e-mail brings informal rebuke," *Tampa Bay Times*, July 28, 2003, A3

"With the 3rd Infantry," *Washington Post*, March 26, 2003, A23. From Gen. Blount's personal archive

Wolffe Richard and Michael Hirsh, "War and Consequences," *Newsweek*, February 2, 2003. From Gen. Blount's personal archive

Wright, George. "US forces battle elite troops," *The Guardian*, March 27, 2003, https://www.theguardian.com/world/2003/mar/27/iraq.georgewright

Zentkovich, Sgt. Craig, "Raiders secure foothold in Kifl," unknown publication. From Gen. Blount's personal archive

Various articles from *The Liberator*, a weekly magazine published by the 3rd Infantry Division's Public Affairs office in Baghdad

SECONDARY SOURCES

Bensahel, Nora, Olga Oliker, Keith Crane, et al., *After Saddam: Prewar Planning and the Occupation of Iraq*, 1st ed, RAND Corporation, 2008, http://www.jstor.org/stable/10.7249/mg642a

Bloomfield, Jr., Lincoln P., "Saudi Arabia Faces the 1980s: Saudi Security Problems and American Interests," *The Fletcher Forum*, Vol. 5, No. 2 (Summer 1981)

Dale, Catherine, *Congressional Research Service Report for Congress: Operation Iraqi Freedom: Strategies, Approaches, Results, and Issues for Congress*, Foreign Affairs, Defense, and Trade Division, March 28, 2008

Dobbins, James et al., *Occupying Iraq: A History of the Coalition Provisional Authority* (Santa Monica, CA: RAND Corporation, 2009), https://www.rand.org/content/dam/rand/pubs/monographs/2009/RAND_MG847.pdf

Dris-Ait-Hamadouche, Louisa and Yahia H. Zoubir, "The U.S.-Saudi Relationship and the Iraq War: The Dialectics of a Dependent Alliance," *Journal of Third World Studies*, Spring 2007, Vol. 24, No. 1

Fontenot, Col. Gregory, *On Point: The United States Army in Operation Iraqi Freedom* (Fort Leavenworth, KS: Combat Studies Institute Press, 2004)

Gordon, Michael R., *Cobra II: The Inside Story of the Invasion and Occupation of Iraq* (New York: Pantheon Books, 2006)

Klare, Michael T., "Political Economy of U.S. Arms Sales," *Social Scientist*, June 1976, Vol. 4, No. 11 (June 1976)

Kyrolainen, Hannu, "An Analysis of New Trends in the U.S. Military Training and Technical Assistance in the Third World," *Instant Research on Peace and Violence*, 1977, Vol. 4, No. 3–4

Lacey, James G., *Takedown: The Third Infantry Division's Twenty-One Day Assault on Baghdad* (Annapolis, MD: Naval Institute Press, 2007)

Marozzi, Justin, *Baghdad: City of Peace, City of Blood. A History in Thirteen Centuries* (Boston: Da Capo Press, 2014)

Polk, William K., *Understanding Iraq* (New York: Harper Perennial, 2005)

Rayburn, Joel D., et al., *The U.S. Army in the Iraq War, Volume 1: Invasion, Insurgency, Civil War, 2003–2006* (Carlisle Barracks, PA: U.S. Army War College Press, 2019)

Razoux, Pierre, *The Iran-Iraq War* (Cambridge, MA: Belknap Press of Harvard University Press, 2015)

Robertson, John, *Iraq: A History* (London: Oneworld Publications, 2015)

Wright, Donald P., *On Point II: Transition to the New Campaign: The United States Army in Operation Iraqi Freedom, May 2003–January 2005* (Fort Leavenworth, KS: Combat Studies Institute Press, 2008)

Index